# Biography and Educ

# Social Research and Educational Studies Series

Series Editor:   Robert G. Burgess, Professor of Sociology,
                 University of Warwick

Social Research and Educational Studies Series: 19

# Biography and Education:
## A Reader

*Edited by*

Michael Erben

UK      Falmer Press, 1 Gunpowder Square, London, EC4A 3DE
USA    Falmer Press, Taylor & Francis Inc., 1900 Frost Road, Suite 101,
       Bristol, PA 19007

---

First published in 1998

**A catalogue record for this book is available from the British Library**

ISBN 0 7507 0752 X cased
ISBN 0 7507 0751 8 paper

**Library of Congress Cataloging-in-Publication Data are available on request**

Jacket design by Caroline Archer

Typeset in 10/12pt Times by
Graphicraft Typesetters Limited, Hong Kong

Cover Printer Biddles Ltd.

*Printed in Great Britain by Biddles Ltd., Guildford and King's Lynn on paper which has a specified pH value on final paper manufacture of not less than 7.5 and is therefore 'acid free'.*

*Every effort has been made to contact copyright holders for their permission to reprint material in this book. The publishers would be grateful to hear from any copyright holder who is not here acknowledged and will undertake to rectify any errors or omissions in future editions of this book.*

# Contents

# Series Editor's Preface

The purpose of the *Social Research and Educational Studies* series is to provide authoritative guides to key issues in educational research. The series includes overviews of fields, guidance on good practice and discussions of the practical implications of social and educational research. In particular, the series deals with a variety of approaches to conducting social and educational research. Contributors to this series review recent work, raise critical concerns that are particular to the field of education and reflect on the implications of research for educational policy and practice.

Each volume in the series draws on material that will be relevant for an international audience. The contributors to this series all have wide experience of teaching, conducting and using educational research. The volumes are written so that they will appeal to a wide audience of students, teachers and researchers. Altogether the volumes in the *Social Research and Educational Studies* series provide a comprehensive guide for anyone concerned with contemporary educational research.

The series will include individually authored books and edited volumes on a range of themes in education including qualitative research, survey research, the interpretation of data, self-evaluation, research and social policy, analysing data, action research and the politics and ethics of research.

This volume provides an insight into leading edge methodological work. All the researchers in this volume have been at the forefront of work on autobiography and biography. In the early chapters there are discussions of theoretical and conceptual issues. These are followed by empirical studies that illustrate the ways in which biographical research can be conducted. All together, the contributions to this volume have the potential to lead to further innovations in methodology.

*Robert Burgess*
*Series Editor*

# Introduction

*Michael Erben*

Within recent years scholarly work in biographical and life-course studies has witnessed considerable expansion in the form of numerous articles, the founding of new journals and a growing number of books. Additionally, courses on biography and life-courses are increasingly being offered at undergraduate and postgraduate levels. In concert with these developments the present edited volume on biography has been produced for those particularly interested in the field of education. The volume represents an early attempt to reflect a variety of research work in this area. Nevertheless, there is a unifying feature to the collection, and that is the recognition that individual motivations and social influences have no easy demarcation. Such a recognition in biographical studies is seen less as a methodological hindrance than a way of observing in the exploration of the *narrative* features of human identity, how the structural and interactional are intertwined. It is further argued in these papers that biographical and autobiographical analyses can examine the significance of selves in relation to general or prevailing values.

While biographical analysis has received novel, contemporary elucidation it is, in fact, a perspective that goes back to early concerns in the social sciences. It is well represented in sociology in the work of the Chicago School, and in psychoanalysis and psychology it had formative elaboration by, respectively, the Freudians and William James. A particularly important text in the history of the biographical approach within social science was Thomas and Znaniecki's *The Polish Peasant in Europe and America* (1918–1920) — the first example of sustained sociological research in which personal documents were used as primary data. In more recent times, one of the most influential texts of post-war sociology, C. Wright Mill's *The Sociological Imagination* (1959) argued that sociology can be defined as the interaction between biography and history. However, it would not be unreasonable to argue that much of this way of thinking, in a welter of abstracted empiricism, was generally lost sight of until the publication of Daniel Bertaux's edited volume, *Biography and Society* (1981). In turn, this publication was supported by the earlier theorizations behind oral history incorporated in Paul Thompson's *The Voice of the Past* (1978). From this time — receiving further fillips from Denzin's *Interpretive Biography* (1989) and a special edition of the journal *Sociology* (1993) — the field of biographical studies has steadily burgeoned in Britain. It has now begun to develop various specialist themes of which the present volume represents a particularly important one — education. The chapters gathered for this book (all specially written for the volume) indicate the range of biographical work being carried out, both theoretically and empirically, in the educational field. A point that all contributions make is that while major, structuring features of the social formation (e.g. class, gender, race) play a clear part in influencing personal identity, they do not in any automatic way create groups with uniform selves. The experiences of the structuring features of the social order are often very differently felt and reacted to even within markedly similar groups.

In echoing some of these points Michael Erben in the first chapter of the volume attempts to outline the methodological issues for biographical research and provide an overview of the ground that most researchers would need to consider when carrying out biographical analysis. A number of related issues concerning the meaning of 'experience' for education are taken up by Robin Usher (Chapter 2) from a specifically autobiographical standpoint in a postmodernist analysis of the relationships between a problematic notion of selfhoods and the discourses that inscribe them. David Scott (Chapter 3) takes issues of theory into the heart of educational practice through a hermeneutical discussion of the relationship between researcher and the researched. In examining in detail a teacher's life amid the constraints of time, changing government policy and class and nationality, he argues convincingly for the utility of a biographical approach. In his attempt to use a non-colonial stance towards his chief respondent, Scott delineates the inherent difficulty of such a procedure and in so doing is able to advance the protocols of the biographical method itself.

Theoretical concerns such as these are reflected in the contributions of a number of the authors. Chris Mann (Chapter 4) in a detailed empirical study, examines the processes by which a number of adolescent girls studying for A levels partly constitute their identities through a complex series of negotiations between home, school, family and personal history. Similarly, Gill Clarke (Chapter 5) demonstrates in discussing the manner in which 'coping' strategies are used by lesbian physical education teachers how identities can (in part) be arrived at through apprehension and anxiety. Clarke, in examining these teachers' attempts to appear 'acceptable' gives their hidden voices recognition while developing a more general method for researching those pushed to the margins of official, mainstream, educational concerns. The contributions by both Mann and Clarke illustrate, as they openly acknowledge, the difficulty and importance of carrying out research that may make a difference to how people are categorized or marked out within the educational system.

These themes have resonance in the contributions of Hilary Dickinson (Chapter 6) and Mich Page (Chapter 7) where once again issues of methodology are seen as inseparable from findings. Dickinson, in a closely textured discussion of the biographies of subjects with learning difficulties utilizes a particular variety of narrative analysis to discuss their lives in detail. Conclusions concerning an understanding of the meaningful educational experiences of her subjects allows her to set the tone for further research in the area. Page is concerned in a wide-ranging empirical study of a further educational college, with the phenomenon of student 'wastage'. Her uncovering of the biographical routes by which students 'drop out' of college has direct implications for national educational policy on student recruitment.

Specific, autobiographical accounts of educational experience are explored by both Brian Roberts (Chapter 8) and Zoë Parker (Chapter 9). Roberts provides a fascinating personal, but generalizeable, account of a (post-1944 Act) journey through the state educational system. In the process he is able to discuss at some length the interaction between the theoretical and the empirical in a grounded examination of his direct, lived experience. Parker is also much involved with the blurred distinctions between the personal and the general in her analysis of how PhDs come to be finalized in the ways they are. She scrutinizes three accounts of how the knowledge that goes towards generating a PhD is constructed to produce an holistic gathering together of what are, in fact, provisional and fragmented ideas and formulations.

The final contributions to the volume by Diana Jones (Chapter 10) and Peter Figueroa (Chapter 11) both indicate clearly the considerable (but underused) strength of the biographical approach for an understanding, and bringing to life, of the history of education. Jones, reveals and exposes in detail (through group biography) the way the lives of an influential few affected those of the many. Her study explores with exactitude how the Nonconformist entrepreneurs of the nineteenth century, in part, shaped and moulded both contemporary and subsequent educational ideology. Figueroa, working in a neglected area of educational history — that concerned with slavery — reveals the inspiring story of a particular African slave, Olaudah Equiano. In using Equiano's own account of his experiences and other source material, Figueroa provides, through the study of a specific person, a disquisition on the relationship between colonial exploitation, educational opportunity and the formation of selfhood.

It is hoped that this purposely diverse volume will be of interest to colleagues working in the broad educational field and may go towards the development of further discussion of biographical approaches to educational research. Any readers who would care to be informed of seminars and other events organized by the Centre for Biography and Education at the University of Southampton are invited to write to: Michael Erben, Centre for Biography and Education, Research and Graduate School of Education, University of Southampton, Highfield, Southampton, SO17 1BJ.

## References

BERTAUX, D. (ed.) (1981) *Biography and Society: The Life-history Approach in the Social Sciences*, Beverly Hills, CA: Sage.

DENZIN, N.K. (1989) *Interpretive Biography*, Newbury Park, CA: Sage.

MILLS, C.W. (1959) *The Sociological Imagination*, New York: Oxford University Press.

SOCIOLOGY (1993) **27**, 1, special issue on Auto/Biography in Sociology.

THOMAS, W.I. and ZNANIECKI, F. (1918–1920) *The Polish Peasant in Europe and America*: *Vols. 1–5*, Boston: Gorham Press.

THOMPSON, P. (1978) *The Voice of the Past: Oral History*, Oxford: Oxford University Press.

# 1  Biography and Research Method

*Michael Erben*

### Introduction

The guiding feature of biographical research is that it attempts to suit its method to its purpose. We may say that biographical research has both *general* and *specific* purposes. The *general* purpose is to provide greater insight than hitherto into the nature and meaning of individual lives or groups of lives. Given that individual lives are part of a cultural network, information gained through biographical research will relate to an understanding of the wider society. The *specific* purpose of the research will be the analysis of a particular life or lives for some designated reason — for example in examining the world of work it may be appropriate to look at the biographical routes by which given individuals become teachers, nurses, prostitutes, librarians, actors, etc. Given the circumstances of the research enterprise such a piece of research may be small-scale or large-scale. What is at issue is not the scale of the research but the *purpose* for which it is required.

Although the methodological considerations that will be discussed in this chapter typically relate to the biographical examination of small populations requiring in-depth, qualitative modes of investigation what is *not* suggested here is that qualitative research is *de jure* superior to quantitative research. Well-judged quantitative research can yield useful results in situations where a qualitative approach would be simply a waste of time or be impossible to use (Erben, 1996). This said, the mode of disclosure characteristic of biographical research will be more textually replete than that conventionally representative of quantitative procedures. Thus, while numbers of respondents may be small in biographical research, the demands made upon the readers of the research involves a degree of vicarious participation not required in quantitative investigation. The validation of such research (in fact, of *any* research) is based upon the degree of consensus among those for whom the investigation is thought to be of interest and relevance. The descriptions, organization, conclusions and formulations represented in the research receive their validation by an experienced group of peers who regard the study as significant, worthwhile and in concert with its aims.

It is clear that one of the advantages of biographical research is that the variety that is the life of the subject will guide researchers against too rigid a view of methodology. As a number of methodologists have commented (e.g. Erickson, 1986; Woolcott, 1992) too concentrated a focus on research techniques can dull the understanding of the relationship between method and the purpose of the investigation.

The useful comment of Geertz's that, 'man is an animal suspended in webs of significance he himself has spun' indicates the reciprocal, constitutive nature of object
and subject (Geertz, 1973, p. 5). As such, the interpretive requirement is that the
complex life-accounts of research subjects be studied, described and appreciated
using as varied a repertoire of investigative approaches as would any cultural texts.

The purpose of this chapter is to introduce some of the points that will need to
be borne in mind when conducting biographical research. Although there is no concrete set of research methods for biographical research there is, nonetheless, a sufficiently integrated complex of approaches that most researchers will need to follow.
The chapter will be divided into three sections. Firstly, the 'Empirical Particularities
of Biographical Research' will enumerate and outline most of the procedures that
will be necessary in carrying out any biographical research, but special reference
will be made to the biographical investigation of small groups or samples. Secondly,
a justification and discussion of the importance of 'Imagination' as a methodological
tool in biographical research will be outlined. Thirdly, there will be a rehearsal of
the importance of the concept of 'Narrative' as an essential requirement for biographical research.

### Empirical particularities

Biographical method will involve the collection of documents from a wide variety of sources from a variety of media. These documents are, typically, likely to be
autobiographies, existing biographies, photographs, videos and films, oral histories,
official records, letters, diaries, postcards, family trees and information (sometimes
fragmentary) located in sources not primarily concerned with the subject. While
these 'life documents' (Denzin, 1989, p. 7) may take many forms, the collection of
contemporary biographical data through interview is one that is especially useful to
educational and other social science researchers.

What the size of such an interview sample should be will be dictated by the
purpose for which the research is being carried out. The exact size of any sample in
qualitative research cannot be ascertained through quantitative methods. It is for
this reason that it is all the more important that the consciously chosen sample
must correspond to the overall aims of the study. This position has now been well
rehearsed in some useful general discussion of qualitative research (e.g. Bogdan
and Biklan, 1982; Burgess, 1984; Glaser and Strauss, 1967). In the case of the biographical analysis of the occupational identity of teachers of a given subject specialism, for instance, informants selected will need to have considerable experience
of and be willing to assist in, the research process. It is therefore 'essential for the
researcher to discover who will be the most appropriate informant before beginning [detailed] interviews' (Morse, 1991, p. 129). The informants' knowledge of the
subject specialism will be the route by which the intricacies of a given occupational
identity will be explored. The characteristics of such selfhood are thus located in
the dialectic between the subject specialism and other features of the informants'
lives. It may be appropriate to use several subjects in such an investigation for

reasons of comparative analysis. However, a single case may be valid given that the respondent is sufficiently representative of a known cohort. Although no two teachers will be exactly alike it is unlikely that they will not echo common themes and concerns in relation to the given demands of an established curriculum (Jardine, 1992; Rampazi, 1996). The appropriate amount of data gained through interview will be determined *both* by respondents' feeling they have made all the observations they feel necessary *and* the researcher ceasing to observe novel cues. Saturation is unlikely to have occurred when only one of these criteria is met (Bertaux, 1981).

An outline of the points that the biographical researcher will need to consider may be represented diagrammatically (Figure 1.1). The diagram indicates a number of stages that any biographical research is likely to consider important in understanding subjects. The term Specific Events is used to describe those events (which may include thought-events) which can be said to provide the researcher with an initial purchase upon the research aims. The term Specific Events is related and embraces Denzin's term Epiphany, but does not necessarily need to be interactional, nor completely momentous (Denzin, 1989). Specific Events are times in a subject's life when they focus upon (reflectively or interactionally) a line of thought that relates to the aims of the research being carried out.

The first of the three columns on the right hand side of Figure 1.1 (Cultural System) refers to the necessity for locating the information gathered in points one to four to ambiences of changing values that are themselves constitutive of selfhood. The second column (Chronology) refers to the dates of important and influential *public* events that will have a shaping influence on the studied lives (e.g. National Service, the 11+, the Cuban Missile Crisis, the contraceptive pill). This column is a reminder that the cultural takes place in particular and identifiable historical time. The first and second columns together alert the researcher that as Lavagatto says, 'time, lived histories, political decisions, and people's habits create an accumulation of historical interventions and cultural usages' (Lambard, 1994, p. 4). The third column (Rehearsals) refers to the reconsideration and refining by the researcher of all the preceding data assembled in the four stages. The arrows between the stages are to indicate that any qualitative research diagram can only be a sensitizing device and that in reality discrete events (from the personal to the international) cannot, in terms of selfhood, be experienced either separately or abstractly. Differing parts of the schema will receive differing emphases dependent upon the nature of the particular research, but all areas will, to some extent, need to be addressed.

For research with a small sample, primarily employing interviews as an approach that deals separately with issues of class, gender, deviance, etc. may prove too categorical an approach for an understanding of the meaning brought to personal accounts. That these issues have influence is beyond question, but the way they may be said to go towards constituting a subject is certain to be myriad (Dilthey, 1961; Sartre, 1971). The biographical subject will always blur the boundaries between the abstract notion of a unique self and the abstract notion of a group identity. Far from being a methodological stumbling block there is here recognition that the self is constituted in the indissolubility of ego and sociality. This indissolubility will take a unique form for any given biographical subject. It is in the delineation of such

*Figure 1.1   Stages in biographical research*

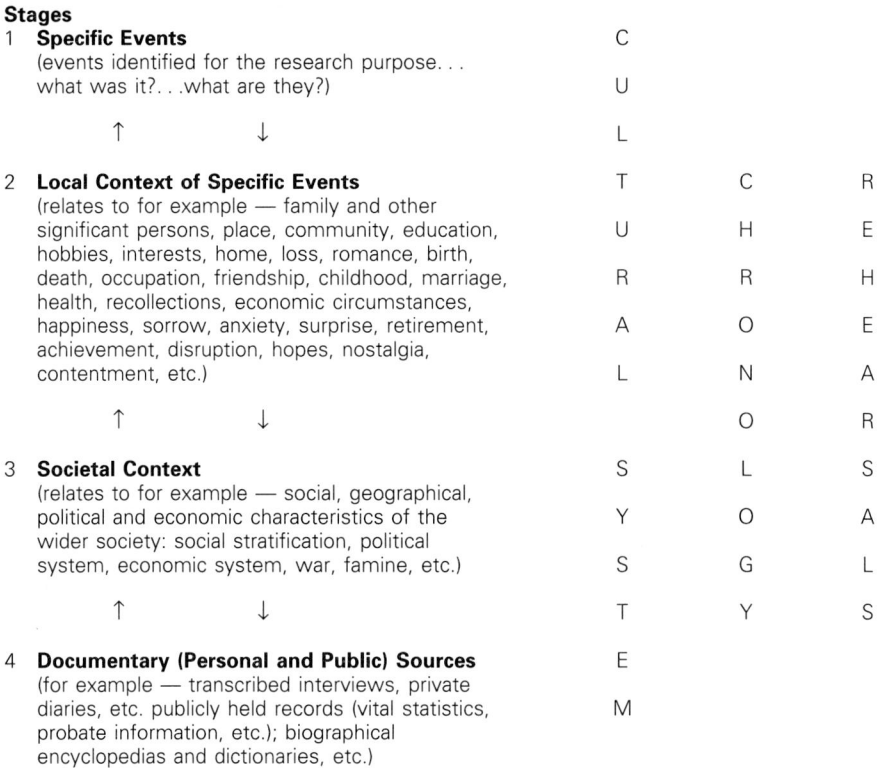

**Stages**

1  **Specific Events**
   (events identified for the research purpose. . .
   what was it?. . .what are they?)

   ↑          ↓

2  **Local Context of Specific Events**
   (relates to for example — family and other
   significant persons, place, community, education,
   hobbies, interests, home, loss, romance, birth,
   death, occupation, friendship, childhood, marriage,
   health, recollections, economic circumstances,
   happiness, sorrow, anxiety, surprise, retirement,
   achievement, disruption, hopes, nostalgia,
   contentment, etc.)

   ↑          ↓

3  **Societal Context**
   (relates to for example — social, geographical,
   political and economic characteristics of the
   wider society: social stratification, political
   system, economic system, war, famine, etc.)

   ↑          ↓

4  **Documentary (Personal and Public) Sources**
   (for example — transcribed interviews, private
   diaries, etc. publicly held records (vital statistics,
   probate information, etc.); biographical
   encyclopedias and dictionaries, etc.)

(Vertical labels at right of figure: **CULTURAL SYSTEM** | **CHRONOLOGY** | **REHEARSALS**)

forms that plausible depictions of individuals can be portrayed. However, what is not being suggested here is that thematic, analytical argument relating to established sociological categories is ultimately precluded. In the general discussion around, and consequent upon, the full data, these categories (social class, deviance, gender, etc.) will offer themselves for comment and interpretation. This can often be a pertinent result of biographical research, for as Ferraroti reminds us 'the effort to understand a biography in all its uniqueness [is also] an effort to interpret a social system' (1981, p. 22).

What may after some initial examination strike the researcher investigating — especially by interview — the biographies of individuals or small groups is that the distinction between hermeneutics (where the emphasis is on the exegetical interpretation of the data) and phenomenology (where the emphasis is on the establishment of subjects' meanings) will not hold. It is possibly useful to suggest a combination of a variety of hermeneutics (most readily identified with Gadamer and Ricoeur) and the sociological phenomenology most associated with Weber in the method of *Verstehen*. To prevent confusion this approach could be referred to as *verstehen hermeneutics* in order to highlight the fact that the explication of subjects' meanings are considered within a hermeneutical perspective. Thus, the information gained through phenomenological analysis is added to the other, accumulated biographical data to form the overall text for interpretation. The only ultimate safeguard of the validity of such a verstehen hermeneutics (along with many kinds of qualitative research) is, of course, good faith and recognizable methodological consistency. This is to say no more than that such a procedure operates in a manner common to most forms of sophisticated cultural evaluation. While hermeneutics has traditionally been employed in the areas of aesthetics and theology it can be used in biographical research to explore (via a broadening of its empirical range through phenomenology) the meanings of 'unremarkable' lives. The authenticity of any piece of biographical research will therefore have its interpretations judged in relation to its degree of internal analytical coherence, referential adequacy and instrumental pertinence.

The complexity of an individual's position in society should, not even for a modest research exercise, be simplified too much. The researcher must attempt to maintain the complexity of a life alongside the research aims. In recent times Sartre has done more than most biographical researchers to stress this point — both in terms of methodology and description — in his own extensive biographical work. Sartre employs the term *totalization*. The initial totalization is the researcher's current understanding of an act, phenomenon, event or *life*. This current totalization on further analysis will lose some of its validity and become absorbed into a second totalization and so on. Laing and Cooper summarize the process thus: a totalization 'is negated as an absolute, conserved as a relative, subsumed in a synthesis and so on' (Laing and Cooper, 1971, p. 13). The way to understand lives for Sartre is through these successive acts of totalization. This point is related to the earlier method provided in the diagram of research procedure (Figure 1.1).

In his work on Flaubert, Sartre attempts to show the process of successive totalizations in order to demonstrate to his reader his methodological procedure while simultaneously attempting biographical description. He attempts to individualize social analysis while employing the seemingly supra-individual methods of the Hegelian dialectic and Marxist materialism. In so doing he uncovers in these methods a deficiency — they have no compass to explain the variety of convoluted ways in which proximate individual lives are both similar and dissimilar, they have no hierarchy of mediations. As Sartre observes: while Valéry was unquestionably a petit-bourgeois intellectual not every petit-bourgeois intellectual was Valéry. In other words, socio-economic features *are* inescapable and causal but *so to* are specific inter-subjective socializing relations.

Biographical investigation must involve the continual examination of the interplay of family, primary group, community and socio-economic forces. To explore one without the others is to impoverish interpretation. Nonetheless, it is legitimate to *accent* or *stress* a single feature rather than another to uncover a particular *route* into a life. Deciding upon the appropriateness of which features to accent or stress among those composing the nexus of social structure and individual identity is at the methodological heart of biographical analysis,

> for a man is never an individual; it would be more fitting to call him a *singular universal*; having been totalized and therefore universalized, by his epoch, he

retotalizes his epoch by reproducing himself into it as a singularity. He is thus at once universal by way of the singular universality of human history, and singular through the universalizing singularity of his projects — he requires to be studied from both perspectives simultaneously. (Sartre, 1971, p. 7–8) [our translation]

As such, while the researcher must contextualize lives within economic conditions, they must also seek to comprehend their specificity. There are too many random features (some of them pre-linguistic) in human upbringing and socialization for particularity not to be characteristic of selves: economic circumstance and genetic predisposition will only ever be part determinants of individual identity. What Sartre calls the internal colouration of individual expectation will always be unique. The interview text is of particular interest to the biographical researcher because it is a specific kind of evidence. In itself it is an objectification of the subject, but has its roots in the life of the subject and it illuminates the life of the subject. However, the context of the subject and information from the subject need to be permanently cross-referenced, but cross-referenced with an objective — that objective being the purpose of the research, without which investigations would remain amorphous and pointless. In such cross-referencing — in relating context to, for example, interview material there may be observed tensions between individual aspirations and conditioning circumstances — these tensions are likely to be a useful source of data for the researcher to offer a commentary upon.

It may be observed that biographical researchers should be aware that there is a far greater similarity between existentialist research procedures and grounded theory approaches than is usually observed. Many of the positions advanced by Sartre can be allied to the qualitative methodology first proposed by Glaser and Strauss (1967). In fact if biographical researchers go even further back they will notice in relation to the study of lives echoes, commonalities and affinities between the work of the early Chicago School (particularly as represented by Cooley), the movement of European phenomenology first propounded by Husserl and the school of biographical hermeneutics inaugurated by Dilthey. One of the virtues of biographical research is that it is possibly more able than some other areas to make manifest the methodological connections between research approaches that have sometimes seemed to have little in common. While, in keeping with earlier comments, a standard research method for biographical investigation cannot be proposed it can nevertheless be suggested, *especially in relation to research involving the in-depth study of small populations*, that a combination of verstehen hermeneutics and grounded theory suggests itself as a highly fruitful research procedure.

## Imagination

The majority of time spent in presenting qualitative research is not used in replicating data but in its interpretation. To perform this interpretation the researcher is required to employ imagination by which we mean the *ability* of mind to speculate upon and to link and assemble ideas related to the research text. Imagination is, here, stimulated into action by the research text — be that text; written, visual, numerical, audial, tactile or some combination of these things. Imagination is the vehicle the researcher employs to aid recognition of significant moments in the data, to relate these to each other and to the overall lives of the subjects under study. In other words imagination very often both fills the gaps within, and develops an architecture for, the research data. At all points, however, the researcher is required to fix imagination in empirical sources — it cannot be allowed free reign and take unwarranted liberties with the lives of subjects. The fact that biographical research findings are imaginative constructions does not mean that they need to be fictitious.

It is unfortunate that the employment of imagination has been played down or ignored in works on social science method. This is a profound mistake because it lies at the centre of qualitative interpretation and is so implicated in epistemology as to be of its essence: 'without it', says Kant 'we have no knowledge whatsoever' (Kant, 1963, p. 103). Mary Warnock declares that 'one must recognise the universality of the imaginative function both in that it belongs to everyone and in that it is exercised by each over all his experience' (Warnock, 1976, p. 202). Similarly, as Hume makes clear, the power of the mind to employ imagination is a necessary, gestalt requirement in apprehending the features of the objective world. Imagination according to Hume can supply the connectedness between observations and features in the world (in this case the research text) that it would be impossible to prove by reason alone:

> Reason can never show us the connection of one object with another. . .When the mind, therefore, passes from the idea or impression of one object to the idea or belief of another, it is not determined by reason, but by certain principles, which associate together the ideas of these objects, and unite them in the *imagination*. [our emphasis] (Hume, 1978, p. 92)

This point forcibly made by Hume in giving imagination primacy in the understanding of others *overrides* for him in all practical matters his own philosophy of empirical knowledge. He argues as far as the self is concerned that there is no rational justification for the assumption that we have a personal identity. However, he also argues, most importantly, that such a philosophical position can only remain a philosophical position because, *in fact*, persons believe that they do have individual identity — i.e. selves. Further, he argues that we cannot live with ourselves, or each other but by having a conception of our selves and the selves of others. Our concept of our self is so powerful and permanent says Hume ('the liveliest impression imaginable') that through it we are able, when given cues, to imagine the lives, sentiments and selves of others (Hume, 1978, p. 317). Hume refers to this ability as *sympathy*, which he argues is the necessary origin of all human relationships.

It is clear that Hume in using the term sympathy means the reconstructive imagination. He argues that,

> no quality of human nature is more remarkable, both in itself and in its consequences, than that propensity we have to sympathize with others, and to receive by communication their inclinations and sentiments, however different from or even contrary to our own. (Hume, 1978, p. 316)

Hume's argument proposes more than an ability to comprehend the feelings of others, it is rather an acknowledgment that a dialectic is set up between our subject and ourselves and that this dialectic deepens and becomes more informative (richer in data) the more purposefully we carry through the aim of our research. This in turn allows the imagination of the researcher to draw conclusions from data that are neither given directly in the data nor arrived at through numerical reasoning — in other words such conclusions are provided by imagination. For Hume this imaginative realm is at its most informative when it is contained and controlled by an empirical referent, by being concerned with an examination of 'common life' (Hume, 1893, p. 162). For the biographical researcher even though the world of the subject may be different from their own there will be sufficient pointers to establish similarity and dissimilarity, and consequently appropriate adjustments to research method can be made and discussed. The importance of using imagination to formally comprehend the meanings of others and to organize that comprehension into a social scientific interpretation of the studied subject goes back to Vico. It was Vico who first called for a qualitative research enterprise where empirical evidence needed the indispensable and crucial accompaniment of imagination. This type of knowledge, claims Vico, is yielded by 'entering into the mental life of other cultures, into a variety of outlooks and *ways of life* which only the imagination makes possible' [our emphasis] (Berlin, 1976, p. xix). With recourse only to positivist techniques for analyzing empirical evidence there is no relaying by researchers of subjects' intellect and feeling combined (Berlin, 1990).

Given the complexity of lives it is all the more important that imagination is employed in the interpretation of such sociological data. In examining the texts of our subjects (be they transcribed interviews, tape recordings, diaries, or similar) the researcher is in a sense contracted to join what we may call an aestheticoimaginative pact. In writing up accounts of lives in terms of imaginative fidelity the researcher is employing methods akin to aesthetic reasoning: the category of the aesthetic becomes a resource through which the research texts disclose the feelings and meanings of subjects. Kant in the *Critique of Judgment* distinguishes between *determining judgment* (based on logical, general rules) and *relative judgment* (based on rules developed from specified particulars). This latter, reflective judgment, requires the same processes as aesthetic apprehension and can 'give rise to new rules by generating new forms of synthesis' (Bowie, 1997, p. 112). For Hume, imaginative fidelity is at the heart of reason itself. To paraphrase him we may say that when we contemplate a biographical research text the vividness and intensity that we may note within it gains such concentration from the purpose of the research and the refining mechanisms we employ to make it aesthetico-imaginatively comprehensible (Hume, 1978). By having a purpose in analysing the research text the researcher sufficiently charges it with meaning to allow analysis. The protocols needed to prevent this imaginative engagement from slipping its explanatory anchor and becoming just fantasy must be its relation to the certainty of the empirical — namely the fact that our subjects exist.

As researchers deliberate upon the life-accounts that is their data they sometimes share a method of analysis similar to that employed by literary analysis (sympathy, speculation and critical distance) in the understanding of fictional lives (Lamarque and Olsen, 1994). The fact that our research data do not necessarily form a neat, completed, unfragmented unit is entirely acceptable, just as it would be in the accounts of selves represented by a Hamlet, an Ophelia, a Lady Dedlock or a Molly Bloom. Thus manifold explanations both by single researchers or a number of researchers examining the same data are acceptable provided that the purpose of the research is central, and that data are judged through *general analytical coherence, internal referential adequacy* and *instrumental utility* (Waller, 1970). In recognizing that the aesthetico-imaginative as a mode of analysis has concerned itself with areas of investigation not open to the evaluative procedures of formal logic the specific strength of the category becomes clear: it can discuss texts in terms of their self-referring features having relation to issues beyond the texts other than by a quantitative link, but by the veracity of it being known that such matters have had, and are likely to have, general significance. We would not wish to argue that examining research texts is primarily a matter of aesthetic judgment — but rather that something of the aesthetic is involved in the imaginative recreation of the quotidian. This conclusion goes some way to address a gap in the qualitative literature concerning the connection between highly focused, small-scale data and wider social issues. Additionally, as Ricoeur argues, *it is not a problem* that the lives we study and examine should remain ambiguous, mysterious, discordant and confused. It is in recognizing this situation in our subjects and in ourselves, says Ricoeur, that we admit an aestheticized and deepened appreciation of the unknowable (Ricoeur, 1988). The researcher in an attempt to approximate the lives of others makes that which can never be fully understood part of a comprehensible mode of enquiry.

It is the case that imaginative reflection upon the research text and beyond form a necessary part of qualitative analysis. However, the data should not be endlessly analysed because a formal, research project must have time-specified limits. It will often be the case that more can be said, but this is as true of quantitative research as of qualitative work. Just as with basic data collection, if the amount of imaginative speculation required strays well beyond the objectives of the research, then the research has been inadequately designed. It is legitimate when imagining what it would be like to be somebody else, or imaginatively constructing a collage of their reflections, attitudes and life-events to set limitations upon how far such research should go. As has been argued earlier, biographical research data do not claim, or seek the impossibility of the exact replication of a life, the requirement is that the research refer to lives in such a way as to illuminate them in relation to a research objective.

## Narrative

It has been argued that the formal particularities of analysis and imaginative engagement are necessary features of biographical research. However, both of these, importantly, can only be employed in relation to the recognition that lives are lived through time and are made intelligible by being composed of narratives. This may at first seem obvious until it is recognized that in attempting to understand the doings of selves narrative has been largely ignored by both social science and philosophy. In social science lives have often been segmented to such a degree that the overall, narrative life has quite simply dissolved (MacIntyre, 1985). Similarly, in philosophy, meanings derived from the conceptualization of actions have more often than not been divorced from the chronological settings in which they occurred (MacIntyre, 1985; Ricoeur, 1992). For biographical research, time and its passage must be seen as *the* inescapable feature of human life. The fact that lived time is finite and that our subjects (and we ourselves) have been born and will die is the backdrop against which all life is lived. In short, *a life that is studied is the study of a life in time*. Further, human beings have a sense of time as an essential part of their mental constitution: persons cannot be cognizant without a sense of occurrences preceding the present or a sense that occurrences will follow what is immediate. Such temporal awareness — accounts of happenings in time — is, as Mink remarks, 'a primary and irreducible form of human comprehension' (Mitchell, 1981, p. 252). In short, human identity is narrational, lives being composed of the narratives by which time is experienced.

These narratives (whether past, present or future) are the cohering mechanisms that make up comprehensible human experience. As such narrative analysis, more intricately than any other method, is able to weave social context and individual life together. It is the surest method of avoiding swamping the personal or subjectivizing the social. This does not mean that the findings of an analysis will be a perfectly replicated life but rather that the project is a serious matter, involving detailed empirical findings, imaginative reconstruction, a sense of history, observations upon morality and the exegesis of everyday existence. Additionally, these features constantly remind the researcher that they themselves are in a sequence of predecessors, contemporaries and successors: that their temporary existence is inexplicable (both institutionally and personally) without a connection (material, cultural and ideological) with their predecessors, and that, once they are dead, so it will be for their institutional and personal successors. If this is true of the researcher it is true, too, of the researched subject and as such deepens the biographical research enterprise.

The philosopher who has done most to stress the importance of narrative for the understandings of lives is, as has been indicated, Paul Ricoeur. Ricoeur is particularly significant for biographical research because he offers, through the concept of narrative, a resolution to a problem central to sociology and social psychology — namely where does individual volition end and societal influence begin. Ricoeur's answer is that both are joined, indissolubly, in the narrative characteristics of human identity and that to attempt their separation is to do methodological and symbolic violence to the understanding of lives. The main formulation of Ricoeur's is that time is 'the structure of existence that reaches language in narrativity' and that narrativity is 'the language structure that has time as its ultimate referent' (Ricoeur, 1980, p. 169). In other words Ricoeur is saying that time is the universal, defining architecture of human existence and that it may only be made comprehensible in terms of narratives. Given that these narratives are inseparably composed of individual volition and social context the research will 'find' the researched life in a conflation of subjectivities and social structure.

Ricoeur characterizes the accounts people provide for themselves of their own lives as emplotment (*mise en intrique*). That is, individuals create plots for themselves out of occurrences in their own lives in order to manage the process of living: they configure a series of events, a chronicle, into the storied nature of selfhood. As such they select from a bewildering array of actions and events those that can compose a sustainable narrative of themselves. In Hayden White's words, to emplot is to, 'effect a mediation between events. . .and the human experiences of temporality' (White, 1991, p. 144). It is these acts of emplotment and the consequent plots that the researcher must engage with. The researcher, in effect, is required to devise a plot to communicate with the plot of the subject. Researchers' plots will no doubt be constructed of individual reasoning, personal interest and employ 'the techniques of analysis developed by the social sciences of their own time to identify the social forces at work in the [subject's] milieu' (White, 1991, p. 145). The researcher, it can be said, redescribes through emplotment the plots of the subject. Biographical research, therefore, regards accounts of lives as allegories of temporality — allegories grounded in empirical fact and employing imaginative reconstruction. It is a palimpsestic process in which the researcher reconfigures the texts of others in terms of a research goal, the authenticity for which is judged by the protocols (scientific or imaginative) sanctioned by the research community.

The biographical researcher is adding to the study of groups a sociology of the individual. The formulation, 'a sociology of the individual' may seem tautologous but as Wilhelm Dilthey early observed, socio-historical reality can be captured and interpreted through an account of that highly singular and complex repository of the cultural — the single person. There have been many instances over the years in the sociology of education in which social divisions and their influences have been theorized, researched, presented and commented upon (e.g. Halsey *et al.* eds (1961 and 1997)). There is, for example, a good deal of evidence that children of lower working-class homes perform less well at school than children from comfortable upper middle-class homes. This we can say is a finding from empirical, quantitative investigation. The complementary results of biographical research will refer to what is unavailable in the quantitative research — that is, how individuals experience the objectively structuring, empirically observable features that place them historically where they are. The experience found in such narratives is likely to be complex. There will be some similarity between subjects, nonetheless, it will be noticeable that no two narratives will be the same. However, this individuality, far from being atomistic allows us to deepen our knowledge of the surrounding social context. The matter is then one of complexity rather than simplicity and the nature of the complexity is 'found in the lack of separation between the inner and the outer, between the interiority of selfhood and the social determination of selfhood' (Erben, 1996, p. 168). The resultant character of this world is expressed in the actions and thoughts through which subjects construct their lives — both within themselves and interactively. As Macmurray points out, not only is the biographical subject a performer of its own thoughts and actions but, further, that such performances constitute the process that make thoughts and actions *per se* possible.

> The Self [the performer of thoughts and actions] is a term whose function is to represent the subject as the object of thought. It is at once a singular and a general term. As singular, it is the unitary centre of all possible experience. At the same time it is a general term [and] becomes the name of something we all possess in common. The Self is constituted by its relation to the Other; that is it has its being in its relationship; [but] this relationship is necessarily personal. (Macmurray, 1991, p. 17–19)

Additional, highly influential echo, of the work on biographical identity represented by Ricoeur and Macmurray is found in the work of Alasdair MacIntrye. In his highly influential treatise in moral philosophy, *After Virtue* MacIntyre devotes a chapter relating narrative to biographical identity and moral purpose (MacIntyre, 1985). This work serves as a further justification for the practice of biographical method. Like Ricoeur, MacIntyre argues for a concept of selfhood the 'unity of which resides in the unity of narrative that links birth to life and to death' and, further, that 'narrative history of a certain kind turns out to be the basic and essential genre for the characterization of human actions' (MacIntyre, 1985, pp. 222 and 208). For the biographical researcher the axiom provided by MacIntyre is that the subject, the individual life, emerges in the dual nature of its distinctiveness (that is person A will never be person B) and its connectedness (person A can 'recognize' the narrative of person B).

It is the case that if an examined life is no longer composed of some form of recognizable narrative it is literally, not possible to be understood. As MacIntyre says, at such points those who are seeking to understand a particular life become 'both intellectually and practically baffled [because] the distinction between the humanly accountable and the merely natural has broken down' (1985, p. 209). Such a position of total estrangement can be observed in some varieties of mental illness, and may be seen in encounters with 'alien cultures or even other social structures within our own culture' (MacIntyre, 1985, p. 120). Although it is likely that the researcher will most frequently choose research subjects who evidence certain kinks of recognizable narratives it is still, nonetheless, the case as MacIntyre indicates that they, like us, are constrained by social circumstance: 'We enter upon a stage we did not design and we find ourselves part of an action that was not of our making' (MacIntyre, 1985, p. 213). The fact that we, and our subject, are constituted as story telling creatures is not, of itself, any guarantee that such stories will be harmonious. MacIntyre reminds the researcher forcibly that while narratives are always conceptually teleological they are also, as lived out in lives, often accompanied by empirical unpredictability. And yet this unpredictability can still, generally, allow both the interpreter and interpreted to share some recognition of fundamental narrational similarity, whether it be related to the mundane and instrumental or the momentous and highly emotional. It is to emphasize this point that MacIntyre quotes Barbara Hardy thus, 'we dream in narrative, day-dream in narrative, remember, anticipate, hope, despair, believe, doubt, plan, revise, criticize, construct, gossip, learn and love by narrative' (Hardy, 1968, p. 5).

*Michael Erben*

It is now clear that in biographical research a variety of techniques garnered from the various disciplines of the social sciences and humanities may be used to look at those complex events called lives. Ricoeur stresses the importance of always subverting the deification of any single disciplinary method with those of other disciplines. The researcher in biographical studies in calling upon a wide range of analytical perspectives is likely, in studying selves, to be constantly reminded that they are not in a closed circle of interpretation. Further, biographical research in not attempting a forensic separation of social structure from subjectivity discloses the researched life or lives as coming about as a network of meanings (emerging from a collage of beliefs, behavioural practices and documentary records) the interpretation of which the researcher is advantageously and ethically implicated within. It is by researchers specifying their research *purpose* and the *scope* of their research that they will find appropriate methods suggesting themselves. This will be so whether the entire research text is a paragraph of interview transcription or a systematic, large-scale survey. No matter what the range of the data and no matter which shade of interpretation the researcher wishes to accent or develop they will nonetheless need to employ, to varying degrees, empirical information, imaginative reconstruction and narrative analysis.

### References

BERLIN, I. (SIR) (1976) *Vico and Herder*, London: Hogarth.

BERLIN, I. (SIR) (1990) 'Giambattista Vico and cultural history', in BERLIN, I. *The Crooked Timber of Humanity*, London: John Murray.

BERTAUX, D. (1981) 'From the life-history approach to the transformation of sociological practice', in BERTAUX, D. (ed.) *Biography and Society*, Beverly Hills: Sage.

BOGDAN, R.C. and BILKEN, S.K. (1982) *Qualitative Research for Education*, Boston: Allyn and Bacon.

BOWIE, A. (1997) *From Romanticism to Critical Theory: The Philosophy of German Literary Theory*, London: Routledge.

BURGESS, R.G. (1984) *In the Field: An Introduction to Field Research*, London: Allen and Unwin.

DENZIN, N.K. (1989) *Interpretive Biography*, Newbury Park: Sage.

DILTHEY, W. (1961) *Meaning in History*, London: Allen and Unwin.

ERBEN, M. (1996) 'A preliminary prosopography of the Victorian street', *Auto/Biography*, **4**, 2/3, pp. 53–68.

ERICKSON, F. (1986) 'Qualitative methods', in WHITTROCK, M.C. (ed.) *Handbook of Research on Teaching*, 3rd Ed. New York: Macmillan.

FERRAROTI, A. (1981) 'On Biography' in BERTAUX, D. (ed.) *Biography and Society*, Beverly Hills; CA: Sage.

GEERTZ, C. (1973) *The Interpretation of Cultures*, New York: Basic Books.

GLASER, B.G. and STRAUSS, A.L. (1967) *The Discovery of Grounded Theory: Strategies for Qualitative Research*, Chicago, Aldine.

HALSEY, A.H., FLOUD, J. and ANDERSON, A. (eds) (1961) *Education, Economy and Society*, New York: Free Press.

HALSEY, A.H. and KARABEL, J. (eds) (1997) *Education, Culture, Economy and Society*, Oxford: Oxford University Press.

HARDY, B. (1968) 'Towards a poetics of fiction: An approach through narrative', *Novel*, **2**, 1, pp. 5–14.

HUME, D. (1893) *Enquiry Concerning Human Understanding*, Oxford: Oxford University Press.

HUME, D. (1978) *A Treatise of Human Nature*, 2nd Ed. Oxford: Clarendon Press.

JARDINE, D.W. (1992) 'The fecundity of the individual case', *Journal of Philosophy of Education*, **26**, 1, pp. 51–61.

KANT, I. (1963) *Critique of Judgement*, Oxford: Oxford University Press.

LAING, R.D. and COOPER, D. (1971) *Reason and Violence*, London: Tavistock.

MACINTYRE, A. (1985) *After Virtue*, 2nd edn., London: Duckworth.

MACMURRAY, J. (1991) *The Self as Agent*, New Jersey: Humanities Press.

LAMARQUE, P. and OLSEN, S.H. (1994) *Truth, Fiction and Literature: A Philosophical Perspective*, Oxford: Clarendon Press.

LAMBARD, P. (1994) 'An interview with Stephano Lavagatto', *Critical Quarterly*, **36**, 4, p. 4.

MITCHELL, W.J.T. (ed.) (1981) *On Narrative*, Chicago: Chicago University Press.

MOI, T. (1994) *Simone de Beauvoir*, Oxford: Blackwell.

MORSE, J. (ed.) (1991) *Qualitative Nursing Research: A Contemporary Dialogue*, Newbury Park: Sage.

RAMPAZI, M. (1996) 'Insegnore la nostra persona ad altri', *Adultita (Il metodo autobiografico)*, **4**, pp. 53–62.

RICOEUR, P. (1980) 'Narrative time', *Critical Enquiry*, **7**, 1, pp. 160–180.

RICOEUR, P. (1988) *Time and Narrative*, Vol. 3, Chicago: Chicago University Press.

RICOEUR, P. (1992) *Oneself as Another*, Chicago: Chicago University Press.

SARTRE, J.P. (1971) *L'Idiot de la famille: Gustave Flaubert de 1821 à 1857*, Paris: Gallimard.

WHITE, H. (1991) 'The metaphysics of narrativity' in WOOD, D. (ed.) *Paul Ricoeur*, London: Routledge.

WALLER, W.W. (1970) *On the Family, Education and War*, Chicago: Chicago University Press.

WARNOCK, M. (1976) *Imagination*, London: Faber and Faber.

WOOLCOTT, H.F. (1992) 'Posturing in qualitative inquiry', in LECOMPT, M.D. *et al.* (eds) *The Handbook of Qualitative Research in Education*, New York: Academic Press.

# 2 The Story of the Self: Education, Experience and Autobiography

*Robin Usher*

A life lived is what actually happens. A life as experienced consists of the images, feelings, sentiments, desires, thoughts, and meanings known to the person whose life it is. . .a life as told, a life history, is a narrative, influenced by the cultural conventions of telling, by the audience, and by the social context. (Bruner, 1984, p. 7)

Experience is always a matter of historicity and discourse. (McLaren, 1994, p. 195)

'Experience' figures as a key concept in educational theorizing, practice and research. Although constituted with many different significations, the common thread is a set of powerful assumptions that the experiences of the self are a source of knowledge and a valuable pedagogic resource which can be harnessed to learning, personal development and the liberatory giving of 'voice'. In this chapter, I am seeking not so much to directly critique these assumptions but rather to consider the pedagogical appropriation of autobiography by an educational discourse of experience. Whilst this provides much potential for the pedagogic enterprise, I should also want to argue that it rests on an overly simplified conception of the structure and effects of autobiography. My argument will be that autobiography is being understood and used in a way that is limited, with little potential for a critical thrust, and which itself is based on a particular way of understanding the educative characteristics of experience, a way that removes its location in history, discourse and power.

## The present self: Two stories of autobiography

. . .there is no clear window into the inner life of a person, for any window is always filtered through the glaze of language, signs and the process of signification [which] in both its written and spoken forms is always inherently unstable, in flux, and made up of the traces of other signs and symbolic statements. (Denzin, 1989, p. 14)

The autobiographical approach has now achieved considerable prominence both pedagogically and in educational research. It has been deployed in both adaptationist and transformative pedagogical practices. It seems to be ideally suited to revealing experience-based learning and in tracking the development of the self as learner. However, it is a deployment with many problematic elements since autobiography as a textual practice of self-representation is actually much more complex in its message and equivocal in its effects than educational discourse takes it to be. Critical questions are raised about education's modernist assumptions concerning the self, experience and the developmental process — what I will call the 'story of the self'.

Autobiography is a special kind of representational practice; a representation of the self through inscription, telling the story of the self through a written text and writing a text through a culturally encoded meta-story. For the purposes of this chapter, I want to highlight how a particularly dominant kind of autobiography works through a metaphysics of presence (Derrida, 1976). Here, the autobiographical process is conceived as a recounting of a fixed, unmediated and preserved, summonable past (the past as presence) by a self conceived as an independently existing person giving meaning to its experience, a meaning which is present (the self as presence) — both the past and the self being representable and knowable and communicated directly and transparently. Autobiography is thus conceived as a practice that must assume a *centred time* and a *centred self*.

Telling the story of the self, as autobiography does, always assumes a certain kind of subject — what I shall call the 'self of the story'. Autobiography itself has more than one story to tell about itself although the most common form tends to be a humanistic story in which the self is invested as a sovereign, unified, rational subject — the source of knowledge and representation. It is a subject enveloped in a story of mastery telling a masterful story — of the problems of life overcome, of the progressive accumulation of knowledge and of self-realization. Through autobiography, subjects make themselves an object of examination, understanding life through modernist notions of ego development, self-assertion and individual accomplishment. In this story, meaning is there, or perhaps more accurately 'in here', waiting to be discovered, unveiled in the telling of the story. The self of the story is embarked on a progressively unfolding journey to discover the unity of the 'real me', the essential self. There is an assumption that the meaning of experiences (the meeting, confronting, passing through and making sense of the events of a life) are transparent, masterable and univocal.

The assumption that a life can be captured and represented in a text 'as it really is and was' has been increasingly questioned and it is now becoming fairly generally accepted that an autobiography is not immediately referential of a life but is instead a work of artifice or fabrication that involves a re-constructing or 'presentation' (rather than a representation) of the self through the process of textual inscription. In the post-structuralist story of autobiography, the subject's mastery of self-construction is questioned. The central character of this story is language and more particularly writing and the production of text. Since, it is argued, language is not simply referential, subjects can only represent themselves in language by creating a 'literary' rather than a 'literal' figure that dis-figures or de-faces as much as it figures (Buss, 1993). Instead of autobiography being a unified representation where an identity is present and fixed prior to language, identity is constituted by the 'play' of language. Autobiography therefore does not record the life and capture the essence of a 'real' subject that exists independently of its textual inscription through autobiography. The subject of the autobiography exists or comes into being *because* of the act of inscription. Furthermore, the fixed and certain self apparently captured by autobiography could be said to be illusory in the sense that changing and shifting identity is only 'fixed' and anchored by this act and even then only temporarily. Language cannot transparently reveal an essential and unified subject. The inscribed subject, historically situated and positioned in multiple and contradictory discourses that shape experience, is an 'I' placed in the world in positions made possible by language. Discourses and positioning shape what and how we experience the world and the humanistic, essentialist view of the self masks the way in which we are constituted in language and positioned differently depending on the discursive practices of gender, race, class, ethnicity and other marks of difference.

Rather than life being represented in a text, it is itself conceived as a social text, a fictional narrative production. Thus how it is produced, the processes of textual production, becomes critical since form and content are not independent of each other but mutually determining (Denzin, 1989). For example, to tell the story of the self in terms of a journey of discovery is not simply to reflect (on) and accurately depict the literal journey of a life and by so doing reveal its meanings but rather to tell a story through a particular kind of modernist discourse, a culturally encoded meta-story. This provides a structure and a set of pre-defined meanings in the form for example, of certain metaphors (the 'journey'), from which the story is constructed and a life thereby emplotted and 'presented'. It is therefore to tell a story which has its justification, its point, its interpretive meaning, in terms of what Lyotard (1984) calls the 'grand narratives', foremost among these being the narrative of human progress. An individual autobiography is then a microcosmic reflection of this big universal story. Thus, as Smith (1988, p. 105) points out — 'autobiography becomes a privileged form of ideological text where the demand that we should consist of coherent and recognizable subjects in relation to a particular knowledge is rationalized'.

In the post-structuralist autobiography the self who writes is not seen as having an unproblematic access to the past but recovers it in re-presented traces and hints. The past is not 'thing-like' and representable as such (past as presence). Both the self and past are constructed and reconstructed rather than being a mimetic representation of entities prior to writing, pre-given and unmediated. Autobiography here therefore involves not only recalling the past but recreating it — and through this re-creation, discovering and re-inventing the self. Thus both are *decentred* — in other words, in this kind of autobiography neither is 'present'. The meaning of the self and of the past are not recoverable in their original, unmediated form — or at least, not as one essential, authentic meaning, even if they ever existed in this form.

The post-structuralist story of autobiography thus poses a set of difficult questions. Is discontinuity rather than continuity of the self more the norm? Are the meanings of a self and its past totalizable and fixed or rather partial, contingent and forever slipping away? Is the self fully in control of events and experience? Is the self always transparent to itself or very often opaque, perhaps even 'unreadable'? Is there a 'core' unchanging self or rather is identity shifting and fragmented? Whilst there are no neat answers to these questions, one thing it is possible to say is that in actuality, autobiographies do not stand at either end of the two extremes posited by these two very different stories. Any autobiography has both humanistic and post-structuralist elements. As a site of interplay between the humanistic vision of autonomous egos and postmodernist decentred selves, actual autobiographies stand at the intersection of the individual and the social, of agency and culture.

At the same time, autobiographies do very often read as if they were simply referential of a life, true representations of a prior self where the past can and does appear fixed, discrete and entire to the mind in the life as told. In other words, an autobiography predominantly *reads* as if it is an account of a centred past by a centred self. In autobiography's dominant humanistic discourse it is the authorial and authoritative voice — the voice that tells it 'as it is and was' — which is privileged, re-presenting the past in its unmediated truth and presenting the self in its full, unmediated authenticity. At the same time, looked at from the other side, autobiographies not only have authors but readers also, who themselves have culturally-encoded pre-understandings and expectations. Autobiographies tend to be read through the need for a 'human' presence in the writing, a need to locate the person 'behind' the text. Once discovered, this presence seems to guarantee both the sincerity and the authenticity of the self of the story. Here, therefore, the autobiographical narrative works in such a way as to make the self essential and its representation 'natural'.

As Graham (1993) points out when markers of an authentic presence are absent, texts appear detached and 'unreal'. He argues however, and in my view rightly, that this very sense of spontaneity, 'reality' or human identity is itself partly a matter of textual production, of how the story of the self is *told* through narrative, plot and character development in such a way that selves become protagonists in their own story and therefore 'real', authentic subjects. It is the very textuality of autobiography, that it is not simply a life as experienced but a life understood and re-presented in a text, that foregrounds 'presence' and thereby *conceals* textuality. Thus although autobiography is always writing in a narrow sense, it actually works like speech in guaranteeing the authenticity of a human presence. Being phonocentric in this way, it is caught in the metaphysics of presence. Autobiography therefore is a literary form which appears to work in a way other than the literary.

But as a literary form autobiography is a genre possessing ideological power and serving a political function. In a culture promoting individualization and empirical knowledge, the inscribed 'I' who functions as a speaking human 'I' has an important validating task. But as I have already hinted, readers are needed with the competence to understand and interpret the significance of genres and literary conventions. The autobiographical text is in an important sense an artefact of Western culture which requires and indeed assumes readers and interpreters who know the meta-narratives and discourses of that culture — who, in other words, are familiar with a particular self of the story and can identify with it. The story of the self is thus bound by 'discourse structures that place limits on both expression and understanding' (Hatch and Wisniewski, 1997, p. 130), constructed, or at the very least mediated, and understood, through socio-cultural interpretive traditions and rhetorical/linguistic practices.

## Decentring time

> For meaningfulness and understanding, stories rely on people's presumption that
> time has a unilinear direction moving from past to present to future. (Polkinghorne,
> 1997, p. 8)

The notion of the decentred self as introduced by post-structuralist writers is now
generally accepted as a significant critique of humanistic narratives of the self. The
notion of decentred time would not however have such wide acceptance. Nonetheless, for my purpose it is a key ingredient in my argument about the need to challenge the pedagogical appropriation of autobiography in the context of a humanistic
account of experience.

The more ready acceptance of time as centred lies in our conventional understanding of time as a flow or succession of 'now' moments, an understanding powerfully shaped by the model of clock time which makes time objective and capable of
measurement. The consequence of this powerful model is that it becomes difficult
to understand *lived* time. The succession model constructs the past as the 'has been'
and the future as the 'yet to be'. Lived time which involves the interfolding of all
three temporal moments of past, present and future cannot then be accommodated.
Heidegger (1962) argues that this is an example of wrongly emphasizing presence
— of understanding human existence or being only in the temporal mode of the
present. The future then becomes a time which is not yet but will come into being
and the past becomes a time, which already having been, has no existence.

Getting away from this model involves recognizing that being depends on all
three moments of temporality where the structure of lived time necessarily involves
their simultaneity — the past and the future are always present. Equally, the present
is never fully 'present' because it encompasses both past experiences and future
possibilities. Being, therefore, is absence as well as presence — what is not now
present as well as what is. We live in time, in the flow of historical time, in the
seemingly unending linear flow of befores and afters but we exist as temporalizing
beings living in the interpenetration of the now and the not-now. Thus Heidegger
argues that human existence is temporal and human beings are embodied time.
Time is neither a 'something' nor something that human beings simply appropriate
into themselves.

Once we start thinking of lived time instead of clock time we can then no
longer understand the past as an object, absolutely separated from the present and
the future. The idea of the past as presence, of seeing the past in terms of itself, is as
we have noted, a common assumption in autobiography. Yet following Heidegger's
argument, the notion of the past-as-in-itself to be recalled contradicts the way the
past is understood in lived time. How we understand ourselves is not just a matter
of here and now present understandings of the past but a product of how we understood ourselves in the past and our anticipation of future possibilities, how we will
be in the future. We can never understand our lives purely in terms of a givenness
of the present or a fixed thing-like past. Our self-understanding is an unfolding into
a future which is enfolded in a past, itself unfolding into a future.

Freud argued that because the present can change the past so the past is not a fixed once and for all 'thing' to be recalled at will. Through 'deferred action', a later event releases new memories of an earlier event. Subjects reconfigure their dispositions thus rewriting their own history and their sense of their previous life. Lacan (1977) following Heidegger suggested that subjects were poised between past and future and their ability to anticipate exerted a pressure upon their actions that was equal and opposite to their ability to remember those actions. He speaks of the 'time for understanding' and the 'moment of concluding' where past and future are indissolubly interconnected. In Lacan's hands the Freudian notion of deferred action renders the status of the past peculiarly fluid. Its internal structure involves the articulation of two moments with a time of delay which lets the first event slip free of its moorings so consequently the second does as well, where this event may not yet have happened if it is a future event (Forrester, 1990). Lacan says of this that it is a matter of reordering past contingencies, giving them the meaning of necessities to come. As Stronach and MacLure (1997, p. 119) point out — 'people don't tell life changes as explicable entirely by fate, chance or external circumstances'. They realize their history not simply in relation to their past but to their future or to put it another way the reorganization of the past goes hand in hand with an anticipation of the future.

Lacan argues that the subject comes into being at the point of intersection between an irrecoverable past and an unattainable future; its structure is that of a ceaseless cross-stitching between what-is-no-longer-the-case and what-is-not-yet-the-case. He speaks of the subject as announcing herself in terms of the 'I shall have been' of the future perfect not simply the 'I have been' of a fixed thing-like past. What this means is that subjects envisage as already complete what has not been fully launched and are placed beyond the goal they have yet to reach. Their horizon moves as they move. Here then is a notion of decentred time in tandem with the notion of a decentred self, a subject in process where the subject's every present moment is a past futurity and a future pastness.

### Development without 'progress'

> There is no plot in this story because there have been none in my life or in any other life which has come under my notice. I am one of a class the individuals of which have not the time for plots in their life but have all they can do getting their work done without indulging in such a luxury. (Franklin, 1974, p. x)

I am conscious that what I have been saying so far could be construed as an argument that selves do not have experiences in the sense of the events and happenings of a life that present themselves to consciousness. This is not what I am arguing. However, I do agree with Ricoeur (1980) in his argument that events and happenings do not occur in a ready-made intelligible order since the world as experienced is chaotic and in flux. This foregrounds the role of narrative practices in ordering the world — consider for example the significance of lives being recounted in terms of beginnings, ends and turning-points. Experiences therefore have an order imposed on them by their emplotment into a narrative, their significance determined by differential placement and emphasis. Thus they are given expression or *meaning*, the autobiographical text being one way of doing this. Even the most apparently informal account or expression of experience cannot escape being 'formed' in this way. But on the other hand, since every expression of experience is a closure, a less than what could have been said, experience is always capable of being re-formed.

Experiences can be expressed or given meaning through the notion of 'development'. However, this is no escape from narrative emplotment for 'development' is itself structured through a narrative (which I shall call developmentalism) and as we have noted earlier it is one which frequently structures autobiographical texts. Following Ricoeur's argument we could say that developmentalism is a narrative which enshrines the notion of order into the plot of a life and by doing so makes the world (experiences) ordered. Thus 'development' is not something found in life, a presence, but instead is something created by certain discursive practices, particularly those of psychology. Development is change storied and presenced in a particular way, for example through psychological discourses centred on universal criteria such as Piagetian stages or life-span phases which at the same time as being universal supposedly reveal an essential truth about individual selves (Morss, 1995).

It is perhaps worth noting at this point that the story of development has many resemblances to the modernist humanistic story of the self. This is no coincidence since both spring from a common Enlightenment tradition; certain cultural notions, for example, that all actions should be aimed at the future and that the world is not fixed as it is but constantly changing — and changing for the better through the operation of reason. The desire to achieve perfection provided a new conceptual framework for human activity, one where activity always had to have a pre-defined direction. Development is thus presented as something inherent, as the unfolding of a 'natural' process. The structuring metaphor of life as a journey, linear and progressive from a known starting-point culminating in a pre-defined end or goal (wiser, liberated, more rational, etc.) that is a 'better' state of affairs than the starting-point, is common to both. What is interesting here is the embedding of a utopian conception of time, a way of seeing selves in terms of a particular conception of 'progress', of their capacity to realize a future which is a positive development from their present circumstances.

Lacan (1977) critiqued developmentalism because it posits a working forwards whilst, in contrast, what characterizes psychoanalysis is that it works backwards to earlier states whose reality and significance is only conferred on them retrospectively. Lacan characterizes psychoanalysis as not being the retracing of a succession of stages into the past but about understanding how positions already taken up are retrospectively reorganized. It is concerned with accidents, where 'development' is narrated as accidental fate. Two notions fundamental to developmentalism are undermined by this critique. First, that of the unbroken, linear process of continuous change over time since this process cannot be made intelligible without drawing on a false and oppressive teleology and second, that these changes can be known in advance because they are entirely maturational in nature and therefore pre-given.

Of course, it would be easy enough to see any critique of developmentalism as simply a denial of change and progress. But as far as change is concerned it is not so much a matter of denying it but of questioning the way in which developmentalism presents change as natural, regular and linear. As I noted earlier this is highly questionable. Furthermore, what this questioning can highlight is the *effects* of developmentalism. Since change is constructed as universal, a norm is created — moreover, a powerful norm since it is couched in the language of scientificity — with the consequence that alternatives to this norm are closed off by being made pathological, marginal and invisible. Thus this story of human development is both totalizing and regulative.

Equally, it is difficult to question the notion of 'progress' so embedded is this in our cultural consciousness. Yet what a questioning highlights here is that 'progress' is not simply a neutral description of reality but that it works textually to normalize the multiplicity and diversity of experience gained in different areas of human activity. Here again we see closure at work but it is also important to note that 'progress' provides an emplotment which satisfies the need to be sure of one's self (a reassuring presence) and of finding an adequate self-referential and heroic description of the current age within which to locate oneself. It is a culturally sanctioned way of constructing 'depth' in terms of a meaningful life, of influencing and controlling one's life-course and of providing coherence for one's life-story. The medium is time in the shape of history as a directed process and a process with direction. Where we are now, the present, is cast as an end-point and each period or stage is narrated as an inevitable move in this direction, every move orchestrated by a particular dynamic. The narrative is linear and unidirectional where one stage leads to another and where each moment — past, present and future — becomes a presence on a line moving in an upward pre-given direction. In the process, difference is repressed and time suppressed (or centred) in a demand for certainty. What is manifested here is a desire for an unmediated, extra-textual presence, a fullness of the present, Derrida's metaphysics of presence. Yet the narrative of development, by fixing upon 'progress' as the transcendental signified (or universal meaning) provides certainty and reassurance but holds still the temporal process of infinite referral and deferral of traces.

If Ricoeur is right about the chaotic nature of the experiential world then the role of narrative practices becomes clear. Developmentalism is a narrative that allows order to be imposed on experiences, their significance determined by their placement in a story. This significance is not found in some inherent quality they possess but rather from the way experiences are narrated and emplotted. Different narratives would give different significances and without emplotment into a narrative experiences would have no significance at all. However, narratives are not just added to an inchoate temporality by interpretive practices since events are already themselves narrative in the sense that they are preformed. They already have a narrative structure in terms of a Heideggerian within-timeness, an anticipated possible future and a pre-interpreted past. Ricoeur suggests that this is an example of the tragic will to totalize, the human need to give meaning to events through narrative closure. Perhaps putting it less essentialistically we can see this as an overarching rationale for a life so that the centred self can preserve a sense of agency (Stronach and MacLure, 1997). But again we can discern the operation of the future perfect where subjects look on their present and past as if from a possible point in the future, and then make sense of experiences in a way that supports this. Of course, our attempts to emplot experiences in coherent narratives do not always succeed but that's the whole point about the future perfect — it leaves room for error and mystery and at the same time resolves the need for retrospective intelligibility.

As a universal story developmentalism treats certain patterns of human change as 'natural' or as the manifestation of progress irrespective of social context. It does not know itself as a story and thus lacking reflexivity it conceals the workings of power in human activity. Exhortations to Progress, History or Reason are often slogans of the powerful who feel themselves in change of a linear history or part of a vanguard legitimized by the direction of progress. But these slogans do not look the same to oppressed groups for whom such slogans have meant the destruction of their values, interests and ways of life (Fischer, 1986).

The narrative of development forces convergence to the 'same' first, because difference is either repressed, marginalized or treated as a threatening 'other' and second, because in structuring the world as a knowable sequence it forgets human open-endedness and unfinalizability. When developmentalism presents itself as 'science', as it so often does for example, in the disciplinary form of psychology, it denies its own narrative form. Developmental discourse makes claims about the world as regularity i.e. that the world is predictable so development is presenced as a knowable sequence. It is totalizing in the sense that its goal is systematic and complete explanation. Furthermore, it not only represses difference but functions as a means of regulating it. If what is done is treated as distinct from its narration this leads to a dangerous distance between the story and the story-teller. It takes the desires of the story-teller out of the picture and saves us from having to explain why one person is telling a story about another but without the other being in a position to reciprocate. Of course, when it presents itself very obviously as 'science' it is easy enough to declare oneself out of sympathy with a story which denies its narrative quality and conceals the workings of power. But most of the time it is not so easy to recognize or problematize, embedded as it is in the powerful codes of Western white patriarchal culture.

### Writing autobiography differently

> The problem that postmodern subjects face is how to produce themselves and give substance to their lives when the means of narrating or documenting the self have lost credibility — when they too become depthless. (Wakefield, 1990, p. 125)

> How can humanity have a figure outside the narratives of humanism? What language would such a figure speak? (Haraway, 1992, p. 88)

Developmentalism is therefore part of a wider story of the self most commonly found in education and defining the self of education's story. It emerges most clearly in those pedagogical situations where students are invited to write their autobiography as a means of reflecting on their own learning. This raises the question of how these autobiographies are to be understood. They can be seen simply as authentic accounts of experience, a means for students to acquire a 'voice', and correspondingly treated as examples of achieved knowledge and the raw material for further learning. Yet I am also aware that these stories are immersed in the narrative of development either in its scientific or more popular form, where for example they are characterized by the 'Hollywood effect' of everything working out all right in the end (Graham, 1993) or the liberatory romance of confessing oneself fully and openly to remove barriers to learning and blockages to personal development. All are stories framed in the narrative of development even as they are presented as stories of how it really is (and was). Of course, I would argue (and indeed have argued in this chapter) that the notion of a 'how it really is' story in an individualistic sense is problematic. Although as a self we each have a unique historical horizon and a particular set of experiences, any story of the self is simultaneously in the story of late capitalism, post-colonialism and patriarchy — stories that emplot lives, often 'behind the back' of individual consciousness.

The narrative of humanism presents a humanistic self that is a meaning-making, coherent and unified individual. This seems problematic in the context of a postmodern world characterized by fragmentation, multiple and contradictory narratives, by globalization and post-colonial conflicts and by the questioning of modernist epistemologies that traditionally provided the grounds for certainty and coherence. In the educational encounter, we are beginning to tell these stories that need to be told and we are all familiar with pedagogies designed to enable their telling. But what concerns me is the possibility that as educators we often (albeit implicitly) tell students the story they must tell — and the story, whether it be located in a pedagogy of individual self-realization or a pedagogy of personal and collective empowerment, is still emplotted through the narrative of development which educators find virtually impossible to critique as narrative.

I have to say that I do not have any definite answers to this although I suspect that part of the answer might lie in harnessing the full potential of autobiography by thinking about how an autobiography might be written differently and how difference might be presented in the writing. Perhaps, a more deconstructive form of autobiographical writing is needed, one which recognizes its textuality. Inevitably, this thinking and writing differently will raise, in their full force, the questions posed earlier in this chapter. As McRobbie (1994) argues the notion of the 'real me' points to the fictive unity of the self which yet once dislodged poses troubling questions of identity. As Haraway asks — what language would a figure outside the narratives of humanism speak? Clearly, a starting point in answering this is to distinguish between 'human beings' and the humanistic self and to 'rethink our notion of the human rather than cling to a view of supposed choice deeply embedded in the ideology of the Enlightenment' (Bergland, 1994, p. 160). Perhaps we just need to get used to living with fragmentation, and rather than endlessly searching for it, accept that the self is in process, continually re-newed and re-invented.

Who knows, this might even prove pleasurable, albeit troublingly so? Here, Baudrillard's texts, *America* (1989) and *Cool Memories* (1990), provide some resonances. The former is a journal of personal experiences in travelling across the USA, the latter a memoir of his reactions to this and to other contemporary events. Interestingly both are accounts of a journey — the powerful structuring metaphor in the narrative of development. But Baudrillard subverts this narrative because his journeys are aimless and non-developmental, they have no point other than themselves — as he says 'the further you travel the more clearly you realize that the journey is all that matters' (Baudrillard, 1990, p. 168). In *America* the experience of travel becomes an end in itself, leading nowhere in particular either spatially or in terms of maturity or self-knowledge. Experience is not presenced, neither is it subjected to analytic reflection and located in a fixed past to be recalled. Rather it is presented as contingent and unfinished, leading to more experience rather than knowledge. In refusing to link experience with knowledge, Baudrillard undermines the notion that underneath the seeming incoherence and disorder of experience there is a deep meaning which once found will enable the coherence and order to be imposed that is necessary for methodical knowledge. Instead he celebrates the pleasurable qualities of the openness and unfinalizability of experience.

Baudrillard presents an analysis of the US through stylistic means by using the literary form of the autobiography but then subverts this to create a feeling of depthlessness. Through his reflexive and non-sequential style of writing he mimics the world he is describing — a world of hyper-reality where reality and sign become one and where the social is endlessly constructed and simulated. He does not so much dent the real as highlights the problematic of the real and of representing the real (Turner, 1993). Thus there is a 'message', or perhaps many messages, at least one of which is about postmodernity and the simulated self, but all are presented allusively.

Here then is an example of a depthless autobiography that tells the story of a depthless world. We may not agree with it, we may even be offended by it, we may want to tell a different story — but at least we know that Baudrillard is telling a story in his 'own' way. Even if we do not believe it, we can get pleasure out of it — and perhaps resonances too which might help us tell our own story. What I get out of his depthlessness is a story that does not privilege presence, either of the self or the past. Writing of *Cool Memories* he says that 'it must fade away even as it is being read' (Baudrillard, 1990, p. 156). The self-present 'I' is dispersed into the interstices of the text and one has the feeling that Baudrillard is, has been, and will be many 'I's. His style of writing reminds us that the autobiographical 'I' is textually constructed, temporally contingent and unfinished. In a very important sense, Baudrillard is not telling it 'as it really is and was'.

Fischer (1986, p. 198) argues that 'the modalities of veracity in our age can no longer (if they ever could) be limited to the conventions of realism'. This is something we need to take account of even if we do not share Baudrillard's vision of the depthless self in a depthless society. At the very least, we need to take seriously the problems raised by the configuring of experience in a mode of autobiographical writing which sits uneasily with the contemporary condition of postmodernity. Postmodernity is a condition which suggests the need to go beyond single dominant narratives into other modes of writing, for example, collage and montage, given that no one narrative, such as for example the narrative of progress, can account for the diversity and multiplicity of human experience. Collage or montage are possible means of writing autobiography differently, in a decentred way, by a decentring of self and time. By subverting the narrative convention of linear progression, utopian time and the discovery/recovery of self, a space can be created that allows a fore-grounding of gaps, exclusions, repositionings, and repressions (Kehily, 1995).

It is significant to note in this connection that marginalized groups have always questioned linear progression and replaced it with texts which interweave tension, contradiction and contingency. As Brewster (1995) points out, migrant writers are commonly thought of as informants rather than writers so they are read as giving 'voice' to their unmediated experience. However, using the example of the Polish-Australian writer Ania Walwicz[1] she shows that the autobiography of the migrant is no pure unmediated voice but just as much framed by literary conventions as any fictional writing. More significantly for the argument I am making, Walwicz writes in collage narrative so the autobiography is neither structured in terms of a linear plot nor are experiences presented as a coherent whole. The story told is unfinished, open-ended and playful, its telling a mimesis of the fragmentary and discontinuous nature of Walwicz's experience, its effect that of randomness, dislocation and uncer-tainty. What is highlighted is a text where meaning 'spills-over', where identity is continually in the process of being constructed and the self presented as a collection of different and disparate voices.

Migrant autobiographical writing reminds us that the centred autobiography although it presents itself as a universal and unproblematic form can actually be read historically as representing and defining white males. The male autobiography tends to present a unitary essentialist self progressing through life with a clear set of aims and ambitions. Male experience, usually relating to professional and work activit-ies, totalizes and normalizes all human experience. The identity created by the act of writing is freed from ambiguity and contradiction, shaped by and for the public domain (Kehily, 1995). On the other hand, the female autobiography as Buss (1993, p. 7) points out is writen in a style that has 'no investment in creating a cohesive self over time' and that exploits 'difference and change over sameness and iden-tity'. It responds to the question — 'how does the not-male human being, perceived in the culture as the Other, represent the self?' (Bergland, 1994, p. 132). The same could be said for autobiographies of members of ethnic minority groups since they too face the question of how to respond to their negative construction in the domin-ant culture. For Hall (1987) the migrant and the colonized exemplify the decentred subjectivity of the postmodern experience. They are forced to find a voice that expresses the multiplicity of their identity. As Fischer (1986, p. 232) points out, ethnic autobiographies make a point of drawing attention to their 'linguistic and fictive nature, of using the narrator as an inscribed figure within the text. . ., of encourag-ing the reader to self-consciously participate in the production of meaning'.

Educators have tended, in the main, to locate themselves in humanistic dis-course regardless of whether their pedagogical intentions have been adaptationist or transformative. Even those who are beginning to use autobiography as a critical resource have tended to construe it within the terms of a modernist narrative that constructs self and time as presence. I have attempted in this chapter to outline what the consequences of this have been and to tentatively suggest a possible alternative. Any alternative would not consist of finding something whether it be experience or the self that is outside the text and independent of inscription. This would be simply to foreground presence once again. What I am arguing for instead is a *re-writing* of the story of the self which deconstructs the dominant self of the story. This would not be a venture ploughing unknown territory — others' stories, the stories of the 'other', are already there.

## Postscript

The past has distended into the present and it is time to bring this narrative to a close. Obviously, a premature closure since much more could be said. Thus this is a text that must necessarily remain unfinished.

This has been a meandering text — a record of a 'journey' perhaps, but more likely a Baudrillardian 'cruise'. Personal experience has been encountered, and mediated by, certain writers who have affected and continue to affect me. This experience has been articulated through a text, written within an academic discourse, but also in a sense an 'autobiography' about autobiography and about how autobiography denies its own being as a text, although hopefully this has not been the case here. There are no resolutions and only a few rather muffled 'messages' but plenty of concerns for the place of experience in the contemporary educational enterprise. Hopefully, there may also be some resonances.

Undoubtedly in telling this story, I have presented myself in a particular way, a way intended to be appropriate to the competences and expectations of the readers of this book. In so doing, I have reconstructed myself yet again, not through a conscious willing but through the demands of writing a text of this kind. But have I told it as it really is or was — and does it matter?

## Note

1 Ania Walwicz's autobiographical works are *Writing* (Melbourne: Rigmarole Press, 1982) and *Red Roses* (St. Lucia, Qld.: University of Queensland Press, 1992).

## References

BAUDRILLARD, J. (1989) *America*, London: Verso.

BAUDRILLARD, J. (1990) *Cool Memories*, London: Verso.

BERGLAND, B. (1994) 'Postmodernism and the autobiographical subject: Reconstructing the "other"', in ASHLEY, K., GILMORE, L. and PETERS, G. (eds) *Autobiography and Postmodernism*, Amherst: University of Massachusetts Press.

BREWSTER, A. (1995) *Literary Formations: Post-colonialism, Nationalism, Globalism*, Melbourne: Melbourne University Press.

BRUNER, E.M. (1984) 'The opening up of anthropology', in BRUNER, E.M. (ed.) *Text Play, and Story: The Construction and Reconstruction of Self and Society*, Washington DC: American Ethnological Society.

BUSS, H.M. (1993) *Mapping Qurselves*, Montreal: McGill-Queen's University Press.

DENZIN, N.K. (1989) *Interpretive Biography*, Beverly Hills, CA: Sage.

DERRIDA, J. (1976) *Of Grammatology*, Baltimore: Johns Hopkins University Press.

FISCHER, M. (1986) 'Ethnicity and the arts of memory', in CLIFFORD, J. and MARCUS, G.E. (eds) *Writing Culture*, London: University of California Press.

FORRESTER, J. (1990) *The Seductions of Psychoanalysis*, Cambridge: Cambridge University Press.

FRANKLIN, M. (1974) *My Brilliant Career*, Sydney: Angus & Robertson.

GRAHAM, R.J. (1993) 'Voice, archive, practice: The textual construction of professional identity', *Journal of Educational Thought*, **27**, 2, pp. 186–199.

HALL, S. (1987) 'Minimal selves' in APIGNANESI, L. (ed.) *Identity: The Real Me — Postmodernism and the Question of Identity*, London: Institute of Contemporary Arts.

HARAWAY, D. (1992) 'Ecce homo, ain't (ar'n't) I a woman and inappropriate/d others: The human in a post-humanist lanscape', in BUTLER, J. and SMITH, J.W. (eds) *Feminists Theories the Political*, London: Routledge.

HATCH, J.A. and WISNIEWSKI, R. (1997) *Life History and Narrative*, London: Falmer Press.

HEIDEGGER, M. (1962) *Being and Time*, New York: Harper and Row.

KEHILY, M.J. (1995) 'Self-narration, autobiography and identity construction', *Gender and Education*, **7**, 1, pp. 23–31.

LACAN, J. (1977) *Ecrits: A Selection*, London: Tavistock Press.

LYOTARD, J-F. (1984) *The Postmodern Condition*, Manchester: Manchester University Press.

McLAREN, P. (1994) *Critical Pedagogy and Predatory Culture*, London: Routledge.

McROBBIE, A. (1994) *Postmodernism and Popular Culture*, London: Routledge.

MORSS, J. (1995) *Growing Critical*, London: Routledge.

POLKINGHORNE, D.E. (1997) 'Narrative configuration in qualitative analysis', in HATCH, J.A. and WISNIEWSKI, R. (eds) *Life History and Narrative*, London: Falmer Press.

RICOEUR, P. (1980) 'Narrative time', *Critical Inquiry*, **7**, 1, pp. 169–190.

SMITH, P. (1988) *Discerning the Subject*, Minneapolis: University of Minnesota Press.

STRONACH, I. and MacLURE, M. (1997) *Educational Research Undone: The Postmodern Embrace*, Buckingham: Open University Press.

TURNER, B.S. (1993) 'Cruising America', in ROJEK, C. and TURNER, B.S. (eds) *Forget Baudrillard?*, London: Routledge.

WAKEFIELD, N. (1990) *Postmodernism — Twilight of the Real*, London: Pluto Press.

# 3 Fragments of a Life: Recursive Dilemmas

*David Scott*

## Introduction

Educational exegesis comprises the study of individuals and collections of individuals living together and immersed in the brute facticity of society. Thus biography or biographical study is the *sine qua non* of understanding how education systems function, of how society is reproduced and constructed through schooling, and of how knowledge of and within such systems is made available. However, biography has to confront two dilemmas. The first of these concerns the relation between autobiography and biography, and the second, the inter-relationship of structure and agency. Biographers come face to face with autobiographical texts situated in time and place. These autobiographical texts, collected in the course of extended interviews, are reconstructions by participants of their own fragmented lives and are thus bricollages. They are made coherent by an act of methodological closure agreed between participant and researcher, these closure devices always having a history and conforming to the arrangements made for textual production at particular moments in time. These methodological agreements are furthermore, negotiated; that is, relations of power enter into these accounts of peoples' lives.

The 'life' is therefore made in terms of the past reconstructed by the participant in the present; that is, past events transformed or re-translated to be narratively coherent, given the epistemological mores of the present. It is never simply enough to understand the process as one of remembering, or of course not remembering (given the frailty of memory), a past life and then representing that account as truthful. It is, as MacIntyre (1988) reminds us, that knowledge of the world and the self is always embedded within traditions of understanding which allow us to say some things and do not allow us to say other things, and furthermore, to say some things in some ways and not in other ways. We therefore literally reconstruct the past with reference to how we understand the present.

We have already conceded that this understanding is social. However, unless we want to take a purely phenomenological perspective, which is that participants' accounts of their lives and activities are always adequate, then we need to go beyond this. Bhaskar (1989) for instance, argues that this phenomenological perspective assumes unjustifiably that participants have full knowledge of the perspectives which underpin their everyday actions. In other words, social actors are not able to transcend the limitations of consciousness. This can be expressed in four ways: human beings do not have full knowledge of the settings which structure their activities; human beings cannot have knowledge of the unintended consequences of their

actions because the translation of intention to fulfilment of project is never unproblematic, and furthermore, what actually happens is the sum of a multitude of human
projects which have unforeseen consequences; thirdly, social actors may not be
aware of unconscious forces which drive them towards projects which consciously
they do not wish to complete; fourthly, social actors operate with tacit knowledge
which they are unable to articulate or unaware of as they go about their lives.

What are the implications of this for the biographer? The latter is complicit
in the production of an account which offers a different perspective on that life,
indeed always goes beyond it. This is so for two reasons: the biographer brings
with them to the act of research both their own biography, that is a set of presupposi-
tions about their own life which is of course transitive and presently constituted *and*
knowledge of the process of doing research. In short, they are positioned both in
terms of their own biography and in terms of those epistemological frameworks
through which they understand the world. For some (cf. Derrida, 1976) the closure
occasioned by the researcher constitutes an act of violence; biography as opposed
to autobiography is always violent. However, the violence of this act is never absolute because, as I suggested above, the power of the researcher to impose unequivoc-
ally their interpretation on 'the life' is constrained and willingly constrained by how
they understand their role. Biographers for example, usually consult and negotiate
about the completed account. They may have incomplete knowledge of the way the
account is constructed and comes to fruition. Fundamentally though, they may be
in sympathy with the project of their participant and thus the types of closure they
mediate may be in accord with those of the participant. What is indisputable is that
the account is constructed by both researcher and participant, and thus conforms to
a greater or lesser extent with particular agendas, and that those agendas always make
reference to the past — both the past of the biographer and that of the participant.
As Erben (1996) notes, this is why the biographical method is frequently referred to
as auto/biographical method. The interpretive or hermeneutical procedure implicit
in the biographical act is necessarily replicative of the process undertaken by the
autobiographer.

We now come to the second dilemma for biographical researchers. Biography
is the study of an individual in society or, in other words, it comprises an understanding of the relations between agency and structure with reference to that individual.
It is complicated by the question of how we can know that context or structure
except through the eyes of the individual participant. We are thus forced back to
accepting a phenomenological perspective, and yet, as I have suggested above, this
has serious flaws. The most compelling problem then for social portrayists is the
precise relationship between structure and agency, which is of course an ontological matter, and then between this relationship and that of the biographer, which
on the surface seems to be purely an epistemological matter. However, the precise
epistemological mode becomes an ontological matter since the text produced has
real material effects, albeit in discursive form. Social life therefore has a recursive
shape or may be characterized by a double hermeneutic (Giddens, 1984). Human
beings both generate and are in turn influenced by social scientific descriptions of
social processes and this introduces an instability into social research which renders

the production of law-like propositions about social activities, and in particular 'the life', as problematic.

Giddens (1984) attempts a reconciliation between the phenomenological and structural. His structuration theory synthesizes structural and agential perspectives. Human beings are neither the subjects of external and overwhelmingly influential forces nor free unconstrained agents, neither controlled nor influenced by those sets of relations and conjunctions which constitute society. Actors continually draw upon sets of 'rules and resources' which, once substantiated, allow social life to continue as they become routinized. Archer (1982, p. 458) adopts a similar approach with her morphogenetic schema, though she disputes the necessity of tying structure and agency so closely together: 'structuration, by contrast, treats the ligatures binding structure, practice and system as indissoluble, hence the necessity of duality and the need to gain a more indirect analytical purchase on the elements involved'.

She also questions whether every human action, every facet of the particular human being, is involved in the ongoing moulding and remoulding of society that is implied by structuration cycles. She writes: 'there are a good many things about human beings and their doings (things biological, psychological and spiritual) which have a precious independence from society's moulding and may have precious little to do with re-modelling society' (Archer, 1982, p. 455). Both Archer and Giddens argue that human beings play an active and intentional part in the construction of their world, though that building activity is subject to structural constraint. Human beings make their world in the context of previous attempts, and at the same time transform those structures and change the conditions which influence subsequent moves to make the world. It is also important to recognize that while agency is responsible for structural transformation, in the process it simultaneously transforms itself (Archer, 1988). Structures then only have substance and then only fleetingly, in the reasons actors have for their behaviours: 'study of the structural properties of social systems cannot be successfully carried on, or its results interpreted, without reference to the knowledgeability of the relevant agents' (Giddens, 1984, p. 329). Data that refer to this are therefore essential elements in any biographical enterprise and their collection is a social and ethical affair.

Social actors' accounts of their agency at particular moments of time are retrospective and delivered in terms of different contexts from which they were originally enacted. The social actor offers an account which has a wave-like form. Past events are construed at different moments in life and then re-constructed again and again in different circumstances; however, it is not the original event which is subsequently reconstructed but the previous reconstruction. Furthermore, as we noted above, the reconstruction which takes place has both a form and a content. Usher (1997, p. 36) suggests a number of important ways of understanding this. Each text has a context 'in the sense of that which is with the text. What is "with" the text in this sense is the situated autobiography of the researcher/reader'. Reference has already been made to this by locating the autobiographical text within biography. Furthermore, each text has a pre-text, a form which is essentially social: 'research texts have a pre-text in the sense of that which is before the text; language as the repository of meaning, discourses as particular ways of organizing meanings, the textual strategies, literary conventions and rhetorical devices of writing' (Usher, 1997, p. 37). Additionally each text has a sub-text and an inter-text. The sub-text refers to the epistemological frameworks which constitute particular arrangements of power in history and which have definite effects. Inter-textuality may be characterized by: 'the structure of the trace. . .the interlacings and resonances with other traces' (Wood, 1990, p. 47, quoted in Usher, 1997).

Thus each reconceptualization of a past event has a context, pre-text, sub-text and is implicated with other texts. For the biographer each text has a recursive element, a bending-back on itself, even if it is always presently constituted. The 'life' is a text constituted in and through history. Social actors make sense of their lives in terms of particular discursive arrangements — how events are understood at particular moments of time. These public events are subsequently understood in different ways. Since they were originally ideological in nature, they are contested not least at the political/policy level, and this changes through time and with it the nature of its embeddedment. The social context is literally transformed before the eyes of participants. The social actor therefore has a number of choices, and these choices refer to how they reconstruct public events autobiographically. They can attempt to conform to how these events are presently understood; they therefore make a conscious decision to renounce their past understanding as inadequate and to view past events in a different way; or they adapt their understanding so that different historical and ideological agendas are reconciled — this of course produces a minimum of dislocation and confusion; or they can be resolute in their beliefs, utterly nonconformist, and understand their life in terms of a relatively intransitive agenda. How they understand the mechanism of the production and reproduction of their 'life' determines its nature.

And for Ricoeur (1984, 1985, 1986) this always occurs within narrative forms. The narrative (or narratives) gives meaning to the expression of self by the social actor; and these narratives are truly social and therefore embedded in time. The central figure in this biographical account is a secondary school teacher in the London Borough of Brent. The narratives which structure it all involve resolution of the personal and the social, and can therefore be said to be dialectical. They comprise three stories: the first is about the child becoming adult; the second is about migration and nationality; and the third is about incorporating public discourses into personal projects. Narrativity therefore allows, as Erben (1996, p. 164) suggests: 'the individual life to emerge in the dual nature, first, of its distinctiveness (person "X" can never be person "Y") and second its connectedness (person "X" can "recognize" the narrative of person "Y").'

### A teacher's life

Mary O'Brien was brought up in Ireland in the 1950s and 1960s in a semi-rural environment, characterized by migration and the idea of betterment through education:

> And I come from an area where, in the fifties and sixties, there was mass emigration and very, very little by way of industry, some fishermen, small farmers, subsistence farming and very few professions in that area, and yet in my generation and the previous generation, the number of professionals that came out of the small National School was absolutely fantastic.

Furthermore, the 'educational' was valued not just as a means of gaining material rewards or pursuing a career but for its own sake:

> There was a great deal of interest in education and, in parts of Ireland, we still have a pretty peculiar vocabulary for instance with people who go to school we called 'scholars' as in Shakespeare's day, but at least they were using the word 'scholar'.

The educational was understood as a form of self-revelation.

However, the narrative which dominated life in rural Ireland at this time was movement or migration — the desire to uproot, explore and even escape from present circumstances:

> Emigration really characterized the experience of the people, there was quite a haemorrhage of the people from Ireland in the fifties.

As we shall see, Mary was to follow this path. However, this did not involve a dissolution of the past, but a reconceptualization of it in terms of different images, discourses, narratives and contexts. Her Catholic upbringing remains an important defining influence:

> The Catholic ethos, which was also tied up with our interest in the historical and cultural past. The Catholic ethos would have been defined in terms of perhaps being a good citizen. . .and also it was a very strong moral outlook in terms of family values and being able to meet responsibilities and also an acceptance of what life might dish out to you. There was within the school that I went to a very strong emphasis on developing potential and there wasn't a ceiling a person might aspire to and not a lot of discussion about the limitations that might affect girls' futures.

Aspirations were nurtured, boundaries dissolved, achievement emphasized, but always within a liberal Catholic framework which stressed the intrinsicality of personal growth and public service:

> I think the emphasis for us in terms of careers would have been very much based on the caring professions. . .I am sure that has deeply affected me in my subsequent career, and I am sure that in terms of occupations which are more geared to the world of finance and business then I am sure that my antipathy or my lack of interest in those professions is very much, has been very much engendered by the teaching I experienced in those schools.

Furthermore, that sense of burgeoning identity, framed within a Catholic ethos, was also specifically Irish, in that it furnished her with a set of literary resources that were to prove seminal:

> I see my identity in terms of my appreciation of the tradition that I am rooted in. That, I think, now gives me a great deal of comfort and it allows me to grow with inner reserves and in all sorts of ways and I very much appreciate the fact that I have been able to learn the language. I am bilingual. I have a good knowledge of Irish history and literature and it gives me a security to perhaps tap in to other cultures and other literatures, especially in terms of teaching in the inner city, that is as an English teacher in an inner city school. It perhaps has also given me that impetus to ensure that writers from, as they say in the exam boards, from other cultures, the Naipauls and the Walcotts, that they actually feature on the diet that is offered to the students in the English classes and that confidence, that diversity and quality, you know, is for the better.

This repudiation of insularity has found expression in her use of sources and resources for teaching from a wide variety of environments.

In addition, the experience of being Irish and colonized engendered a sense of identification with oppressed minority groups and has been an important influence on her perspective, beliefs and notions about education. Once again we see how events in the past have been reconceptualized as present discourses and influence public stances at different moments in life:

> So there was that feeling perhaps of injustice which was very conditioned by my own experience in the Irish system. I think my understanding was further engendered by the notion that we had to succeed in the educational system largely on account of our imperial past, that the draining of the economy which we were led to believe, as students, owed a lot to our colonization, that my attitude to education was very much conditioned by my understanding of colonization and so it was relatively easy for me to relate the experiences of Irish people in the education system to those from other colonized areas.

This sense of injustice is reinforced by personal experiences, the more compelling because they were unexpected. She had expected to find that professional teachers would be committed to anti-racist and anti-discriminatory policies and that they would be sophisticated enough not to indulge in crude racism and discrimination:

> I was aware as a young teacher that the sort of anti-Irish feeling that I would have been aware of in a detached way, perhaps in an academic way, I was actually shocked when they began to impinge on me as a professional in a London school and I was acutely aware of it on two occasions; one when a teacher referring to Marilyn was offering some creative excuse for being late and this tutor turned to me, this was my first day of teaching which will give you some idea, this tutor turned to me and said 'How Irish of her,' and I was scandalized, not really from a racist front, but in a snobbish sort of way. I expected this teacher to be able to articulate in a different mode and I remember being taken aback at the quality of her expression. . .

Personal experiences, remembered and then reconceptualized at different moments in life, provide compelling reasons for action.

Furthermore, her notions of how professionals should behave, nurtured by her experiences in the Irish educational system, were such that she was surprised at the low levels of professional behaviour which she found. Again the image of succour or nurture is foremost and this is contrasted with a relative lack of care given to trainee teachers and with how they subsequently behaved:

> In terms of Irish professionals within the education system, I think the point I would want to make is that because of the economic situation the teacher training colleges and, perhaps, the universities could demand a very high level of entry and therefore I equated that context with the English system and when I moved from perhaps a selective, for it was a selective system, that I knew in Ireland to the comprehensive system in England, I was expecting to find perhaps colleagues who had perhaps been through a very rigorous education system. I did not find that it was a very general characteristic although clearly there were pockets of it, very definite pockets of it, and so I suppose I was disappointed to find myself as a new teacher in a system where perhaps teachers were not nurtured or perhaps the quality of training given to teachers was not on a level that I might have expected from the selective system in Ireland. . .

This found its most vivid expression in the low levels of their commitment to the children. Paradoxically, within a selective Irish educational system the ethos she experienced was inclusive; whereas in an English comprehensive system her initial impression was that it was exclusive, in particular with regards to working class and black children:

> But I was mindful that working-class kids were just not given the sort of opportunities that working-class kids in Ireland had been given and these were kids who were further disadvantaged by being black kids and that. . .

Her idea of professionalism also comprised two further notions: first, that the community would award high status to teachers; and second, that reward had attached to it a corresponding obligation of best performance from the teachers themselves. The conjoining here of reward with public duty is echoed elsewhere in this account:

> Yes, the teacher would have respect, perhaps not status as an accountant might have status or be a member of the golf course or attend, you know, these sorts of social functions that others in the community might, but in terms of the sort of respect that was afforded to priests, there was some of that respect was given to school teachers, definitely, and the antipathy that the bad teacher in fact would have been afforded. . .

Social pressures were brought to bear on those teachers who failed to live up to the standards expected of professional people.

This discrepancy between her professional values and her experiences teaching in an English comprehensive school was given expression by the need to resolve the crisis she felt when she first started teaching in England. The resolution was achieved by personal endeavour and the learning of coping strategies and also more importantly by making use of supportive agencies:

> Funnily the worst point in my teaching career was my first couple of years teaching at a school in an inner city, and the problem there was just the lack of transparency, just the total, the indifference that I felt that was given to teaching and learning. It was perhaps the contrast between the very different systems in Ireland and England.

These outside influences comprised the advisory service from the borough in which she worked. Its officers became an important influence not just because they provided strategies and techniques for overcoming the crisis she felt in her classroom management, but also because she was able to sublimate her personal vision, nurtured in Ireland, into a public vision of education as it was espoused by the borough in which she worked:

> But I am positive that the drive for comprehensive schools in the early seventies was only augmented due to the efforts of very competent advisers who had the vision, who had strategies for developing the techniques and the resources that teachers could develop in the classroom and I am very mindful of that, but the system as a whole had not delivered. . .

This resolution of earlier difficulties in the classroom left its mark. Her present success has to be understood in terms of how she now understands her past, both cognitively and affectively:

> I think that I've striven for those standards on account of those early experiences when I was so frustrated, and now find classroom management very, very interesting when I work on it. I find teaching in a class absolutely stimulating, even after twenty-five years and I am convinced that it's not just, you know, a natural development, I'm convinced that I am still harping back to the days when I could not do it and that it is almost a relief when I can.

The important point here is that she is dealing with a notion of the past self as it is understood in the present and the reconciliation that is achieved is a reconciliation of remembered experiences.

Her vision of education was and is public and political: a fair and just society can in part be achieved by the work of the education service. What happens in classrooms has a profound effect on society in general. Teachers therefore have a responsibility to nurture the best instincts of the next generation, and teaching can therefore never be just another form of employment:

> I think that what I was unconscious of, when I stand in front of a class I am still conscious of, or perhaps sub-conscious more than conscious, is that it matters what is happening here in this classroom. It does matter and that the sum total of these learning experiences in the classroom will matter and the pupils need to know that as well.

This stress on providing beneficial experiences for children in schools leads her to express it in terms of managing learning experiences, which on the one hand taps into current discourses about education; but on the other, allows her to feed into a discourse of empowerment:

> I think that the emphasis on management and the opportunities for teachers to tap into knowledge and ways in which good management works, I think that that has to be an enormous advance. We were very much speaking the language of more effective management, there is no doubt about that.

Again, there is an attempt to reconcile past and present understandings.

Empowerment remains for her the dominant motif of her professional life, given expression as it was by influential public bodies, in this case, the advisory service which had a responsibility for the school in which she worked. These influential sources were to be neutralized by policy enactments and legislation in the 1980s, but while they existed, they were enormously influential and empowering:

> We were, as young mid-scale teachers, we were very conscious that in the late seventies and early eighties we felt empowered and we also were mindful, perhaps, of the sort of experiences that we had as young teachers in classrooms where black kids were not able to attain much. We were drawing on our immediate experience and this was, finally, a way in which we could see opportunities for black kids you see and we were the ones, and I talk about this in the grass roots movement, pretty much empowered by leading advisers in the borough and also tapping in to elected members and to community groups and to other sources of academic research, so it was quite a developed movement.

However, this discourse of empowerment, which though led by the local education authority, was essentially a grass roots movement also tapped into current discourses about effective schools. The notion of effectiveness however is understood as inclusive, and it comprises a particular responsibility to low achievers and the economically disadvantaged:

> On the basis that the management structures were not functioning and that management was not taking consideration of their responsibilities and so we were very mindful of management roles and responsibilities. . .So these were the avenues which enabled us then to look at perhaps what constitutes, or what constituted, effective schools because, you know, we were very clear in our hearts that kids were not attaining largely because of the inefficiency of schools. . .

She incorporates the past into current discourses of education:

> But in those days, pre-equality days, there wasn't much, to my mind, much emphasis on good schools either, or what constituted good schools.

And this resulted in a neglect of those things which mattered to her.

However, there is a feeling of loss, a reverting back to a vision of education nurtured by her experiences in the past. Those least able to cope would be neglected:

> The focus, what I'm emphasizing here, that those people who were part of that, you know, race or gender culture movement of the mid-seventies and eighties, that a lot of what they were focusing on was what constituted things interestingly, that is now what has moved forward, but perhaps in a different direction, in some ways a different direction of what we understood things might be, and the emphasis on race and general equality has been lost.

There is also a sense of regret that her professional ethos has been subverted by new arrangements for teachers. As we have seen, notions of professionals engaging with each other to provide good practice in schools is, as she sees it, largely a thing of the past. What it did was to engender a feeling of empowerment, a belief that professional activity could have an impact on public life and that national policy could be responsive to those grass roots practitioners who provided the service:

> There was a feeling at the time that, as professionals, we needed to network outside our own immediate profession, and there was a real sense of that taking place . . .That actually was a fact. And any number of conferences, mostly conferences, would suggest that, you know, the real networking had taken place but there was also, going back to the theme of being empowered, there was also the idea that, perhaps, we could impact on national policy. . .

She was quickly disillusioned of this conceit.

Her defence of past activities by her and her fellow professional teachers in Brent is unequivocal, coupled with a sense of regret:

> It has made a difference because what I have been talking about is ways which show our adherence to an anti-racist approach. We were convinced by it because to us it equated with good education, so basically in this area in Brent you would find, you know, many thriving examples of good education so the kids who have come through the system have entered the work force as, you know, on a level playing field, so at that minimum level we succeeded.

Indeed, for her, the present drive to make schools more effective can be reconciled with past emphases on race and gender equality, even though the rhetoric of conservative policy reforms of the 1980s and early 1990s comprised concerted attacks on anti-racist and anti-sexist initiatives:

> It's not something that we can quantify in some cases, but perhaps, in 1997, more failing schools would have been on the hit list about to be closed down in the borough of Brent, if we hadn't had that tradition and I would suggest, yes, that there was no reason why Brent, given, you know, the number of variables that characterized the traditions in which failing schools exist, that the fact that there is an absence really, there is no secondary school in Brent on that failure list.

And this is a source of professional pride.

Teachers in England and Wales had to confront a series of educational reforms in the late 1980s and early 1990s which changed both their practice and their sense of professionalism. In some ways, these new discourses were disempowering, both because of what they were and because of the speed of implementation. Mary, in common with other teachers, had to make sense of a set of reforms which did not fit, at least on the surface, with her long-held beliefs about educational processes. Though she voiced opposition to them through her professional association, this, she felt, had little effect:

> We were so concerned with coming to terms with the reforms and changes, trying to make sense of it and trying to see how our practice could accommodate it that we were overwhelmed, and though we voiced resistance to the negative impacts of it, we were as English teachers able to voice our opposition to the stance etc. but in common with many practitioners I was just taken over by the tide of change.

The failure to oppose effectively these reforms was exacerbated by the dissolution of the local authority power-base, which as we have seen, provided her with much support in the early years of her career. Interestingly, that same sense of professional pride which characterizes her practice was now being brought into play to implement the new reforms:

> But, of course, National Curriculum also corresponded, you know, with LM and with the local management, so with a lot more powers being vested in heads, the people who, perhaps traditionally, looked to the LEA and other sources for backing, and moral support and real support, and could no longer rely on that sort of area of expertise and so that would have been an added reason for the acquiescence. Admittedly classroom practitioners, you know, have only so much time on their hands, so by the time they have assimilated the new ideas into their practice, there wouldn't have been much time left over. . .and of course there would have been the professional pride of coming to terms with all the nuances of the National Curriculum, so by the time you have conducted that. . .because of the sheer force of the innovation and the overall attention to detail that was necessary, that just in terms of time that would be left over there wasn't much, and at the same time, because of local management, there were no longer the opportunities to attend courses and specialists outside of the school, you remember staff development. . . Much, much more insular.

Furthermore, the competitive nature of the reforms undermined any real attempts to resurrect past arrangements and necessitated the need to reconceptualize her idea of what it means to be a professional:

> And a little later on, not very much later on, we were so mindful of the competitive nature of the market place, so colleagues that we would have quite happily shared experiences and the resources with, colleagues that we would have networked with — that source, you know, our power-base or whatever — but they were no longer

our natural allies as they were in the early days. Nowadays, it is all about competing and we all have to be concerned about the school's image, and there are very, very crude marketing ploys that we have to implement, very crude.

These are fragments of a life, continually being re-made.

### Concluding remarks

They are moreover, fragments of a particular life as it is presently understood. As we have seen, this text is constructed in terms of four notions:

1   The interpretative process involves an interweaving of two different agendas: those of the person and their biographer; or as Gadamer (1975) puts it a 'fusion of horizons'. By this he meant that we cannot step outside ourselves even for a moment. We are always immersed in our perspectives and frameworks, so that the act of research constitutes a joint act of exploring these positionings. As Usher (1996: 22) suggests:

> A fusion of horizons is the outcome of intersubjective agreement where different and conflicting interpretations are harmonized. By comparing and contrasting various interpretations, a consensus can be achieved despite differences — indeed because of differences. Hermeneutic understanding is therefore a learning experience involving 'dialogue' between ourselves as researchers and that which we are trying to understand.

This means that any autobiographical text has to be understood in terms of the context of its construction and this includes the situated autobiography of the researcher.

2   The past is organized in terms of the present; that is present discourses, narratives and texts constitute the backdrop to any exploration of the past. It is not that a biography refers to actual events which are then imperfectly recollected, but that past events are interpretations undertaken by the person whose 'life' it is, and that these interpretations always have a pre-text. Furthermore this pre-text, comprising as it does the means by which meanings are organized in the present, always makes reference to other pre-texts in the past and indeed supersedes them. Wood (1990) refers to these resonances as traces; that which the past leaves to the present.

3   The public and the private can never be disentangled. For the biographer, it is the way the social actor interacts with the structures of society and the way this contributes to their continuation or modification that is of interest. Private acts are therefore also public acts.

4   The 'life' is always fragmentary, comprising parts as opposed to wholes, narratives that never quite come to fruition, disconnected traces, sudden endings and new beginnings. What gives it its meaning is the act of methodological closure agreed between the person and her biographer.

However, the depiction of the 'life' as fragmented and the agreement reached with the participant about it do not take away the responsibility of the author for producing an interpretation. It follows that this account is one of many that could have been made. Indeed, the closure occasioned by the researcher necessarily treats the evidence as fixed and reliable and glosses over ambivalence and uncertainty. This is a 'privileged' reading of the 'life'. Perhaps, as Stronach and MacLure (1997, p. 49) argue,

> the problem is not what will count as an authentic portrait, but the assumptions we make about personhood. We think of the problem as one of representation (the person as given, the portrait as problematic) and we struggle with forms of ethics, social interaction, data analysis and reporting that will 'express' the person, squeeze his (sic) essence from the body of data.

They go on to suggest that the problem is how we actually conceptualize the 'life': 'making problematic what we mean by a person' (ibid.). Throughout the account above, the author has had to continually confront this dilemma; that is, the use of narrative devices, tropes, metaphors and other rhetorical forms to sustain the integrity of the person to whom they refer. Even though the commentary is brief and rarely goes beyond the data, it is there to make sense of those data — to provide the reader with the means to recognize that person as a person. In doing this, it is doing no more than that person would do anyway and again here we see the close alignment of autobiography with biography. The biographer however, stands apart. They cannot own the account in the way that the autobiographer can. They always impose a view, follow a particular direction, make sense of an event in one way rather than another. They are therefore complicit in the account and have to take responsibility for it. This, as I have suggested, refers to both its content and its form; indeed, the notion of a biographical account is part of that imposed structure. And yet, the solution to this problem is not easy to find. Stronach and MacLure (1997, p. 57) argue that: 'One goal must be to produce accounts which deny the reader that comfort of a shared ground with the author, foreground ambivalence and undermine the authority of their own assertions'. How we do this and whether we do it successfully or not are key elements in the construction of any 'life', let alone that of Mary O'Brien.

## Acknowledgments

My thanks go to Mary O'Brien for allowing me access to her life. This is of course not her real name.

## References

ARCHER, M. (1982) 'Morphogenesis versus Structuration', *British Journal of Sociology*, **33**, 4, pp. 455–483.

ARCHER, M. (1988) *Culture and Agency*, Cambridge: Cambridge University Press.

BHASKAR, R. (1989) *Reclaiming Reality*, London: Verso.

DERRIDA, J. (1976) *Of Grammatology*, Baltimore: Johns Hopkins University Press.

ERBEN, M. (1996) 'The purposes and processes of biographical method', in SCOTT, D. and USHER, R. (ed.) *Understanding Educational Research*, London: Routledge.

GADAMER, H-G. (1975) *Truth and Method*, London: Sheed and Ward.

GIDDENS, A. (1984) *The Constitution of Society*, Cambridge: Polity Press.

MACINTYRE, A. (1988) *Whose Justice? Which Rationality?* London: Duckworth.

RICOEUR, P. (1984) *Time and Narrative, Part One*, Chicago: University of Chicago Press.

RICOEUR, P. (1985) *Time and Narrative, Part Two*, Chicago: University of Chicago Press.

RICOEUR, P. (1986) *Time and Narrative, Part Three*, Chicago: University of Chicago Press.

STRONACH, I. and MACLURE, M. (1997) *Educational Research Undone: The Postmodern Embrace*, Buckingham: Open University Press.

USHER, R. (1996) 'Telling a story about research and research as story-telling: Postmodern approaches to social research', in MCKENZIE, G., POWELL, J. and USHER, R. *Understanding Social Research: Perspectives on Methodology and Practice*, Lewes: Falmer Press.

WOOD, D. (1990) *Philosophy at the Limit*, London: Unwin Hyman.

# 4     Adolescent Girls Reflect on Educational Choices

*Chris Mann*

The aim of this chapter is to explore initial findings from educational life histories written by 17-year-old girls, currently taking advanced level examinations (A level) in the United Kingdom (UK). A life history methodology was adopted to give insight into the thoughts and feelings that might underlie the educational choices of female students in late adolescence. The girls were invited to address the question 'How did I get to here?'; the question alluding to their sixth form status. Life histories were also appropriate as they illuminate how people 'articulate, comprehend and shape their lives in relation to public narratives' (Thomson, Hoar, Lea, Stuart, Swash and West, 1994, p. 177). This is particularly important at a time of change, when social frameworks may be unstable and constantly shifting. For instance, in the 1990s, stereotypical gender patterns have been challenged by an unprecedented increase in female employment which has developed alongside increased economic uncertainty for men. It is against this backcloth of gender transformation, that the working-class and middle-class girls in this study sought to reconcile their educational choices with the contradictions in their lives. Family context and interpersonal relations are often a key feature of female life-explanation and this clearly applied to these girls. Almost all of the 60 scripts prioritized relationships, and most refer to the family. The texts gave insight into the relationship between family educational history, developing identities, social context, and use of language. I shall describe some of the ways in which these elements inter-relate, and then elaborate by drawing on two specific narratives.

Family life trajectories in the 1990s are complicated. Relationships rarely stand still: parents move away from grandparents, parents separate, families are split and reconstituted. However, the educational life histories suggested that for many girls, particularly from rural working-class families, traditional forms of femininity are still rewarded and high levels of female academic achievement are often viewed with ambivalence or antagonism, especially by the older generation. As a result, working-class girls often discuss their educational success in terms of doubt and uncertainty (they 'suppose' they 'might' carry on); in terms of 'proving' themselves (sometimes to friends and teachers, sometimes to the family itself); and in terms of earning (or forcing?) family acceptance: 'I want to make them proud of me'. However, girls acknowledge that 'appropriate' levels of academic achievement are welcomed. GCSE success may be considered momentous, the cause of excited family telephone calls: 'My mum rang my dad at work then my grandparents and aunts'. Indeed, as family pioneers in *further* education, some working-class girls plot their success as an important, potentially catalytic contribution to the wider family circle: 'I was the first child and grandchild in the entire family to take A levels so it was automatically me who was to go through everything first!' However, ideas about *higher* education might be a cause for alarm: 'No one in the family has ever gone to university and I am not expected to be the first'.

It is often grandparents, above all, who remind young women that their new identity as an 'achiever' may be laudable in a secondary school but higher aspirations would not be appropriate in the community life they have been part of: 'Gran wants me to be a straight-A student, setting an example as the eldest grandchild, but she says a woman's job after schooling is to get married and have lots of children'. Narratives suggest that many grandparents expect girls to act in 'acceptable' ways, or emotional support and solidarity may be moderated or withheld. Girls who have started to believe that women should have the same opportunities as men find their strong — and valued — relational bonds with grandparents at risk.

The power of the third generation, and the 'tradition' that stretches behind it, can also influence views of femininity within many families. Some girls were quick to identify paternal grandmothers as the source of 'the problem' of the traditional views held by many fathers. Few traditional working-class girls in this study look to their fathers for encouragement in orientating themselves as 'academic achievers'. When educational life histories refer to working-class fathers there is frequently a bleak note. They present fathers as 'always bunking off school'; 'leaving school at 15 having been at secondary modern school'; or leaving school at 17 'because he got his girlfriend pregnant' and 'his parents made him get married'. There were fathers who modestly hoped 'we were going to get a decent education and not bunk', who 'didn't really encourage' and who didn't 'take a great interest in education'. There were also fathers who were seen to refuse support for reasons of envy and fear: 'he didn't want any of his children to do better than him'. While fathers might display a lack of involvement in education whatever the gender of their children, their views on femininity socialize girls into an understanding of traditional gender norms: 'Dad says that women are best at answering phones and doing secretarial things as it's a man's world'.

The ways in which girls from traditional working-class families talk about their mothers is noticeably different from their accounts of their fathers. While many working-class mothers have been forced by financial pressures to take a significant role in the labour market, gender equalities within the home rarely keep pace. With traditional patterns under strain, many working-class mothers intervene, urging their girls towards an achievement orientation that may secure their future. Teaching daughters to read and write at home was seen to be a key contribution of working-class mothers, and many girls in this study described feeling competent and confident in their early school years because of this 'head start' to their education. In addition, some mothers shared their experiences of lost opportunities, feelings of being cheated, or a future of 'dead end' jobs: 'Mum sees school as something important and really pushes me. She met my dad when she was 14 and left school for him when she was clever enough to be a nurse and that's what she wanted. Because she missed out she really wants me to have a career'. However, some mothers may feel unable to disturb the flow of tradition in working-class homes and the norms often held by husbands (and grandmothers) may still take precedence in a girl's socialization. Thus, daughters may experience ambivalence: 'Mum says go to college — and then she changes her mind. I don't know what she thinks really'.

However, in many homes, the changing work patterns, revised gender expectations and adult learning experiences of the 1990s are leading working-class parents to become highly involved in the education of their children. Parental educational or career advances have frequently been hard won and some parents have an empirical understanding of the challenges facing young people from working-class roots. The strong sense that many adults have consciously reviewed their life experiences is found in reported language use. While traditional families talk to girls in terms of what 'has always been' or what 'ought to be', other working-class families talk of what 'might have been', 'should have been' and 'still could be'. Girls' narratives plot the wistfulness and longing of family members who have 'wanted to break the chain' of working-class life trajectories; the urgent encouragement of those who have done so. Most girls admire and wish to emulate the drive and persistence of family educational pioneers, and they approve of, and identify with, their aspirations: 'They stuck it out even though they haven't enjoyed a lot of the stuff they've done. They've done it for us. And you know, it's been worth it, so I'm going to stick it out too'.

Above all, girls from working-class families in transition talk about their mothers' past lives and can often identify with the value judgments their mothers are transmitting. Mothers frequently stress the gender aspects of lost opportunities. A great number of girls evoke mothers who 'didn't have the opportunity to continue', 'gave up A levels to marry my dad' or 'missed out on further education' because of marriage and children. A few girls referred to mothers who had been excited by the success of brothers who were 'the first' to go to college — only to find that the tantalizing vision would be denied to the daughters of the house. The girls frequently evoke their mothers in language that suggests a mother's retrospective annoyance at the passivity, or resignation she showed in the face of the limited expectations of her family: 'she was never given the chance to go to university', 'her father plonked her in secretarial college', 'she was always expected to get married'. The language of diminutives was used to show the mother's reported frustration with female positioning: 'the little housewife sort of thing', 'she was always made to look small by everyone', 'just another little woman'.

Many mothers (and older sisters) are then described as active agents in the family's recent history. They subsequently made things happen, sorted things out, made decisions, 'proved' themselves. The mothers' experiences of pitching their female selves against the expectations of society is seen to give them a status that gives weight to their advice. These mothers stress education and achievement, not femininity. Mothers who may have married early now stress: 'It's not only looks that matter, I should build my own character and personality — my mum thinks that issues like how I look are very trivial'. A girl may identify completely with the mother's desire to educate herself and position herself as the triumphant culmination of the mother's story: 'She's got a lot of hopes in me getting through. Because I'm doing what she never did. And I think it's really important for her'.

The support of working class *fathers* who intervene in their children's education may place a strong emphasis on class, rather than gender transition. Many girls describe such men as being 'held back', 'left behind' and marginalized in public life. Often politicized by recent study, or difficult life experiences, these fathers are subsequently seen to relinquish traditional male control of a girl's femininity, while intervening positively in the education that will foster her social mobility. Their daughters are often aware that traditional expectations of masculinity are being challenged by their fathers, and express gratified amazement at the unexpected advice they offer: 'As for marriage dad says it's *up to me* when, where, if!, how!!!, what to!!!

The life histories of working-class girls drew attention to a fairly distant relationship between school and home. Family support for education was frequently presented as ambiguous, unassumed, striven for, involving human cost. In contrast, middle-class girls used language that flagged familiarity with, and expectation of support for, educational success. It was 'naturally assumed'; 'a natural path'; 'I always expected to go on'. In a later discussion, one girl reflected on how the autobiographical theme I had provided revealed the depth of her assumptions: 'When you said, "Why are you here? Why did you *decide* to do A levels?", I thought — I *don't know*, I just never asked myself that question before' [*interview*].

For middle class girls the intergenerational inheritance of educational success was seen to be a strong factor in determining the 'naturalness' of achievement. Grandparents might feature as role-models. Grandfathers might be 'very artistic and musical'; 'a historian'; able to 'speak five different languages'; while grandmothers might do, 'loads of sculpture and paintings and stuff' or set up a tradition of female aspiration: 'All the women in my family have careers — thanks to Grandma. My mum says "You're no good without that piece of paper" — the same message she got from her own mother. They have indirectly shown me what women can and should achieve'. Parents continued with these traditions. In contrast to the narratives of many working-class girls, middle-class parents were frequently discussed as a unit, so far as educational values and career trajectories were concerned. This suggested some similarity of lifestyle between the sexes — and by extension similar aspirations for male and female children. Many parents were seen as a 'team', discussing interventional strategies, rewarding achievement or 'freaking out' together, depending on the situations they were faced with in the girl's progress through school[1]. Support for education generally remained a stable factor regardless of disagreements about other issues. It was not unusual to hear that, in separated or reconstructed families, parenting adults would continue negotiations to support children and step-children in a wide range of school-linked activities, even if their personal relationships were described as 'difficult'. In contrast to working-class girls, there was evidence of a wide range of practical support mechanisms available, including private tutors, payment for extra-curricular activities and extensive knowledge of how the education system works[2].

However, while many daughters benefited from the energy, acumen and sophistication of parents acting on their behalf, others felt swept away in the process. While educational life histories identified the absence of practical support in many working-class homes, middle-class girls expressed different concerns[3]. Girls wished parents would: 'not expect so much of me'; 'give me more breathing space'; 'stop nagging me'; 'leave me alone to get on with it rather than trying to run my life'; 'not always expect me to get straight As'; 'stop comparing me with themselves or friends'; 'stop being so persistent and pushy'; 'stop putting so much pressure on me'. It became clear that some forms of intervention were experienced as a form of control which overwhelmed autonomy. It is hard to avoid the conclusion that in some middle-class families acceptance is seen to *depend on* being academically successful — and success for these middle-class girls referred to levels of achievement that were often beyond the most tentative aspirations of (particularly rural) working-class girls.

Many middle-class girls used words centred on being judged and failing, 'feeling terrified' to disappoint. They described the 'awful' feelings that followed the news of 'mediocre' marks: the heightened emotional atmosphere at home; the anger and disappointment. Educational involvement for middle-class girls could be experienced as personally stressful, particularly if parental acceptance was an issue. Achievement was sometimes felt to be a performance that would be 'judged' against the prowess of those who had gone before, both older generations and siblings. The overwhelming pressure from high family expectations can be felt at an early stage, 'tracking' a girl throughout her school life. In this context gaining acceptance in the family might require a level of achievement that not all girls could attain: 'I was following in the footsteps of my two very successful sisters. This has always put me under quite a bit of pressure to succeed like they've done, and when I've failed to reach their standard, I've always felt a failure to my parents and teachers'. Intensely felt family expectations that lead to excessive intervention in a girl's education is not limited to middle-class families but it is more commonly found there. Family members *may* provide well-informed educational intervention but benefits could be counterbalanced by excessive educationally-focused *control*.

While such influences may prevent middle-class girls from imagining an identity that does not include academic achievement, working-class girls often have to reconcile contradictions in their lives before they can develop an identity as an academic achiever. I shall now present a more in-depth analysis of the educational life histories of two working-class girls in order to demonstrate the ways in which they struggled to incorporate educational achievement into a sense of self. The analysis that follows each of these two, uncut, previously hand-written, educational autobiographies was constructed from the viewpoint of my own history. I am a white middle-aged woman, born working-class, educated into the middle-class, and attempting to conduct research according to feminist principles. The young women quoted here will have known about these characteristics (and will have registered a lot more about me than I dare imagine!). They wrote these autobiographies after a series of eight, hour-long, group discussions that I facilitated. I cannot estimate the effect that these factors have had on either the form of the narratives, or the form of the analysis, but, without doubt, there has been an effect. Accordingly, neither the narratives, nor the analysis, can claim to take a 'final and authoritative' position (Weiler, 1992, p. 40).

### Emma's educational life history

For as long as I can remember I've always loved school, when I was little my mum taught me to read and write etc. at home, so I was always ahead at school and I suppose that has always inspired me to try and keep top of the class. As far as doing A levels is concerned my mum has had a lot to do with it because she gave up A levels to marry my dad and although she doesn't regret marrying dad she really wishes she had waited and done her A levels and so she really persuaded me not to throw away any opportunities I get and I suppose I've always remembered that when doing my GCSEs. The type of person that I am, though, knowing what I have to do and actually doing it are two very different things and I am very easily distracted. So far I've made it sound like everything has been really easy but my fourth year (the start of GCSEs) was a complete disaster. I made a new friend and she was a bit on the wild side, we used to skive lessons etc. and I got really behind. I eventually realized what I was doing and started to catch up, but then I started going out with my now ex-boyfriend and I spent all my time with him as he had left school and didn't think much to education, and again fell behind. Luckily though, at the start of the fifth year I had new friends and a new boyfriend who were very supportive, and my experiences of the year before made me even more determined to do well. So I worked really hard and in the end got the results that I wanted. I decided that after all that work it would be a shame not to carry on education so here I am doing A levels. There have been other things that have affected me getting here to do A levels. One major thing was my weight problem that I suffered in the second year and again in the fourth year. This is because I am very vain and always worry about what other people think of me. I made myself very ill both physically and mentally and that took me a long time to get over and obviously my school work was greatly affected but, I feel that I came out of it a lot stronger and that it has given me more confidence which has helped me through the start of sixth form. I can only think of one time that I have considered not doing A levels and that was the day I got my GCSE results. I was really pleased with what I had achieved under the circumstances, but my dad didn't seem bothered at all, he just muttered 'well done, but you could have done better' and that was it. I felt that there wasn't any point in doing A levels as I wouldn't get support from him, but we sat down and talked it out and as I said here I am.

Emma sets about presenting ways to explain how someone with her claimed identity — the 'type of person I am' — a person who has 'always loved school' — can reduce her first GCSE year to 'a complete disaster'. The child of a white working-class family, she presents her mother as a strong encouraging presence, teaching her to read and write at home, and 'inspiring' her to 'keep top of the class', and to take up post-compulsory education, 'because she gave up A levels to marry my dad and although she doesn't regret marrying dad she really wishes she had waited and done her A levels and so she really persuaded me not to throw away any opportunities I get.' Emma then adds, rather doubtfully, 'I suppose I've always remembered that' and goes on to reflect, 'So far I've made it sound like everything has been really easy', which in her own terms it had not.

To start with, Emma acknowledges that spending time with a girlfriend, and a boyfriend who had left school, contributed to her 'falling behind' in her schoolwork. Within the narrative her language moves backwards and forwards between the perspective of home and peer group. She contrasts herself who has 'always loved school' with her boyfriend, who, in a colloquial phrase that captures adolescent contempt 'didn't think much to education'. Using this syntax suggests a reluctant respect, as does the phrase 'on the wild side' describing her girlfriend, which conjures up an untamed, non-circumscribed lifestyle, more admired than despised. She then goes on to admit to another 'problem' that she was experiencing at this time, and which she talks about as a discrete event for which she takes personal responsibility as a character flaw. Losing weight, 'I made myself very ill both physically and mentally [pause] because I am very vain'. There is no evidence here of awareness of counter-narratives that highlight social pressures concerning 'femininity'. In Emma's terms this cluster of events is presented as the errant behaviour of a nature 'very easily distracted' from 'what I have to do'. Emma's awareness of obligation to a given academic course seems to be the context within which actions of her own autonomy and experimentation are described as distractions, worse 'a disaster'.

Apart from the 'distractions' at school Emma has an extra complication. It was the attitude of her father who, she suggests, made her feel that, 'there wasn't any point' in her continuing with her A levels, as, 'he didn't seem bothered' about her success, and seemed unlikely to offer support for her academic work. It is possible that in their different ways each parent may be asking Emma to be passive and compliant; accepting both her mother's wish that she should succeed where the mother did not, and the father's wish that she, like her mother, should return to a traditional working-class female position by giving up her schoolwork. Emma's narrative suggests that she has internalized contradictory parental positions towards school work that constrain her agency in complicated ways. On one hand, there is potential for issues of class and gender to restrict her. On the other hand there is the possibility that a struggle between parents over their conceptions of what a girl 'should be', combined with the daughter's own sense of what she might be, may lead the girl to anticipate loss — either of her own voice, or of one parent's approbation — whatever course she takes. There is considerable evidence that such confused messages may contribute to anorexia; the strategy of 'privileged girls struggling with the demands for competitive achievement and the conventions of femininity' (Debold, 1991, p. 179). In addition, in this case, the mother's ambivalence about the direction taken in her own life, may also have been internalized by her daughter. To feel connected to her mother might mean that Emma would also approach education with contradictory feelings, fearing the risk of abandonment by her mother *whichever* path she took. Zimmerman (1991, p. 229) suggests that a situation of this type is like asking a girl to cross a desert alone 'with insufficient water and no navigational aids' as 'mothers, constrained by their own experience, cannot provide these supplies'.

It took Emma a long time to get over her eating disorder but she feels that she has 'come out of it a lot stronger' as the fight, with the support of new friends, had given her confidence, which she hopes to put to use in tackling her A levels. She is proud of her success here, wrenching her health back from the contortions she had put her body through to appease what 'other people think' and in a sense wrenching her identity back to its earlier course. Emma finishes her narrative in a way that brings her story neatly back to resonances of her mother's history and perhaps demonstrates that the strength she has developed in the detours of her 'disaster' year may have also played its part in preventing history repeating itself. Her father's apparently dilute reaction to her GCSE level results nearly resulted in her giving up her studies, like her mother before her, but on this occasion 'we sat down and talked it out and as I said here I am'.

Emma's autonomous acts of experimentation with the life styles of her friends, may not have been the 'disaster' she names it, but a necessary exploration of life style alternatives before reclaiming her education in her own terms. She returns to her studies 'a lot stronger', gets on top of her eating problem, gets 'the results *I* wanted', and, crucially, engages her father in a positive talk about her future.

### Vicky's educational life history

How is it that I am here doing these A levels?
Since I have been in secondary school and further education my family and I have moved a few times. I feel this has influenced my education attainment and decisions. Although making new friends is not a problem for me, the attitudes of people in different areas has been quite hard to contend with. Not only are the people around me constantly changing in their views on life but I am too. Unfortunately I have never made up my mind on a career for the future which does trouble my family. I am not so worried because 'whatever will be, will be'. Whilst I was doing GCSEs peer pressure was very predominant in choices and decisions made. As I have grown up this factor has lessened greatly, it no longer applies to me. I found secondary school the hardest mental time of my life. Where I lived at the beginning of my education (the first year of secondary school) was a small village where 'everybody knows everybody else's business'. This didn't suit us at all because we, as a family, keep ourselves to ourselves. There was also a small percentage of racism that I had to contend with. Although I was not completely alone as my older sister, of three years, had also gone through this and experienced prejudice alone. She helped me come to terms with their 'ignorance' and I gradually ignored the verbal abuse. Then we moved again and I had only one experience of prejudice against me at this school. It seems strange, looking back over this part of my life even though it was not long ago, it doesn't seem part of me. (It feels like it happened to someone else and I was just a voyeur.) I felt that I was the only one experiencing this racism because I was the only half-caste person in the whole school (apart from my sister). I couldn't understand what I could have possibly done to them for them to hate me so much. My sister would say 'just ignore them

and they'll stop' or 'I know what you're going through and it won't last forever', but to me they were just words falling on deaf ears. She said she understood but how could she when it was happening to me! Only now when I look back on those events do I understand what she meant. I do believe that racism has lessened but it will never completely go away. I do believe that boys' views of girls on a whole has influenced me greatly. When at secondary school, sports were a major part of my life. But the boys would always put us down no matter what when it came to playing together. On one occasion, a girls' soccer team was set up and the boys wouldn't stop 'taking the piss!' until eventually it was stopped and taken off lunch-time activity timetable. Not only did I feel put down by the boys on the field but also in class. I took Computer Studies at GCSE level which is supposed to be a stereotypical 'male' subject. There were only a few girls in a class of about twenty boys. We were hassled a lot for being girls and better than them in class. My mum and nan were (and 'are') always there for me when I needed them. And I really love them for that. When it comes to my Pop there's a big gap in my mind. I hardly ever see him because he's at work all day. In the mornings I'm out of the house before he's awake, to go to college. When I get home he's at work. When he gets home I'm in my room (making a very poor effort to revise for exams), he sits downstairs, I stay upstairs or go out and then the routine repeats again. Day after day. . .He often says that we (me and my three sisters) 'don't know him'. As scary a thought as it may be, I think he's right. I love my Pop. My Pop's the one that's geared/pushed me and my sister to A levels. He says that 'without education you're nowhere'. Whereas my mum has just given me the advice of 'it's your life, you're only going to do what you're going to do, it's purely your own decision, I'll stand by you whatever you want to do'. I love my mum. I think the *main* reason I did A levels was because I didn't know what I wanted to do as a career so I chose A levels in subjects I enjoyed at GCSE or that I was interested in. Also my father's influence added to the choice of A levels. BUT now I wished I hadn't done three essay subjects because my life has become just work and no play! Being situated in this college has really changed my outlook on life and education. Because there's so many different types of people passing through, I've realized there's a real world other than education. After my A levels, no matter what my results are I hope to go to New Zealand for a year to live and work. Then I'll leave my life up to destiny and follow whichever path in life is mine.

Vicky, is a working class girl, with a Nigerian father and an English mother. Starting at her sixth-form college involved travelling into town from a rural area and this is seen as a catalyst, changing her 'outlook on life and education'. As she says, 'the attitudes of people in different areas has been quite hard to contend with. Not only are the people around me constantly changing in their views on life but I am too'. Vicky uses her narrative as an opportunity to take stock of the volatile nature of her current state of mind at this time of personal development and institutional change. She is well aware of the constraints that have affected her earlier educational career, recognizing that factors of gender and, above all, race, have been particularly significant. She is familiar with the discourse of sociology, using concepts and language that make connections between 'educational attainment' and 'racism'; 'peer pressure'; and the behaviour of 'stereotypical "male" subjects'. She can also address gender issues in the more pungent language of the female adolescent, recognizing that boys 'put us down' in sport and in the classroom, by hassling and 'taking the piss!'. But she is lost when it comes to finding language to support her in the actual experience of racism. Her sister has attempted to address racism in the terms of lay psychology, constructing it as infantile behaviour, 'ignore them and they'll stop', and attempting to diminish its power by labelling it as 'ignorance'. Vicky is not comforted. As she says, in this area, *all* words are 'just words falling on deaf ears'. If she has a counter-narrative to racism it is one of uncomprehending despair, 'I couldn't understand what I could have possibly done to them for them to hate me so much'.

These examples show how, in her own terms, and using various linguistic codes, Vicky has started to interpret the influence on her education of the over-arching defining identities of race and gender that have helped to structure her life experience. However, while she is making sense of her past, she is also attempting to frame her present and future. At this time of change and re-assessment her narrative begins to grapple with other issues that highlight some of the underlying complexities and contradictions in her situation.

Aware that her sixth-form experience has 'changed' some of her views, Vicky is using her narrative to re-evaluate her life. The collective cultural understanding of her peers at the new college have presented challenges to messages about life and education she has brought from home. She has started A levels in a friendly, accepting college where there are, 'many different types of people passing through'. Before, she had accepted her father's view of life as a kind of siege situation where the family kept apart, and kept their heads down — studying for future success. She speaks (still in the present tense) in the language of collective familial identity when she says 'we, as a family, keep ourselves to ourselves', as it is the family's experience, and her own as, 'the only half-caste person in the whole school. . .that racism has lessened but it will never completely go away'. No doubt galvanized by his own experiences of racism, Vicky's father has asserted that, 'without education you're nowhere' and he 'geared/pushed' Vicky and her sisters into A levels. Bruner has argued that the family continues to influence life stories, 'by posing the thematic structures in terms of which life can be accounted for, by setting the linguistic contrasts and defining the dilemmas' (Bruner and Weisser, 1991, p. 146). Vicky's father has provided a framework for life that uses the thematic contrast of 'somewhere' and, 'nowhere', with education as the key to getting 'somewhere'. But the new linguistic contrast gleaned from her peers seems to set the stifling atmosphere of 'education' ('I'm in my room making a very poor effort to revise for exams') against the invigorating possibilities of 'real life' (going to New Zealand). In addition, the adolescent perspective sees new dilemmas beyond that of the family's struggle to cope with racism. The educational study, that in the latter framework represents a strategy of resistance to oppression, becomes seen itself as an oppression — 'my life has become just work and no play'.

Vicky may have begun to absorb the new thematic structure of her peer group but she also attempts to incorporate this new framework into her allegiance to her family. It becomes clear that she is in process of negotiating her way around two opposing meaning systems while struggling to integrate her emotional and intellectual experience into a coherent self that can survive what are, in effect, multiple identities. Her identity has been created and re-created in the family's shared experience of prejudice and isolation — she 'identifies' with them. No doubt until fairly recently she had identified with her father's aspirations for herself and her sisters. In contrast to her experience of the negative aspects of gender dynamics at school, all the daughters had received strong positive affirmation in their educational endeavours from the authoritative male in the home. But now Vicky is finding this influence irksome. Her use of language — he 'geared/pushed' the sisters into A levels has an ambiguous tone. It suggests pressure rather than encouragement. His influence in her choice of A levels is represented as contributing to her sense of being overworked. Perhaps seeking a way to reconcile her past and her present she reviews her relationship with her parents in a process that seems to seek out opportune contradictions in the family 'script', that have the effect of marginalizing her father in the family. She reflects, 'My mum and nan were (and "are") always there for me when I needed them'. On the other hand, 'When it comes to my Pop there's a big gap in my mind. I hardly ever see him. . .He often says that we (me and my three sisters) "don't know him". . .I think he's right'. And while the 'absent' father may indeed suggest that without education a person is nowhere, the 'supportive' mother has given the currently more palatable message that someone is 'only going to do' what they are going to do. A truism that Vicky could more easily integrate into a new meaning system.

Vicky shows signs of wanting to wriggle out of a school life she is now beginning to see as limiting and restrictive but the narrative suggests that she will not openly challenge her father about this. Instead she draws on linguistic clichés that will put a protective gloss over her strategy of inaction. Glossing over her mother's assurance that she will support her whatever her '*decision*', Vicky concentrates on the possibly fatalistic aspects of 'it's your life' and seems to be re-interpreting this into an assurance that there will be a familial seal of approval, from at least one quarter, if she decides to half-consciously let her educational aspirations slip away. She finishes her narrative with her identity apparently left to chance, 'whatever will be, will be', and in her final sentence, 'I'll leave my life up to destiny and follow whichever path in life is mine'. It is possible to see this as just another case of a hard-working student being wooed from her labours by the heady distractions of youth, but a close reading of the narrative reveals the range of power conflicts and competing meanings that Vicky is attempting to reconcile. It can only be conjecture but it also occurs to me that the bruising experiences of racism may have contributed to a splitting of the identity in ways that go beyond multiple options of being and become psychologically profound. Unable to find language to effectively process these experiences there is a suggestion that Vicky has cut off from an integral part of herself 'it doesn't seem part of me (it feels like it happened to someone else and I was just a voyeur.)'. It is possible that this detachment from a previous painful reality is still preventing Vicky from engaging fully with the present — in which case New Zealand may represent a further flight from the present rather than an alternative future.

## Conclusion

These educational life histories suggest that the negotiations girls are involved in, and the strategies they adopt as they make choices about education, are all part of the process of defining identity. The language a girl may use to represent her educational experience and the ways she has dealt with that experience may vary, depending on the variety of life perspectives the girl is attempting to incorporate in her personal world view. The life histories suggest that while identity may be conceptualized within large collective social identities such as class, race and gender, these elements work together in unexpected and subtle ways. In addition, as girls negotiate interactions between the triangle of school, home, and friends, personal relationships give a psychological undertow to the struggle to find an educational identity. Educational life histories offer a means of exploring such complexities. They also offer a methodological approach that may map *changes* in social meanings. Although some working-class girls may still be struggling to see themselves as high achievers, there has clearly been a 'genderquake' (Wilkinson, 1994) in terms of the unprecedented levels of girls' educational achievement nationally. This is linked to a fear that both middle-class and working-class boys may underachieve in the current social climate. Educational life histories show us how young people invest their sense of self in their educational choices. Such in-depth understanding may help inform policy initiatives that seek to help all young people to meet their potential.

### Notes

1   These middle-class processes are described in detail in Allatt, 1993.
2   Middle-class families have more input into decisions about kids' course choice and level — possibly reflecting their greater sense of entitlement and efficacy in dealing with school officials (Useem, 1991).
3   Walkerdine (1996) has found similar patterns in her recent research on middle-class girls.

### References

ALLATT, P. (1993) 'Becoming privileged: The role of family processes' in BATES, I. and RISEBOROUGH, G. (eds) *Youth and Inequality*, Buckingham: Open University Press.

BRUNER, J. and WEISSER, S. (1991) 'The invention of self', in OLSEN, D. (ed.) *Literacy and Orality*, Cambridge: Cambridge University Press.

DEBOLD, E. (1991) 'The body at play', in GILLIGAN, C. (ed.) *Women, Girls and Psychotherapy*, New York: Hayworth Press.

THOMSON, A., HOAR, M., LEA, M., STUART, M., SWASH, V. and WEST, L. (1994) *Life Histories and Learning*, University of Sussex: Conference Papers.

USEEM, E. (1991) 'Student selection into course sequences in mathematics: The impact of parental involvement and school policies', *Journal of Research on Adolescence*, 1, pp. 231–250.

WALKERDINE, V. (1996) 'Transitions to womanhood: Social constructions of success and failure for working-class and middle-class young women', *British Youth Research*, Glasgow: The New Agenda.

WEILER, K. (1992) 'Remembering and representing life's choices' in *Qualitative Studies in Education*, **5**, 1, pp. 39–50.

WILKINSON, H. (1994) *No Turning Back: Generations and the Genderquake*, London: Demos.

ZIMMERMAN, J. (1991) 'Crossing the desert alone', in GILLIGAN, C. (ed.) *Women, Girls and Psychotherapy*, New York: Hayworth Press.

# 5    Voices from the Margins: Regulation and Resistance in the Lives of Lesbian Teachers

*Gill Clarke*

This chapter explores the radical potentialities of biographical methods for making difference visible. In so doing the life stories of lesbian physical education teachers are utilized to illustrate not only how difference is disguised by the ability to 'pass' the heterosexual presumption, but also to demonstrate how their stories are about resisting the hegemony of heterosexual lifestyles. Narratives from interviews with white secondary teachers are interpreted to reveal how these women may appear at times to be complicit in and colluding with heterosexual discourses whilst at the same time resisting and challenging both from within and without. Further to this through an analysis of the contemporary socio-political and cultural context and in particular Section 28 of The Local Government Act 1988, it will be claimed that heterosexual regulation and domination is never entirely successful and that wherever there is power there is resistance. Finally, it will be argued that the task in this biographical project is not only to listen to the voices from the margins but to recognize that difference is a civil rights issue, which requires a change in laws to reflect and acknowledge all our realities. As such we need to pursue the goal of social justice, thereby eliminating the privileging of heterosexual identities and creating a social landscape that allows us all to define our lives.

### Sexuality and surveillance of the self: The introduction of Section 28

In order to understand how these lesbian teachers live out their lives it is necessary to situate them within the wider socio-political and cultural context. Analysis of the circumstances leading up to the passing of Section 28 reveals much about the power of the new moral right and about attitudes towards lesbians and gay men. Attitudes and resultant discourses that I will argue remain exceedingly powerful — and especially so within the conservative world of education and more specifically that of physical education. During Margaret Thatcher's premiership the 'campaign for family values' was pursued with much vigour and concerns were expressed about the sanctity and well-being of the institution of the family. This traditional patriarchal institution was seen as being under attack particularly from homosexuals whom it was believed 'could undermine the basis of our society' (Boyson, 1987, pp. 1002–3). These fears were to lead, in part, to an increase in state involvement and to a greater regulation of sexuality. Alongside these concerns must also be seen central government alarm over the growing power and autonomy of some local authorities and, in particular, the activities of some local Labour councils — the so called 'loony left'. Haringey in north London was seen as one such example: their policy of 'positive images' of homosexuality led to clashes between parents and gay rights supporters. Dame Jill Knight (1987, p. 1000) speaking in the House of Commons commented: 'Hundreds of thousands of pounds are being spent by some councils in promoting sexuality in our schools. All of that money could be far better spent'. In the same debate, Dr. Rhodes Boyson (the Minister for Local Government) stated:

> The government share the view that a society is defined by its shared beliefs and habits. There are some kinds of behaviour that Christian charity may lead us to tolerate, but there is no reason why public funds should be spent on promoting that behaviour and no reason why we should tolerate those who spend public funds in this way. Undermining the common standards of society, flaunting behaviour that the overwhelming majority of those brought up in this country and its traditions find revolting, unsettling the minds of the coming generation is one way — a subtle way — of changing the society in which we live. (1987, p. 1002)

It was against this political landscape that the supporters of Section 28 were able to mount a passionate and vociferous campaign against homosexuals who were depicted as sick, sinful, predatory individuals who were a threat to children and the continuance of society. The Earl of Halsbury (1986, p. 310) spoke of how he had been 'warned that the loony left is hardening up the lesbian camp and that they are becoming increasingly aggressive'. In support of the Local Government Act (Amendment) Bill [H.L.] 1986, Lady Saltoun of Abernethy (1986, p. 317) summed up the views of many of those in the House of Lords by stating: 'This is a small Bill — a David of a Bill that sets out to kill a Goliath of an evil'. Thus the Conservative moral crusade was mobilized and orchestrated around the twin threats of local government autonomy and homosexuality, each in their own way viewed as a potential threat to public safety and the security of the state. Section 28 of the Local Government Act 1988 was therefore an attempt to fuse the two 'evils'. It stated:

1    A local authority shall not —
    (a)   intentionally promote homosexuality or publish material with the intention of promoting homosexuality;
    (b)   promote the teaching in any maintained school of the acceptability of homosexuality as a pretended family relationship.

2    Nothing in subsection (1) above shall be taken to prohibit the doing of anything for the purpose of treating or preventing the spread of disease. (Smith, 1994, p. 183)

The discourses of Section 28 were an attempt by its supporters to restore the family to its rightful, 'natural' place at the heart of British life, and to protect it from attack by lesbians and gay men. The intention was also to reassert the 'moral' high ground in schools and to maintain cultural conformity and the omnipotence of heterosexual identities, values and institutions, whilst at the same time defining, regulating, policing, and enforcing sexual boundaries. In order to do this not only were local authorities targeted as potential purveyors of homosexual propaganda, but so too were teachers, both it was argued could use their influence to threaten the authority of the state and the sanctity of the family (see Evans, 1989–90). This repressive legislation exemplified not only legal disapproval of lesbian and gay lifestyles but it also illustrated the power of the Conservative New Right to dictate what constituted 'acceptable–normal' sexual identity and despite large-scale protests it passed into the legal statute books in May 1988. Although summarily dismissed as ambiguously worded, it continues to be dangerously open to misinterpretation, and as such its implications are potentially far-reaching (see Colvin and Hawksley, 1989). Despite these legal paradoxes and the fact that its provisions have yet to be interpreted by the courts (see *OutRage!* and *Stonewall*, 1994) it still carries powerful and prejudiced messages about homosexuality, serving as it does to legitimize hegemonic discourses of heterosexuality. Undoubtedly, the passing of Section 28 has had a marked effect on the teaching of lesbian and gay issues in many schools[1] as well as creating a climate of fear and self-censorship amongst lesbian, gay and bisexual teachers (see Clarke, 1996). The newly elected Labour government before the election promised to repeal Section 28 — as yet there has been no indication about how or when this will happen (see *Stonewall*, 1997).

Whilst Section 28 may only be of symbolic power and significance, it has nevertheless contributed to the situation whereby all the lesbian teachers in my research feared for their continued employment should their sexuality be revealed. Hence, as is later illustrated, the compulsion that many feel to employ heterosexual passing strategies so as to conceal their 'real' sexual identity. Thus it is possible to begin to see how their 'true' voices are constrained, silenced and deprived of authority by not only the state, but also by the legal and educational system. As such, their very presence is often erased from the social and political landscape, for some at best they may have a presence on the margins but for most, as we shall see, invisibility becomes a measure of their survival. The task then in this biographical project is to make these largely invisible lives visible, in doing so I draw on the voices and storied lives of the marginalized as a means of challenging and exposing sexual oppression and domination.

## Locating lesbian lives

The life stories which frame this chapter are drawn from questionnaires, personal correspondence and in-depth interviews conducted with eighteen white lesbian physical education teachers during 1993–5. All names are pseudonyms, the first woman interviewed chose a name beginning with the letter 'A', the second a name beginning with 'B' and so on. The interviews focused on: lesbian identity, activities of teaching, and relationships with teaching colleagues and pupils. These discussion areas arose from my reading of other researchers' work on lesbian teachers (Griffin,

1991; Khayatt, 1992), together with my own experiences of teaching physical education for seven years in secondary schools. The interviews were tape recorded, transcribed and returned to the women for comments, corrections, deletions and so on. I also sent them copies of some of the papers that I have written about their lives for comment, though it would be naïve and simplistic to think that these small and partially collaborative actions have solved the problems of representation, power and exploitation.

The interviewees were white, able-bodied and aged between 23 and 47 years old. Some were single, some had been married (all retained their 'Mrs' title), some were currently in long-standing lesbian relationships, none had children, they came from a variety of working and middle-class backgrounds. The length of time they had taught for varied between just over a year to twenty-five years and all worked with pupils aged between 11 and 18 years. At the time of the research they were teaching in a variety of establishments from: mixed comprehensive schools, girls' schools, church schools to independent schools. These were located variously in inner cities, urban and/or rural areas.

## Performing heterosexuality — just a passing phase?

None of the teachers were completely open in their schools about being lesbian, for some their sexual identity was known only to a small number of colleagues, but for most their identity was a closely protected secret. As I have already claimed Section 28 has done much to keep these teachers locked within the (heterosexual) closet of the 'classroom', indeed Ivy when asked what Section 28 meant to her stated: 'It means that a lot of people are frightened about those of us on the edge, who rock the boat and challenge the status quo. It means a lack of freedom to be who I am'. This lack of freedom is compounded by the fact that education is by nature and tradition a conservative profession. It is a profession that is seen to be entrusted with the education of young and potentially vulnerable minds, and as such, the profession has always had a moral responsibility to uphold high standards of behaviour and conduct in order to fulfil one of its functions, that of being a role model for young people. Physical education has a specific tradition of its own, again not only markedly conservative but also highly gender differentiated, since historically the subject has developed around two distinct and separate male and female sporting cultures built around particularly narrow ideologies and stereotyped visions of heterosexual masculinity and femininity (see Fletcher, 1984; Scraton, 1992). Thus within the male domain of sport and physical education the heterosexuality of women participants has often been open to question. Indeed, research by Harris and Griffin (1997, p. 49) sought to assess the cultural stereotypes and personal beliefs held about women physical education teachers. Their findings indicated that their 'Respondents felt that most Americans stereotyped women physical educators as masculine, aggressive, athletic, lesbian and unintellectual'. From my own experiences in physical education and sport I would suggest that similar beliefs would not be uncommon in England. To participate in the physical education and sporting arena openly as a lesbian is to run the risk of harassment and intimidation (see Clarke, 1995; Lenskyj, 1991). What is also pertinent to this discussion is that the very subject matter of physical education, that is the centrality and the physicality of the body, creates additional anxieties, fears and pressures for lesbian teachers. As Fay stated:

> it is different for PE teachers because you are involved with the physical side of things. It has got to be worse. . .there has got to be a different stigma attached to it and everything else that goes with it, and I think that is what people are frightened of. Ginny often says if I taught something else it wouldn't matter, but because you teach PE it is different, and I think it frightens a lot of people that if that was found out they would think you were molesting or you were some kind of pervert. You know, the only reason you are teaching PE is because you can see all the kids undress. I used to go through all sorts of strategies in the changing rooms so that I was never near the kids when they showered. When I taught with somebody else I always left it up to them, and I would kind of be in the background.

Gabby also felt that physical education teachers were targets for homophobic suspicions and accusations, she said: 'the impression I get is that if I was a history teacher it would matter less, but because I am dealing with young girls getting changed, then I'm immediately a paedophile'.

Whilst I acknowledge that teachers of other subjects may be forced to deny their sexual identities, what I am arguing for here is a recognition that the gendered bodily culture of physical education and sport creates a unique context for denial that might not be experienced by teachers within other subject disciplines. Sullivan (1993, p. 99) in writing about her own experiences of oppression as a lesbian teacher in an inner city comprehensive school in the United Kingdom wonders:

> How lesbians who teach girls' physical education cope I don't know. I would be paranoid that my sexuality would be discovered and that the tabloid press would have a field day fabricating salacious headlines.

Coping for these teachers is the daily reality of their lives in schools and this is not without its personal costs, for them it means that if their lesbian identity is to survive then they must engage in a variety of camouflage strategies so as to pass convincingly as heterosexual. Fay described how:

> When you go into school you know it is different. . .I find it very difficult to cope with, because you know my sexuality to me is a very important part of me and then all of a sudden you are faced with here we go, back again to the conservatism of it all and we are covering our tracks by not saying who we live with, who we go out with, what we do at weekends. You are only choosing to tell the bits that aren't going to tell a story. I did find the change very different (compared to the 'freer' environment of college) and I think that's partly why I moved from the school I was in because I couldn't cope with people you know, I felt I was living a bigger lie there and so when the job came up that I could come back to. . .where I had all my friends around me it was far better.

'Covering our tracks' was a strategy employed by many of these teachers to disguise the reality of their home lives, for Caroline it meant that when other staff were talking 'about their husbands or children or whatever' she would also 'get this urge to talk incessantly about my homelife' (but it was) 'something that I really do have to suppress, and if I'm feeling that way it can really get me down'. Conversations in staffrooms that revolved around personal relationships were regarded with some unease since they could potentially be sites where their heterosexual cover might be blown. Hence most of these teachers either felt the need to censor what they said or to steer the conversations to safer topics, however, in some cases it was felt that it was simply easier to avoid them. Other topics of conversation that were viewed as 'risky' were those that revolved around homosexuality, here the fear was the belief that by engaging in debates too vociferously around issues like the lowering of the age of consent for gay men, then attention would be drawn to them with the result that questions might be asked about their sexuality. Not all the women felt so disempowered, Ivy felt more able to enter into debates and to challenge homophobic jokes but this she said was because she was the Equal Opportunities Officer for her school — this, she reasoned, afforded her a kind of legitimacy and protection. Other strategies that were employed to disguise the self were revealed by Gabby when she disclosed how she protected her sexual identity 'by not getting involved in anything socially at school where staff would be taking their partners'.

As these women's partners were not of the 'right' and publicly sanctioned sex, when asked by pupils whether they had boyfriends they felt pressurized into inventing mythical male figures in order to deflect suspicion. Thus these mythical males were also dropped into conversations so that these lesbian teachers appeared 'normal', that is heterosexual. Harriet described how she 'openly lied' to pupils, she said: 'I felt terrible about it. . .but I do really feel put on the spot'. Pressure also came from some colleagues who were often urging them to find a man, for as far as these colleagues were concerned they did not have any sort of visible partner. Caroline revealed how she responded to questions about whether she had 'a fella',

> I lie through my teeth quite frankly, I much prefer them (the pupils) to think that I
> might have a fella, or even that I might have a fella and wasn't saying, than they
> think that I didn't. . . .I try to be secretive and mysterious but make it clear that
> there is somebody.

Being secretive or in some cases ambiguous was a way of conforming to the institutionalized discourses of compulsory heterosexuality. Deb remarked 'I don't deny anything, I am ambiguous in what I say to them, just because I don't want them knowing my lifestyle. . .'. Knowing about their lesbian lifestyles was seen as being extremely threatening to the continuance of their teaching career, consequently it was felt by some of the women that it was necessary to publicly and openly portray to their colleagues and pupils that they were interested sexually in men. Harriet, for instance, acknowledged that she 'was overtly flirtatious with young male staff' in order to convince others of her heterosexuality, she also revealed how one of the male staff was 'very tactile' and always giving her a hug, she said:

even though I hate to admit it, it does my image good at school and it's just nice to have him as a friend and I think I'm pretty sure it would change things signific-antly if I told him. But I'd love to tell him so that he realized that we haven't got two heads.

Harriet was not alone in wanting to reveal her sexual identity to teaching col-leagues, but this desire to tell was not felt to be worth the risk of 'losing friends and being exposed to people, ridiculed I suppose. It shouldn't matter if people are going to say things' (Annie). Clearly differences do matter but in these specific cases it seems that the risks — be they real or imagined — are just not worth taking.

### Passing as an act of resistance and subversion

Passing as heterosexual in the workplace for these lesbian teachers is as we have seen manifest in a number of different ways including: the inventing of boyfriends, and being flirtatious with men in order to establish their heterosexual credentials. The main form that these strategies appear to take is through the censorship and removal of the self from potentially hazardous situations, i.e. non-attendance at staff socials, avoidance of certain conversations/debates in staffrooms. What is evident from these narratives is the way that work, that is teaching, shapes and constrains how lesbian lives are lived out in the environment of the school. These passing strategies involve in many instances the performing of a particular heterosexual part. In con-ceptualizing these 'acts' as performances I draw selectively on Butler's (1990, 1991, 1993) concept of gender performativity. This notion of performance provides a useful metaphor to play with since schools are rather like theatres where all sorts of performances are engaged in. Inasmuch as I am claiming that heterosexuality is being played at I would not want to dispute that these women are not 'really' lesbian or that being a lesbian is something that you slip into and out of like some sort of sexual tourist. Rather it is that the nature of schooling and the socio-political con-text requires that they perform their heterosexual parts convincingly so as to be able to deflect attention and/or scrutiny when necessary. Additionally, their scripts are severely constrained (even compulsory) if their performances are to be socially sanctioned and publicly approved. Whilst this notion of performance provides cru-cial insights into the public ways that lesbian lives are largely lived out in schools it would be a gross mistake to fail to recognize that for these teachers they *have* to perform in order to survive in a heterosexist and homophobic world, therefore these performances should not be trivialized. The costs for these teachers should they not play their part are all too real to be denied. Their lives are more than a game (Clarke, 1997). As Esterberg comments:

> lesbian performances are serious play; that is, while there is an element of play, of fun, in the slippage of categories, this is serious play because it has to do with deeply important aspects of the self. Lesbian identity — and our playing out of it — *matters*. (1996, p. 261)

Esterberg's claims are borne out by Harriet who saw her attempts at concealing her lesbian identity as a game, for her it was 'quite a nice game to play, it's about the only game that I can play that I know I'm going to win because I've got an ace under my sleeve. There's something they don't always know about me'. Several of the women also admitted that they 'like(d) part of the secretiveness, and the fact that going against the norm is quite thrilling in a way' (Deb). Barbara also described how she found 'it quite exciting in a way getting away with it, fibbing. . .I just laugh to myself because they have no idea'. 'Getting away with it' becomes a means of resisting and challenging albeit in perhaps a rather hidden way. This too is another paradox of their identities. For some this 'getting away with it' has become an almost enjoyable pursuit: Deb disclosed how: 'In some ways it is a game. . .it is just a bit of fun. . .let them wonder'. This refusal to reveal their sexual identity and the non-challenging of comments is for these teachers a way of resisting. Consequently it is important that these silences are not misread as 'women's allegedly more passive, reticent and non-aggressive verbal and bodily habitus' (Luke, 1994, p. 218), but rather as a conscious discursive strategy to contest the hegemony of heterosexuality.

Allied with these strategies for resisting, performing a particular part can also be viewed as a subversive and resistant act, insofar as the performance is a way of throwing heterosexuality back in your face! Since where the part is successfully performed then the point is made (albeit largely privately) that heterosexuality can be copied, faked and bought without it being realized that it is merely an imitation.

Furthermore this performing and passing as lesbian as Inness (1997, p. 161) claims 'calls into question the distinction between heterosexual and homosexual'. What this also demonstrates is that sexual boundaries are not as fixed as some might have us believe, rather they are social and cultural constructs that can be crossed. Indeed Deb stated that she knew some women who were 'blatantly unhappy in a situation and you know why, (she believed they were lesbian) but they won't do anything about it, because they haven't got the courage' because she claimed 'going against the grain (that is being lesbian) is quite a hard thing to do'. Caroline also thought it was difficult for lesbian women, because as she said 'you don't have convention on your side. . .and people don't think women ought to be together anyway'. Like Cheryl Clarke (1983, p. 128) who writes about lesbian women in North American society, I want to argue that just being:

> a lesbian in a male-supremacist, capitalist, misogynist, racist, homophobic, imperialist culture, . . .is an act of resistance. . . .No matter how a woman lives out her lesbianism — in the closet, in the state legislature, in the bedroom — she has rebelled. . .

These varied conceptions of resistance are important as they allow for the recognition that these women are not just passive, subjugated people but active agents engaged in struggles in different locales and at varying levels, be they ideological or structural. Thus how their voices are (re)presented and interpreted is crucial if they are not simply to be portrayed and read as victims of a heterosexist and homophobic society. Joy makes the case that she does not want to be presented as 'bound down', she believes that:

it's quite important that we are not seen as victims, that people recognize that there are problems for other lesbians. To get it in perspective one of the worst things of our lives is the fear, quite often it's unfounded, . . .the silences keep us oppressed, keep us down. The more of us that can do it (come out), the people you work with will have to realize we are just ordinary folks. . .

## Missing voices: Hearing what 'we' have to say

As we have seen, one of the strengths of biographical methods is that it offers possibilities for making visible (and central) those whose lives have been erased from the landscape and for those who have been silenced it offers the platform for them to speak in their own words about their experiences. Thus it can provide a powerful platform for advocacy for the oppressed and marginalized as well as contributing 'to the destigmatizing of sexually stigmatized groups' (Faraday and Plummer, 1979, p. 792). Hence it is imperative that the story-teller engages with the moral responsibilities that such a biographical project entails insofar as they are also speaking for and about 'them'. Therefore how we write stories and locate ourselves will impact not only on how lives are subsequently viewed and interpreted but also on the authority of our claims. Additionally, embedded in the telling of these stories are issues of privilege, power and the potential for exploitation and abuse (see Alcoff, 1991).

For those who have been denied a place to speak from, the narratives presented here provide this group of teachers with the power of a collective story. For one of the consequences of their successful invisibility in schools is that they remain isolated from other lesbian teachers and this can make for feelings of insularity and loneliness. This lack of collective identity/presence is also potentially problematic for their working together to create social and political change. Nevertheless, these narratives offer possibilities for transformation and social change through making visible the social and political injustices that force these teachers to deny their sexual identities. For those who are isolated and feeling 'in a world of one' (Ivy) it provides them with a link to and a solidarity with others, insofar as they are able to see that they are not alone. Caroline, for instance, said that she 'was extremely pleased' to be involved in the research because

> I think that it is something that is very important. . .I know that I would like to read it because I would be fascinated to know what other peoples' experiences have been and what their thoughts are. . .I think it is extremely important and it's probably not given the respect it deserves. . .there are a lot of people living an extremely lonely inner existence and they are living a lie at school and often they are living a lie at home as well, and where do these people find out how other people are feeling? . . .and equally there are a lot of. . .staff that you live a lie to, who don't know you are living a lie. It would be nice to say if only you knew, and I think this is an opportunity to let people know, and people do need to know.

Telling collective stories can 'let people know' and moreover they can as Barone (1992, p. 143) argues 'prick the consciences of readers by inviting a re-examination of the values and interests undergirding certain discourses, practices and institutional arrangements found in today's schools'. In connection with this Fay, when asked what she hoped might come out of the research, alludes to similar points:

> I suppose from my point of view that sometimes I have got a little more courage you know to say 'this is what I have to put up with', you know 'I am a lesbian and I am having a relationship with another woman and this is what I have to put up with every day when I come to school. . .'. And at some point in the future maybe I have got enough courage to come up and say 'look this is me, this is it and this is part of me that I want people to realize that this is part of me'. And like you say, in publishing something like that maybe people will read it and maybe next time they will think twice either about what they say or if there is somebody else on their staff that they think might be gay they give them the opportunity to talk about it. Sometimes in a way I feel very angry that they don't give me the opportunity to say 'yes'. You know if somebody said to me 'are you having a relationship with another woman, are you gay?' I suppose they feel it is not their place, but maybe next time if somebody reads it, it might give them the courage to ask. Because sometimes it is very difficult to say, it's easiest to be asked because then you have got the option of opting out.

The collective story also offers further transformative possibilities, for as Richardson (1990, p. 26) argues:

> At the individual level, people make sense of their lives through the stories that are available to them, and they attempt to fit their lives into the available stories. People live by stories. If the available narrative is limiting, destructive, or at odds with the actual life, peoples' lives end up being limited and textually disenfranchised. Collective stories that deviate from standard cultural plots provide new narratives; hearing them legitimates replotting one's own life.

For these women hearing other stories and knowing that others would read them was a positive and empowering experience. Ivy revealed how for her it is also 'a visibility that I didn't have, it's a voice I wouldn't normally have. . .like any isolated group you feel vulnerable, but if you know there are other people you know that are in same position as yourself. . .it's quite positive. . .'. The importance for these women of having 'a voice to the outside world' (Ivy) should not be underestimated and furthermore it appears to have provided them with some sense of community. Thus as mentioned earlier, how these stories are told is crucial if these seemingly private issues are to become public issues. Since how we write creates a particular and partial view of reality it is essential that in writing about these lesbian women that the stereotypes that are often held about female physical education teachers are challenged. Therefore as Richardson (1992, p. 108) reminds us, it is crucial that we continue to ask ourselves: 'What consequences does our work have for the people we study, and what are my ethical responsibilities for those consequences?'

One of the positive consequences of this biographical project was revealed by Fay who had read a paper I had written based around the first five interviews I had conducted (see Clarke, 1993). She described how:

> Both Denise and I read it through. You know I think it is good to voice it. . .and I also think it helps people, because you know you talk amongst yourselves, but you don't very often talk to somebody you don't know, completely from outside about things that are going on, and I think that it does make you feel better that at least somebody else is listening.

Harriet found the interview a positive experience, for her it was 'therapeutic thinking about it and talking about it. And it's interesting talking to someone like minded'. However talking about life experiences can also be at times unsettling, Fay towards the end of our conversation revealed how:

> doing something like this puts you into thinking whether you should be more open. Sometimes I think I would like to be more out and for everybody to know because I am not bothered really. I say I am not bothered, yet I don't do anything about it. . . .I mean it does make it more difficult for you because it brings up all sorts of things and you start chewing things over and when I sat and read your paper, you know, I was like going to Denise 'look, listen to this' you know and I think it does churn you up, but I don't necessarily think that is a bad thing. I think it is some-thing people have got to say 'why am I so angry, and why is it churning up so many things?' because if it is I have got to do something about it and at the end of the day you are kind of like the medium for everybody to throw all this informa-tion and feelings at, and I think people have got to sort out, you know if they are not happy with it they have got to do something with it. It can make things more confusing, but only because you are raising the issues of things.

Creating a space for these women to speak is clearly no panacea, but as Harriet commented 'even if it doesn't get anywhere, at least you feel like somebody knows now'. Whilst it is crucial that people do know, what has concerned me (and con-tinues to do so) is that in making these women's lives visible through lifting the veil of secrecy that surrounds their lives, has their 'safe' cover now been removed? Will their lives now be less anonymous, will they now be looked for, will they face reprisals? Has their and my speaking removed the safety of silence? Is this counter-productive? These are difficult questions which illustrate the paradoxes that surround the need to make sexual differences visible. For in spite of the risks, unless we name ourselves we will continue to be ignored and remain an invisible and largely silent presence in the educative system — yet paradoxically by naming ourselves we may be bringing unwanted attention to many.[2]

### Concluding remarks

Like Denzin (1989, p. 82) I believe 'that biographical work must always be inter-ventionist, seeking to give notice to those who may otherwise not be allowed to tell their story or who are denied a voice to speak', but as I have illustrated this is no easy task. Furthermore, for those who are denied the spaces to define and articul-ate their sexual identities, 'simply' giving them a voice will not in itself lead to the wholesale transformation of the socio-political landscape that is long overdue. In order to attain full sexual citizenship in British law and policy the normalizing and privileging of heterosexuality over other sexualities must be recognized, contested and changed. Sexual and social justice requires, therefore, not only a recognition of the ways that institutions such as the state and the educative system legitimate and reinforce a particular form of sexuality, that is heterosexuality, but it also necessitates a change in laws. As Kaplan (1997, p. 3) states 'the achievement of equality for lesbian and gay citizens is part of the unfinished business of modern democracy'. There is much still to be finished.

## Notes

1   The discourse of Section 28 has impacted negatively on the content of school sex education programmes. The British Medical Association's (BMA) (1997) recent paper on 'School Sex Education: Good Practice and Policy', makes it clear that schools have a responsibility to teach about homosexuality if they are to meet the needs of all young people. Furthermore, the BMA is also calling for the repeal of Section 28.
2   The National Union of Teachers (NUT) stated in 1996 that it will give full support to those NUT members who choose to come out at school. What impact this will have on the lives of these lesbian teachers remains to be seen.

## References

ABERNETHY, LADY SALTOUN OF (1986) *Official Report*, House of Lords, 18 December 1986, col. 317.

ALCOFF, L. (1991) 'The problem of speaking for others', *Cultural Critique*. Winter, pp. 5–32.

BARONE, T.E. (1992) 'Beyond theory and method: A case of critical story-telling', *Theory into Practice*, Spring, **31**, 2, pp. 142–46.

BOYSON, R. (1987) *Official Report*, House of Commons, 8 May 1987, col. 1002/3 and 1002.

BRITISH MEDICAL ASSOCIATION BOARD OF SCIENCE AND EDUCATION (1997) *School Sex Education: Good Practice and Policy*, London: British Medical Association.

BUTLER, J. (1990) *Gender Trouble: Feminism and the Subversion of Identity*, London: Routledge.

BUTLER, J. (1991) 'Imitation and gender insubordination', in FUSS D. (ed.) *Inside/Out Lesbian Theories, Gay Theories*, London: Routledge.

BUTLER, J. (1993) *Bodies that Matter: On the Limits of 'Sex'*, London: Routledge.

CLARKE, C. (1983) 'Lesbianism: An act of resistance', in MORAGA, C. and ANZALDUA, G. (eds) *This Bridge Called my Back: Writings by Radical Women of Color*, New York: Kitchen Table: Women of Color Press, pp. 128–137.

CLARKE, G. (1993) 'Towards an understanding of the lives and lifestyles of lesbian physical education teachers', unpublished paper presented at the North American Society for the Sociology of Sport Annual Conference, Ottawa: Canada.

CLARKE, G. (1995) 'Outlaws in sport and education? Exploring the sporting and education experiences of lesbian physical education teachers', in LAWRENCE, L., MURDOCH, E. and PARKER, S. (eds) *Professional and Development Issues in Leisure, Sport and Education*, Eastbourne: Leisure Studies Association, pp. 45–58.

CLARKE, G. (1996) 'Conforming and contesting with (a) difference: How lesbian students and teachers manage their identities', *International Studies in Sociology of Education*, **6**, 2, pp. 191–209.

CLARKE, G. (1997) 'Playing a part: The lives of lesbian physical education teachers', in CLARKE, G. and HUMBERSTONE, B. (eds) *Researching Women and Sport*, London: Macmillan, pp. 36–49.

COLVIN, M. with HAWKSLEY, J. (1989) *Section 28: A Practical Guide to the Law and Its Implications*, London: National Council for Civil Liberties.

DES (1988) *Education Reform Act: Local Arrangements*, London: HMSO.

DENZIN, N.K. (1989) *Interpretive Biography*, London: Sage.

ESTERBERG, K.G. (1996) '"A certain swagger when I walk": Performing lesbian identity', in SEIDMAN, S. (ed.) *Queer Theory/Sociology*, Oxford: Blackwell Publishers Ltd., pp. 259–279.

EVANS, D.T. (1989/90) 'Section 28: Law, myth and paradox', *Journal of Critical Social Policy*, Winter Issue, **27**, 9, 3, pp. 73–95.

FARADAY, A. and PLUMMER, K. (1979) 'Doing life histories', *Sociological Review*, **27**, 4, pp. 773–798.

FLETCHER, S. (1984) *Women First: The Female Tradition in English Physical Education 1880–1980*, London: Athlone Press.

GRIFFIN, P. (1991) 'Identity management strategies among lesbian and gay educators', *Qualitative Studies in Education*, **4**, 3, pp. 189–202.

HALSBURY, EARL OF (1986) *Official Report*, House of Lords, 18 December 1986, col. 310.

HARRIS, M.B. and GRIFFIN, J. (1997) 'Stereotypes and personal beliefs about women physical education teachers', *Women in Sport and Physical Activity Journal*, Spring, **6**, 1, pp. 49–83.

INNESS, S.A. (1997) *The Lesbian Menace: Ideology, Identity, and the Representation of Lesbian Life*, Amherst: University of Massachusetts Press.

KAPLAN, M.B. (1997) *Sexual Justice: Democratic Citizenship and the Politics of Desire*, London: Routledge.

KHAYATT, M.D. (1992) *Lesbian Teachers: An Invisible Presence*, Albany: State University of New York Press.

KNIGHT, DAME, J. (1987) *Official Report*, House of Commons, 8 May 1987, col. 1000.

LENSKYJ, H. (1991) 'Combating homophobia in sport and physical education', *Sociology of Sport Journal*, **8**, pp. 61–69.

LUKE, C. (1994) 'Women in the academy: The politics of speech and silence', *British Journal of Sociology of Education*, **15**, 2, pp. 211–230.

OUTRAGE! AND STONEWALL (1994) *Sexuality and the State*, London: National Council for Civil Liberties.

RICHARDSON, L. (1990) *Writing Strategies: Researching Diverse Audiences*, London: Sage.

RICHARDSON, L. (1992) 'Trash on the corner: Ethics and technography', *Journal of Contemporary Ethnography*, April, **21**, 1, pp. 103–119.

SCRATON, S. (1992) *Shaping up to Womanhood: Gender and Girls' Physical Education*, Buckingham: Open University Press.

SMITH, A.M. (1994) *New Right Discourse on Race and Sexuality: Britain, 1968–1990*, Cambridge: Cambridge University Press.

STONEWALL (1997) *Equality 2000*, London: The Stonewall Lobby Group Ltd.

SULLIVAN, C. (1993) 'Oppression: The experiences of a lesbian teacher in an inner city comprehensive school in the United Kingdom', *Gender and Education*, **5**, 1, pp. 93–101.

# 6    Perspectives on Learning Difficulties through Biographies

*Hilary Dickinson*

## Introduction

A conventional conception of biography sees a life story primarily as a record, usu- ally written, of events in an individual's life, though explanation and interpretation are frequently included. Recent sociological development of the genre of biography is broader (for example Bertaux, 1981; Denzin, 1989; Dickinson and Erben, 1995; Erben, 1993 and 1996) and highlights the range of forms that may be considered to be biography. Such developments also draw attention to biographies as a source of understanding of cultural processes as much as of individual lives, and to the complex relationship that exists between the account of a life and the 'reality' of that life.

Biographical accounts by parents of people with learning difficulties, and auto- biographical accounts of learning difficulties are worthy of attention partly because they are stories of those who are generally denied a voice in history. But such accounts also have features of intrinsic interest. Learning difficulties are develop- mentally and biologically real; but they are also socially constructed, labelled, valued and devalued in ways which have been subject to historical change. Parents of people with learning difficulties have, in the contemporary context, a number of difficult and different things to deal with. There is the feeling, at any rate initially, of personal and social failure; there are practical educational problems to con- front; and there is the question of what learning difficulties are and what they mean. These mainly negative experiences can be transformed in narrative, and it is sug- gested also in life, into positive ones, of a sense of achievement, self-fulfilment and satisfaction derived from supporting others. In the transformation of experience culturally available narrative genres and tropes are utilized. The experience which is transformed is not simply the arrival of practical difficulties in the environment, such as additional time needed for basic socialization (though these can be substan- tial) but is a major disruption of assumptions about personal and family identity and a taken for granted life plan. It is the active process of adjusting and reassigning meaning through narrative that gives these accounts their particular biographical interest.

The perspective that will be used to interpret these biographies draws on the work of Paul Ricoeur on narrative. This perspective sees an account of a past experi- ence not only as a record of the experience, but as an active process that remakes and reshapes past events in order to bring them into line with perceptions of the present. Ricoeur's work stresses the connection between a life story and a life lived: 'we are justified in speaking of a life as a story in its nascent state, and so of life as *an activity and passion in search of a narrative*' (emphasis in original) (Ricoeur, 1991, p. 29). Seen in this perspective the genre of biography — narratives about the lives of individuals — is a specialized aspect of an activity central to human life. For Ricoeur this central place for narrative follows from his views about the importance of temporality — time and the passage of time — in human life. 'There is nothing more real for human beings than the experience of temporality' (White, 1991, p. 151). The constant flow of time means that the here and now is ephemeral to the point of non-existence, with the result that our lived lives are inevitably constructed as stories since the moment of 'real' existence can never be caught. Such a perspective alerts us to the continuum between lives as they are lived, and as they are recounted, either orally and informally or in the genre of biography; it alerts us to the active, performative elements in life stories. The account of the experience is not separable from and external to the person giving the account, but becomes part of the experience and the meaning of that experience. Narrative discourse then is as much 'performative' as 'constative' (White, 1991, p. 150). 'Constative' from the French *constater*, to notice, to state, refers to the record of events in a narrative. The performative element refers to the active living and reliving of the events of a life; through this process the narrator is able to remake and reshape past events and experiences and give them new meaning in relation to the present. In this process, for example, what was at the time a terrible misfortune can later be seen as a stage in a meaningful series of events. Ricoeur's work reveals, by means of examining the performative element of a narrative and by means of showing the importance of temporality in human life and narrative, the similarities between a 'real' life and a narrative of that life.

The written autobiographical accounts I discuss are four books by parents about a daughter or son with learning difficulties: *'Why me?' 'Autobiography' of Sheenagh Hardie* (Hardie, 1991); *Mummy, Why Have I Got Down's Syndrome?* (Philps, 1991); *Peter, My Son* (Fletcher, circa 1992) and *My Life is Worth Living* (Creasey, 1993). (The 'why me?' in the title of the first mentioned book refers to Sheenagh's remark when she learned that she was the first winner of the Kyle Apter Award for Achievement; the inverted commas round 'Autobiography' in the title are appropriate since it is the parents writing in the persona of their daughter). These accounts were selected since they are recent works and readily available to their principal intended readers — families newly experiencing a member with learning difficulties. Three of the four are about people with Down's syndrome. Since Down's syndrome, first described by John Langdon Down in 1866, is the commonest single identifiable cause of learning difficulties, this may explain the predominance of accounts of this condition — or it is possible that the highly active Down's Syndrome Association has encouraged people to feel it is worth writing about. These four written accounts were written by a parent or parents of a child with a learning difficulty so the experience of learning difficulties is seen at one remove. There are similarities between the four accounts in respect both of constative and performative features.

An important explicit constative purpose in all four is to inform and help others experiencing learning difficulties. The performative element — which is partly explicit, and partly emerges from the narrative form in which events are situated — is connected with the reliving and reshaping of past events to show how difficulties have been overcome and positive meaning found in events that initially seemed wholly negative. A narrative of a life is not constructed only from unique experiences of individuals, but also from the cultural repertoire of the narrator. A cultural repertoire contains knowledge and beliefs (for example on what learning difficulties are 'like') and framing devices through which experience can be understood (such as narrative forms) and this repertoire will tend to shape in particular directions a narrator's understanding of unique events and individual experiences. In two of the biographies considered here (Hardie, 1991; Philps, 1991) there was a more comfortable fit between unique experiences and the cultural context than in the other two (Fletcher, circa 1992; Creasey, 1993). For the latter two the events and experiences described fitted less comfortably into available cultural frames.

I also include extracts from an interview with David (not his real name) whom I contacted through People First, an organization run for and by people with learning difficulties which provides information, training (for example in self-advocacy) and advice ('People First' Information Pack, circa 1991, p. 1). People First, a new organization, contrasts with the long established Mencap (the Society for People with Learning Disabilities) in that it is run by as well as for people with learning difficulties. The focus of this article is on parents' accounts of children with learning difficulties, but David's account is of interest because of the contrast he provides with the parents' accounts; the issues that are important in his life are different from theirs. David's story was given in an interview in contrast to the written parents' accounts; and the tiny numbers mean that no claim for generalizability can be made. Nonetheless it is interesting to note that there seem to be constraints, albeit self-imposed, at work in the parents' accounts which are not present in David's. He is able to fit his narrative into a cultural context about what learning difficulties are and should be 'like' that is not so easily available to the parents. The focus in this chapter on parents is not because I regard them as more important than those who themselves have learning difficulties. They are as important; and they are also interesting because constraints on the performative aspects of the parents' narratives are illuminating for the study of biography. (For some first hand accounts by people who have learning difficulties see Burnside, 1991; Deacon, 1974; Hunt, 1982).

## Constative and performative purposes of written and oral narratives

The following explicit purposes are found in the narratives used here (the four written autobiographies and the interview with David):

1    To support, encourage and educate other families where someone has learning difficulties or (in David's case) other people with learning difficulties.

2   To shift public perception of learning difficulties — for example to remove negative definitions and low expectations.

3   To show how the writer (and his/her family and friends) or the speaker has overcome difficulties and achieved a sense of fulfilment.

4   To show how an event or condition that might be perceived negatively is part of a wider meaningful destiny or divine purpose.

These purposes are listed in order of frequency of occurrence — purpose 4 is found only in Philps and Hardie, and 3 is found in its most developed form in these two and in David's interview. In Creasey and Fletcher purpose 3 is present, but the end condition of fulfilment has been attained after great pain. The book by Fletcher is unusual in that it provides no explicit rationale, and deliberately avoids any claim to speak for the family as a whole.

However, in listing the purposes of an account, important elements conveyed by the form of the narrative as a whole are left out. In the Introduction reference was made to the importance of narrative as 'performative' as well as 'constative'. The list of purposes for which someone wrote an account would constitute part of the constative — the merely chronicling — element in a narrative. But the performative elements of a narrative are as, or more, important than the constative in understanding the totality of its meaning and these are found in the form rather than the content of the narrative. Chanfrault-Duchet describes the importance of the respondent's own ordering of a life story:

> the narrative encompasses not only the temporal and causal organization of facts and events considered significant, but also the value judgments that make sense of this particular life experience. In turn, such a view implies that the most crucial information resides not in the answers given to specific questions, but rather to the narrative organization itself. (1991, p. 77)

Here Chanfrault-Duchet touches on the dimension of a narrative that the word 'performative' conveys. Any narrative organizes the actions and events it tells of into a meaningful whole. Whether implicitly or explicitly, it explicates the meaning of the events and sets them into a social framework of regular expectations and obligations, into a moral framework (and I would include here devices which indicate the narrator's rejection of a conventional religious moral framework), and (frequently) into a cosmological framework involving ideas about destiny and the Fates or a divinity (Kelly and Dickinson, 1997, pp. 267–70). Thus in the 'Autobiography' of Sheenagh Hardie, before Sheenagh's birth her mother was out with her elder brother as a baby and she:

> was stopped by a clean, old gypsy woman, who looked inside the pram. 'You have a lovely baby there Ma'am. Some day you will have a house of your own. . .You will have. . .a little daughter. . .' And she broke off suddenly in the middle of a sentence, a strange look in her eye. . .[It seemed] an old woman's ramblings. . .until about three years later. (Hardie, 1991, p. iii)

This part of the narrative encourages the reader to infer that the birth of the child with Down's syndrome was not a mere chance event, but was foretold and so part of some greater scheme of things. Performative elements in a narrative do not merely organize for the reader or listener events which are finished with from the narrator's point of view. Rather they provide a 'living through' of the events — I hesitate to call it a reliving — in which fresh meanings can be attached to them. Thus at the time when the old gypsy woman spoke to Sheenagh's mother her remarks were not seen to have any special meaning; it was only in the light of later events that their significance could be properly perceived and reflected on.

### Congruity and incongruity between narrative and context: The search for a narrative of learning difficulties

In order to take on performative meaning, the narrative must use existing cultural conventions and genres. The meaning of the old gypsy woman's remarks can only exist for narrator and reader if both understand notions of destiny and know that old gypsy women often have second sight. A narrative unfolds in a cultural context. As Denzin observes (1989, p. 73) 'No self or personal-experience story is ever an individual production. It derives from larger group, cultural, ideological and histor-ical contexts'. In the case of these biographies there needs to be congruity between the conventions and assumptions of the narrative, and those of the 'real' world as experienced by social actors. For these parents an important cultural context is that of what learning difficulties are 'like'; the parents are not solely concerned with a private experience (as if, anyway, it were possible to separate purely private experi-ences) but with how learning difficulties are construed in the social and public world. I argue that there are problems for the parents in producing congruity between their own experiences and what learning difficulties are 'like', and that this is in part caused by a lack of a widely accepted public narrative that defines and places learning difficulties satisfactorily. This produces constraint on the parents' narrat-ives which is not, by contrast, to be discerned in David's narrative. There are two further, related, features of the parents' contexts which constrain their narrative forms, which again, are not an issue for David. One is the constraint of writing on behalf of someone who does not speak themself — or whose speech is differently privil-eged; and the other the intensity of the pain occasioned to the parents by the birth of a child with learning difficulties.

The parents early experienced the problem of the absence of a widely cur-rent and satisfactory definition. There are uncertain and unhelpful notions — 'Is she going to be one of those kiddies who are stout with slanting eyes and are not quite right?' (Hardie, 1991, p. 2) — and the wholly negative — 'Don't you realize how badly retarded Paul is?. . .How could my son have a child like that?' (Creasey, 1993, p. 44). There are, however, two positive, and publicly endorsed narratives about how to perceive learning difficulties. There is on the one hand the image of the Innocent, affectionate and docile, happy to receive paternalistic care. This was a commonly endorsed public narrative, accepted by parents and professionals until challenged by a more recent, and currently more favoured view which sees people with learning difficulties as having the right to be fully adult persons, exercising responsibility and autonomy. People First embodies this 'rights and responsibilities', or 'citizenship' perspective. The citizenship view owes much to the disability movement generally and can be dated at least from the 1970s (see for example Brechin and Swain, 1987; Ryan, 1987, pp. 153–164).

The parents, in order to transform a negative experience into a positive one, need to discover a positive narrative, and to bring their own experience into line with that positive narrative. Some illuminating parallels can be drawn between the biographies examined here and accounts of religious conversion. The convert needs to bring his or her private experience into line with religious definitions of appropriate kinds of conversion. Thus Beckford (1978), studying Jehovah's Witnesses, shows how a convert went through the stages that were, for Witnesses, evidence of a 'proper' kind of conversion — not emotional, but cognitive and reflective. Stromberg (1993, p. 82) discusses how the nature of religious reality as perceived by an informant justified, even required, a particular kind of behaviour from him. The parallel between conversion narratives and the parents' narratives is not perfect. In narratives of conversion, the convert seeks to make the process explicit — it is of the nature of conversion that it is a spiritual journey which shows the stages by which the narrator rejects or outgrows a previous, erroneous self, and forges a new self congruent with the desired religious world. In the parents' stories the process by which they developed a 'correct' understanding of learning difficulties is largely implicit.

To a great extent it is revealed by their distancing themselves from people who have incorrect perceptions. Caroline Philps describes the difficulty of getting her daughter a place at a mainstream primary school:

> It seemed ironic to me that at the same time as parents of 'normal' children were allowed to send [them] to the school of their choice, we [parents of handicapped children] had to beg on bended knee. . .Many 'normal' children had behavioural problems or learning difficulties, but [had no problems getting a school place]. For handicapped children, various assumptions were made about their level of ability before they were given the opportunity to develop at all. (Philps, 1991, p. 66)

Gordon Fletcher reports a similar experience: 'After being told by a teacher, yes, a teacher. . .that I would never teach Peter to say his name and address. . .that was a challenge I could not ignore' (Fletcher, circa 1992, p. 37). A source of 'correct' understanding can be the child him or herself: 'Lizzie was becoming less frustrated and Bolshy; her speech was improving; she was successful at reading and was able to be more grown up' (Philps, 1991, p. 57) or the unprejudiced reactions of others: 'Joe and Annette [other children] helped me, and although they were disappointed that he couldn't play with them yet, they always spoke to him and never gave up trying to attract his attention. . ."We love him anyway. He's our brother!" I was told' (Creasey, 1993, p. 36).

Earlier in this section mention was made of two constraints on the parents' stories in addition to the search for a positive narrative of learning difficulties. The first of the two is the intensity of the pain experienced by the parents on first becoming aware that their child had learning difficulties; and the second the problem of speaking for someone else. All the parents write of the pain, and for some, feelings of guilt, on learning of the child's disability.

> But *I* knew [that her daughter had Down's syndrome]. I bravely said I was a Christian and God must have a good purpose in giving her to us. . .Mark [husband] came as soon as [he could]. . .I felt guilty. . .I felt I'd failed him. (Philps, 1991, p. 13)

> What a cruel, horrible way it was for my folks to find out about me. [They read the letter the clinic doctor wrote referring the daughter to a paediatrician]. . .It was heartbreaking to them. Dad's immediate thoughts were then 'Why must Sheenagh live in this world?'. (Hardie, 1991, p. 3)

> All this time I had this feeling of inner despair, the hopelessness of it all, because all of this time there was no response from Peter at all. (Fletcher, circa 1992, p. 7)

> I tried not to let them [other children] see that I was upset. . .I would have outbursts of weeping, so I shut myself away in the bedroom. (Creasey, 1993, p. 41)

The pain felt by the Philps and Hardie families came very soon after the birth, before any experience of the real practical or emotional difficulties of bringing up a child with disabilities; this chronology suggests that a part of the pain comes from the disruption of a predicted, taken for granted and desirable life event — the birth of a healthy child — and a consequent loss of self-respect, rather than from the experience itself of bringing up a child with disabilities. The interruption of an expected life course is immediate and traumatic, the practical and emotional difficulties that follow are also part of the pain experienced by the parents. The guilt that all the families with the exception of the Hardies express (Creasey, 1993, p. 42; Fletcher, circa 1992, p. 6; Philps, 1991, p. 13) is probably connected with loss of self-respect in so far as respect is an attribute that, on an implicit level, we feel we *earn* — and its loss something we construe as our own fault. Writing of serious physical illness Howard Brody connects loss of self-respect to the interruption of a 'rational plan of life' (see Brody, 1987, pp. 41–58, also Bury, 1982). This pattern fits the experience of the families considered here. It is illuminating to note that Philps and Creasey (women) assume that the 'fault' that gives rise to guilt is from the mother's side of the family, while Fletcher (man) assumes it is from the father's (Creasey, 1993, p. 42; Fletcher, circa 1992, p. 6; Philps, 1991, p. 13). The significance of the degree of pain felt to the search for a positive narrative of learning difficulties is that of the great distance, metaphorically, the parents have to travel from early — and for Creasey and Fletcher long-enduring — pain to the re-establishment of self-respect and sense of self worth.

The second of the two additional constraints arises from a tension between the fact that the biographies are primarily about a child with learning difficulties, yet manifestly, the parents' feelings and experiences are important. Implicitly though, the structure and performative thrust of all the written biographies is to minimize the parents' pain and hurt, and to move on to the positive experiences, foregrounding the development of the child. Part of the constraint then seems to come from some degree of suppression of pain. A second part stems simply from not knowing exactly what another person (the child) thinks or desires. In *Peter* Fletcher stresses that the story is his story and he cannot claim to speak for his wife; it remains implicit that similarly he may not know what his son feels. A third aspect, related to the second, is that it seems that the responsibility of speaking on behalf of someone else — an other who has a differently privileged voice — also produces constraint. This is hard to exemplify since by its nature constraint or inhibition suppress something. However a common narrative device, that of humour, is interestingly almost entirely absent. It might be said that the events related are not by their nature humorous — but this is no argument since humour as a defence against misfortune has an honourable history. It can be found in narratives about severe illness (Kelly and Dickinson, 1997, pp. 268–9). But humour as a defence mechanism in the parents' narratives would be hard for the narrator to present acceptably. Self mockery (Kelly and Dickinson, 1997, p. 261) is fine; but anything that could be construed as mockery of a person with disabilities would be opprobrious. But a fourth, and possibly most important aspect of constraint attendant on speaking for another, is that it is hard to avoid a subordinated position for the person spoken for. It is hard to present a narrative structured thus as one of rights and responsibilities rather than paternalistic care.

There is, it has been argued, a search for congruity in written accounts between the parents' experiences and their views on what learning difficulties are like or ought to be like. This search is not explicit, but it exists as a constraining factor in these narratives. Philps's book straddles a 'rights and responsibilities' and a 'protectionist' narrative while the Hardie story is more clearly in a 'protectionist' mode. The awkwardness (an issue to be explored in the final section) of the books by Creasey and Fletcher comes from their inability to fit their experiences to existing conventions.

Having looked at constraining or inhibiting factors in the parents' narratives, I go on to use some extracts from the interview with David to show an absence of inhibiting factors in his story. The cultural context that is available to him — a narrative of 'rights and responsibilities' which sees the person with learning difficulties as an autonomous adult — fits comfortably with his experience and aspirations. After the look at David's narrative there follows a section which examines how the overall structure of the narratives, both written and oral, helps organize experience into a framework of meaning; that is to say the structure is an important part of the performative element of a narrative.

### The oral account — David's story

As David's story is given in an interview (also to be found in an earlier working of some of these ideas, in Dickinson, 1994) its performative elements are less evident than in an independently produced account; but nonetheless they are clearly present. I have selected David's oral account rather than one of the written first hand accounts of learning difficulties because it is so thoroughly cast in a 'rights and responsibilities' rhetoric of learning difficulties, so showing the possibilities of this mode of expression. Hunt (1982) was first published in 1966, before a 'rights and responsibilities' rhetoric was possible. For different reasons the other two written accounts were not selected for analysis; Joseph Deacon (1974) had severe cerebral palsy but his cognitive impairment was slight or non-existent and Burnside's (1991) was initially tape recorded and gives little information about the amount of revision and correction by the amanuensis.

Here follows a transcript of part of the interview with David, starting at the beginning. Square brackets [ ] indicate inaudible sections, and dots. . .indicate short sections omitted.

H   You tell me where you'd like to start from.
D   Well I don't mind — I don't know which one you want because I've got quite a lot. See, I've got a life story. I've been in hospital so a long time, fourteen years, and I come out of the hospital in [ ] and then I been in [ ] group homes, hostels, you name 'em. . .
H   Tell me about some important bits of your life story.
D   My life story — from way back?
H   Well no — any bits that you feel were important for you.
D   I think it's — going out of the hospital. If you'd been in a hospital like I've been — how they treat you. Then got out. . .
H   How did you manage to get out?
D   I got married and got out. Then my marriage broke down.
H   That was someone who was in the hospital?
D   [ ] This person lived in the hospital and she'd been somewhere else — another hospital and then she moved into this hospital. Then I got married in the hospital itself. And that's why I got out — I didn't been married I wouldn't be here. I would have been dead.
H   And you'd still be there?
D   No, I'd be dead.

D and his wife lived in a council flat when they left the hospital. The marriage broke down because of his wife's violence. D left her and went back to the hospital for a few months, and then went to a group home which he didn't like. The tape is not clear here, but I think D was contrasting people who had never lived outside hospital and found a group home acceptable compared with D who had experienced independent living.

D   I like to be independent. I like to live on my own.
H   What is it you like about living on your own?
D   You can go out when you want to. You go out in the morning — and you come back when you want to. Then you have your own key. And that's — and you have to cook your own meals — when you're wanting to. . .
H   And in the group home you can't go out when you want to?
D   Not that you can't go out when you want to — people check on you every five minutes. You have to be in at a certain time — say six o'clock and you don't

have to go out. When you're on your own, you're allowed to go out when you wanna.

H   Can you tell me what are the nice features of your life at present?

D   Nice? I like living on my own. I like coming here [i.e. to People First] — to help people. Like if I was — had a bad experience like I done — then I'd teach other people to speak up for themselves — and learn — to do things for themselves — instead of the other way round [ ] When I went first to People First meeting in Lambeth. . .[ ] There were people who'd never speak up for themselves at that meeting.

H   And how did you first come across People First?

D   I'd got [ ] that means a person who helps you do a job when you've finished your training. And she said to me [ ] got a People First Meeting down in Lambeth that you can go to.

H   And when you went to this first meeting — how did you feel?

D   I feel — I don't know — I feel anxious. I don't know what to expect — of me — I feel — other people with learning difficulties there — I can't explain it. When I went there — three or four times. . .great in the end. Got learning difficulties like you are — and feel good — can speak. Then I start off trying to run the meeting [ ] Then I went for an interview for a job [with People First] — and I don't got it. They want a lady. They had — all men there. Then after that I went to this job here. And I don't got it. But since then I been a volunteer — here [ ] answer the phones — open the letters like I done here [referring to what he was doing when I arrived] — fold leaflets up. . .

H   Do you think you've changed [since being at People First]?

D   Yeah — more confident — more, speak up — more — Tell people [ ] to set up groups in different boroughs. . .I'm working in Newham now. They set up a [youth?] group. The hospital's closing down. . .What we do is set up a People First Group — not People First — a User Group — I got an Open Day coming up shortly — May 3rd. [ ] I've been on the telly three or four times.

H   What programmes?

D   People First programmes. They phoned me up — on BBC 2 — [ ] and I'm going — supposed to be four people on it — care worker — people in the community.

The BBC had David's phone number but haven't yet contacted him. He told me he had been to Canada for a People First Conference, that he had had to be careful while away about taking his medication for epilepsy, that People First was great, and that there was a paid job as care worker coming up with them which he thought he had a good chance of getting. He explained how he helped people to speak up for themselves:

D   You sit down with that person to explain that you can talk — you can speak up — if you take your time. That's what we do. . .Some people can't talk anyway. And what we do is — body language — drawing — or eye contact — or even if they got a hand language. We had a meeting yesterday and one person couldn't talk at all, and I talk hand language to him — and he understand . . .Reports — trying to put it in language we can understand.

The constative elements in David's narrative tell of moves towards independence and autonomy — marriage, leaving the hospital, managing the breakdown of his marriage, more independence — and helping other people to be independent. There are also performative elements of this narrative. Particularly of note here is the start where David, in response to my desire to hear his life story, asks me which one I want. This suggests a practised and self-aware narrator accustomed to bearing in mind the wishes of different audiences and the different presentations of self which are possible. Other performative elements include the values expressed and affirmed — autonomy, development of confidence, helping others. As the interview goes on, David introduces related performative themes himself — the TV programme contacting him, the conference in Canada, the way he has learned to help people with little or no speech to communicate. These too are performative (as well as constative) elements of the narrative, in that they both demonstrate and reaffirm the values of independence and autonomy. The language in which David expresses himself is also part of the performative element and here the idiosyncratic grammar plays a part; it gives a sense of individuality to the narrative, and more than that, it adds weight to David's claim to be able to help people who are inarticulate, in that he evidently knows what it is like not to be able to communicate with absolute ease. The most important performative aspect of David's narrative, and in contrast to parents' narratives, is that he has no special notion of learning difficulties. His values — independence, helping other people — could be and often are applied to other situations than his own. He, and other people he has been helping, have problems they need to overcome, but these are not 'special' problems and 'special' people. It is the ordinariness of David's narrative that is its most interesting feature.

## The role of narrative structure in expressing performative meaning

Philps's *Mummy, Why Have I Got Down's Syndrome?* and Hardie's *Why Me?* most completely shape their narratives into a coherent whole, showing how the families successfully fostered the achievement of their Down's syndrome members and found meaning in their lives. The introduction to Philps's book is worth quoting at length since it encapsulates this very well:

> It is difficult to describe any person adequately. It is even harder to describe someone who is so much an essential part of our lives as Lizzie is. . .Lizzie has enriched our lives in a unique way. . .Growth into parenthood. . .[can be painful] . . .For us there was also the pain of coming to grips with what having a handicapped child might mean. But it is not through gritted teeth, but often with amazement and laughter. . .She has helped us see the world through new eyes and our other children — who are equally special to us — are part of that world. So this book is for anyone interested in children. But perhaps it is especially for the many parents who share our own particular experience in the hope that it may bring encouragement as they face the future. I hope that, as you read this book, you will meet Lizzie through its pages. I hope that you will find in it reflections of yourself and of the God who made and loves us all. (Philps, 1991, p. 7)

The biographers shape the stories into a meaningful whole; a whole which employs recognized cultural texts. Cultural texts of how learning difficulties are to be construed have already been discussed. But the overall temporal structure of the story, its progress through time, also draws on existing cultural forms. A narrative pattern found by Victor Turner (cited in Mishler, 1986, p. 151) in a wide range of cultural contexts is that of breach, crisis and redress, followed by either reintegration or schism. This schema can be seen to have similarities with Gergen and Gergen's (1983) typology of narratives as being connected to desired goals in terms of stability, regression and progression. David's narrative is one of progression, from being controlled by others to being in control of his own life and able to help others gain control of theirs. The parents' narratives are of regression (the birth of the child with learning difficulties) followed by a progressive narrative describing how difficulties were surmounted.

Turner's more precise specification, however, provides additional illumination of the performative elements of the parents' stories. The breach (of an expected and desired life-course) is the birth of the child with learning difficulties; the crisis the emotional pain resulting from loss of the expected kind of person one was — a 'proper' parent and member of a family — and consequent feelings of guilt. Also part of the crisis stage are the emotional and practical problems of bringing up a child with learning difficulties and the negative and unhelpful behaviour of (some) friends, relatives and professionals. The redress is the process of (i) dealing with the negative feelings and guilt, (ii) the mobilization of appropriate support and education for the child, both through the actions of family members and through professionals (e.g. schools, hospitals, group homes) which includes, (iii) the separation of supportive or 'good' individuals and organizations from negative and rejecting ones (Fletcher, circa 1992, pp. 12, 14). A family might find that some relatives and friends would 'melt away' (Fletcher, circa 1992, p. 6), or worse, openly express hostility (Creasey, 1993, p. 42); conversely and more positively a friend who had not seemed particularly close would be a staunch support. The most important stage in the process of redress is (iv) — growing recognition and acceptance of child with learning difficulties as an individual and a member of the family.

The reintegration runs along with the redress phase in these accounts. As the parents — or rather whole families — are successful in (i), (ii), (iii) and (iv) above they are reintegrated into a state of being participating and self-respecting members of society; not a state the same as before the birth of the child but one equally, and in some respects more, rewarding. Only one family experienced a schism. Carol Creasey's husband was unable to accept that their son had learning difficulties. This caused a rift between husband and wife which was a significant influence on the separation and divorce which followed. The reintegration (without the first husband) only fully took place after Carol met and eventually married her second husband.

Overall then, the written biographies follow similar trajectories which can be described in Turner's terminology as breach, crisis, redress and reintegration. The performative richness of such a structure is that those involved are taking part in a recognized and approved life drama in which right triumphs after difficulties confronted, and participants are tested by hardship but emerge with flying colours. Yet only two of the written accounts (Philps and Hardie) match what might be termed the spirit as well as the outward form of a progressive narrative of this kind. Both Philps and Hardie provide a narrative which moves progressively to fulfilment, contentment and calm. Both have stated purposes (what could be termed the constative purposes) that include support and encouragement of others. But a performative purpose of showing how the writer and family overcame difficulties (the redress stage) and achieved fulfilment has equal, or indeed more importance. The process of redress is mediated by other people:

> The father [of a Down's syndrome acquaintance] told my Dad that his son was 'the greatest thing since sliced bread'. . .he has learned a great deal from his son and feels he is a better parent and man as a result. I am sure my Mum and Dad agree. (Hardie, 1991, pp. 44–5) (See also the quote from Philps at the beginning of this section.)

The contentment and fulfilment of life's purpose following difficulties successfully surmounted is one of the elements that makes a religious conversion narrative an appropriate parallel, and is central in these two books in constituting their performative aspects. In contrast while both *Peter* and *My Life* contain final sections in which a satisfactory present situation and hopeful future are recorded, the convincing air of contentment of Hardie and Philps is absent; the satisfactory ending of Creasey and Fletcher doesn't soften the reader's memory of the hardships of earlier parts of the accounts. *Peter* is often an angry book, mostly with the agencies and authorities who dealt with Peter and his parents. It is as if the writers are unable wholly successfully to bring off the performative meaning they seek.

In looking for features of the books that might account for the differences between Creasey and Fletcher on the one hand, and Philps and Hardie on the other, four call for consideration — the literary quality of the books; the severity of the children's learning difficulties; the religious outlook of the families; and the character of family life depicted in each book. Judgments about literary quality are subjective, so this section will be brief. Philps and Hardie strike the readers as works by authors accustomed to writing (which judgment is supported by the fact that Philps's book is her second about Lizzie, the first having appeared when Lizzie was two), while both Fletcher and Creasey are less fluent. Though the occupations of the parents are only specifically given for Philps — the father is a minister in a Christian church — Fletcher and Creasey give an impression of less education than the others. Thus a less convincing handling of performative elements of the narrative might spring from lesser skill. However, it is probable that the second issue — the differences in the abilities of the children of the four families — is more important than literary skill.

Paul's (Creasey) and Peter's (Fletcher) learning difficulties were far more severe than Lizzie's or Sheenagh's. In Paul's case (unlike the other three who had Down's syndrome) there was the additional problem of diagnosing what was amiss. While at Peter's birth there was no question of his parents seeking permanent institutional care for him, quite early in his life he experienced 'phased short stage care' in a hospital because of the severity of his problems (Fletcher, circa 1992, p. 11).

By contrast Lizzie and Sheenagh were little behind 'normal' children as far as toilet training and mobility were concerned. Sheenagh won the Kyle Apter Award; and on p. 131 of Philps's book there is an impressive drawing by Lizzie, aged only eight and a half. These differences of ability suggest that it is more difficult for Creasey and Fletcher to recast their experiences in a positive narrative of learning difficulties.

The remaining differences between the Creasey and Fletcher families on the one hand and the Hardies and Philpses on the other are those of religious belief and character of family life. A religious perspective is absent in *Peter* and occasional and conventional in *My Life*. By contrast in both *Why Me?* and *Mummy* a religious perspective is integral to the accounts. Both the Philps and Hardie biographies show religion as a part of everyday life: 'For this [church service on TV] Grandma brought out two old well-thumbed hymn books. We looked up the hymns in them . . .and blended our voices in the choirs which sang' (Hardie, 1991, p. 75). Additionally religion, or in Sheenagh's story perhaps more precisely a quasi-religious destiny (the old gypsy woman) is seen as a framework both of cause (things were 'meant' to be) and meaning (bad seeming events are not just random bad luck, but part of a greater order). Such a perspective is most elaborated in Philps who presents a carefully argued theodicy on pp. 134–5 of her book. A religious perspective as found in *Why Me?* and *Mummy* may make it easier for the writers to interpret the child's learning difficulties, both constatively and performatively, as part of a meaningful and ultimately benignant order.

The Philpses and Hardies appear as exemplars of an ideal family — Christian in these instances, but the idealized family life might easily be that of another religion. There are mother, father, several children, and mother doesn't work in paid employment. The perfect family image is very much a part of these narratives of a happily integrated Down's syndrome person. The idealized conventional family unit of Philps and Hardie, the sense even that the books are family narratives rather than those of individuals, is absent in Creasey and Fletcher. Carol Creasey experienced a broken marriage and remarriage and had paid work outside the home. *Peter, My Son*, unlike the other books is by Peter's father, not mother. It is interesting that Fletcher explicitly rejects any notion that it is a product of a family authorship; as the Foreword makes it clear that the thoughts and feelings in the book are the author's: 'I write this as a clear distinction, as quite likely my wife. . .would, and does, have various opposite opinions' (Fletcher, circa 1992, p. 4).

### Concluding remarks

In the autobiographical accounts of learning difficulties analysed here I have concentrated on the interplay between the 'constative' and 'performative' elements of the narratives — that is, between the record of what were perceived as significant events and the reordering and reliving of these events. This latter is the performative element, and provides opportunities for reshaping events and interpersonal relationships wherein the telling of the story can validate the past and reveal a meaningful whole which may not have been apparent at the time. The two elements are inevitably closely interlinked. Another issue explored is the significance of the wider context of what it perceived 'to be like' to have learning difficulties. The performative aspect of the narratives is most evident in relation to two issues; the social construction of what learning difficulties are 'like' and secondly, the reordering of events into a temporal frame of meaningful stages. David, the author of the oral, first hand account, fits his narrative comfortably into a 'rights and responsibilities' construction of learning difficulties. The parents have more difficulty in the search for an appropriate construction of learning difficulties and their narratives include some elements of an older, paternalistic view.

Where the temporal ordering of the narrative is concerned the four written biographies have a similar structure, that of a struggle, ultimately rewarded by successful re-establishment of the family and its members to self-respect and a sense of having a worthwhile social position. While all four written biographies have this structure, two of them fail to establish this narrative structure with conviction. Possible explanations for the differences between the four books are sought in different family structures, religious orientation and the severity of the child's disability. The structure of David's story is similar to the written ones in that it is a progression from a low point — but not so severe a crisis as the parents experienced — to control over his life.

## References

BECKFORD, J. (1978) 'Accounting for conversion', *British Journal of Sociology*, **29**, pp. 249–62.

BERTAUX, D. (ed.) (1981) *Biography and Society*, Beverley Hills: Sage.

BRECHIN, A. and SWAIN, J. (1987) *Changing Relationships*, London: Harper & Row.

BRODY, H. (1987) *Stories of Sickness*, New Haven and London: Yale University Press.

BURNSIDE, M. (1991) *My Life Story*, Pecket Well College, 36 Gibbet Street, Halifax.

BURY, M. (1982) 'Chronic illness as biographical disruption', *Sociology of Health and Illness*, **4**, pp. 167–182.

CHANFRAULT-DUCHET, M-F. (1991) 'Narrative structures, social models and symbolic representation in the life story', in GLUCK, S. and PATAI, D. (eds) *Women's Words: The Feminist Practice of Oral History*, London: Routledge.

CREASEY, C. (1993) *My Life Is Worth Living!*, Cornwall: United Writers.

DEACON, J. (1974) *Tongue Tied: Fifty Years of Friendship in a Subnormality Hospital*, London: Mencap.

DENZIN, N. (1989) *Interpretive Biography*, London: Sage.

DICKINSON, H. (1994) 'Narratives in the experience of learning difficulties', *Auto/Biography*, **3**, 1, and 3, 2, (double issue) pp. 93–104.

DICKINSON, H. and ERBEN, M. (1995) 'Bernstein and Ricoeur: Contours for the social understanding of narratives and selves', in ATKINSON, P. et al. (eds) *Discourse and Reproduction: Essays in Honor of Basil Bernstein*, Creskill: New Jersey. Hampton Press.

ERBEN, M. (1993) 'The problem of other lives: Social perspectives on written biography', *Sociology*, **27**, 2, pp. 15–25.

ERBEN, M. (1996) 'The purposes and processes of biographical method', in SCOTT, D. and USHER, R. (eds) *Understanding Educational Research*, London: Routledge.

FLETCHER, G. (circa 1992) *Peter, My Son*, London: Privately published.

GERGEN, K. and GERGEN, M. (1983) 'Narratives of the self', in SARBIN, T. and SCHEIBE, K. (eds) *Studies in Social Identity*, New York: Praeger.

HARDIE, S. (HARDIE, H. and HARDIE, A. (1991)) *Why me? 'Autobiography' of Sheenagh Hardie a Down's Syndrome Girl*, London: Excalibur Press.

HUNT, N. (1982) *The World of Nigel Hunt: The Diary of a Mongoloid Youth*, Norwich: Assett.

KELLY, M. and DICKINSON, H. (1997) 'The narrative self in autobiographical accounts of illness', *Sociological Review*, **45**, 2, pp. 254–278.

MISHLER, E. (1986) *Research Interviewing: Narrative and Interpretation*, Cambridge, MA: Harvard University Press.

PEOPLE FIRST (circa 1991) *People First: New Starter Pack*, London, 207–215 Kings Cross Road: People First.

PHILPS, C. (1991) *Mummy, Why Have I Got Down's Syndrome?*, Oxford: Lion Paperback.

RICOEUR, P. (1991) 'Life in Quest of a Narrative', in WOOD, D. (ed.) *On Paul Ricoeur: Narrative and Interpretation*, London: Routledge.

RYAN, J. (1987) *The Politics of Mental Handicap*, (Revised edition) London: Free Association.

STROMBERG, P. (1993) *Language and Self-Transformation: A Study of the Christian Conversion Narrative*, Cambridge: Cambridge University Press.

WHITE, H. (1991) 'The metaphysics of narrativity: Time and symbol in Ricoeur's philosophy of history', in WOOD, D. (ed.) *On Paul Ricoeur: Narrative and Interpretation*, London: Routledge.

# 7    Collecting Slices of College Dropouts' Lives

*Mich Page*

## Introduction

> To know yet to think that one does not know is best;
> Not to know yet to think that one knows will lead to difficulty
>                    (Lao-Tzu, Sixth century BC Chinese proverb)

This chapter is based on my doctoral thesis on student withdrawal from a college of further education. For those interested in the complete method and underpinning methodologies I would refer you to the original work, *A Framework for Understanding Student Dropout in the Further Education Context* (Page, 1996). The research was undertaken at the college where I was employed. When I first asked for permission to do the study, no one was particularly interested in student dropout. It was so unimportant that the management information systems did not even try to measure student withdrawal. Obtaining permission was therefore quite simple; everyone thought the investigation was 'harmless', although they had the good grace not to say so directly.

I was dissatisfied with the current thinking on, and acceptance of, student dropout. I therefore set about this research in an attempt to throw some light on the sources of my own dissatisfaction. Since that time, student retention has become something of a 'buzz' word as government funding is now in part, attached to student achievement. Colleges now recognize the need to keep students on course, otherwise they risk going out of business in today's 'market forces' driven educational climate. This climate change forms a significant part of the historical context in which the research took place.

I began to take a personal interest in the stories I was hearing from dropouts when it became apparent that there was a conflict of interest, in need of resolution. On the one hand, college staff believed students were entirely responsible for choosing to leave prematurely, referring to them as 'self-selecting failures', the student deficit model, as I call it. On the other, I was listening to dropouts telling me that they had no choice, it was forced upon them, it was the right decision, their route to success, and an opportunity too good to miss. The research faced the task of unravelling this conflict by collecting empirical evidence and using it to explain why students leave college. Both numeric and narrative data were collected and used in a complementary fashion, by triangulation, to develop an understanding of a phenomenon so long ignored by educators.

The narratives have been given verbatim in a *reportage* form, uncensored, unimproved. Meaning has emerged from these stories as they were told, and I have used this emergent understanding to explain what these individuals were doing when they decided to dropout. In this respect I have acted as editor rather than interpreter of their words. Thus these dropouts have not only spoken to me but through me, to a wider audience. Inevitably, the study is subjective but I make no apology for this, because as Burgess (1982, p. 1) points out, the researcher is 'the main instrument of social investigation'. I simply acknowledge that the easiest way to gather data on people is to interact with them, working alongside them, talking to them and most of all, listening: thus objective distance and impartiality are made impossible.

> No matter what methods we use in our social investigations, we have to make a choice about where we will position our selves. (Berg and Smith, 1988, p. 9)

My position was firmly in the thick of it; right in amongst everyone I was interested in, working within the field but sufficiently detached from the day to day beliefs of my colleagues to enable observation. Field researches carry this dilemma to an extreme. As an 'insider' Burgess (1982) recommends that we have to be both self-critical and self-aware, thus superimposing an 'outsider's perspective' onto the 'insider's view'. Certainly working within the field allowed me easy access to people without the added impediment of having to negotiate gatekeepers. But there were also disadvantages, the main problems are highlighted by Van Maanen (1983, pp. 51–52) who says,

> Culture is itself an interpretation and therefore most of the facts one goes into the field to discover are themselves already known about and interpreted in a particular light by the people one talks to in the setting. The results of ethnographic study are thus mediated several times over — first, by the fieldworker's own standards of relevance as to what is and what is not worthy of observation; second, by the historically situated questions that are put to the people in the setting; third, by the self-reflection demanded of an informant.

The method I have chosen uses 'slices of life stories' as Denzin would call them (1987b, p. 22). The words (data sets, narratives made into text) have come directly from the dropouts but the questions were mine. These questions have both a personal and contextual aspect: my dissatisfaction with the current explanation of student dropout and the growing need to make education efficient, respectively. By choosing to make student dropout problematic, I have taken the first steps recommended by Denzin (1987) that record the transformation of individual actions into collective, social interaction. Each dropout acted on their own, making a personal decision based on the choices and options open to them. Together, these dropouts create a significant problem, particularly in terms of expenditure within the further education system, approximately £500 million per year (AUDIT Commission, 1993). Thus the personal becomes the social and as Denzin (1987b, p. 7) says 'these personal experiences' are related to 'the larger contexts in which they have emerged'.

The recognition of the difference between the psychological consciousness of the individual prompting a unique action and the multiplying effect of many such similar responses being made by a number of individuals, all acting in the same way, distinguishes the psycho-analytic from the social (Durkheim, 1964, pp. 1–4). It is at both the personal decision making moment and this larger social context that this research is focused. The pivot for all this has been the self, which recognized and chose to enquire into the nature of this particular problem at this specific time.

## Words and meanings

> For a large class of cases — though not for all — in which we employ the word 'meaning' it can be defined thus: the meaning of a word is its use in the language. (Wittgenstein, 1953, p. 20)

This study also seeks to debunk some of the negative attributes associated with the word, dropout. Listening to what dropouts have to say has changed my understanding of what a dropout is. I have deliberately let them explain themselves. This strategy was preferable to the continued application of a negative classification imposed by the perpetuation of the self-selecting failure myth. Thus Van Maanen's warning of interpretations already being in place has been used so that these prior interpretations are recognized and made problematic in their own right, as part of the historical context which gives rise to student withdrawal.

### *The missing population*

Student dropout can be defined in many ways, but for the purposes of this study it has been identified as premature withdrawal from a course of study. Although statistics vary considerably between institutions, dropout is a ubiquitous problem. The variations in data on retention are due entirely to the different ways in which students are counted and withdrawal defined. In Britain, non-completion accounts for between 30–80 per cent of all post-compulsory student outcomes (The AUDIT Commission, 1993; Bale and Parkin, 1989; Dearing, 1994; Roberts and Webb, 1980).

A mythology seems to surround the concept of dropout since many college staff believe that dropouts are self-selecting failures. Because of these 'student deficit' beliefs, no one was particularly interested in finding out what dropouts really thought, or their reasons for leaving college. It is easy for these myths to arise since dropouts, by virtue of having left college, are no longer available to challenge these notions. Dropout has only become an issue of importance since incorporation (1 April 1993) because a proportion of FEFC funding is now linked to student achievement.

The research design involved the systematic identification of, and collection of internal management information on all students who dropped out over a four-year period in one of the twenty largest colleges in the United Kingdom. A total dropout population of several thousand individuals was eventually compiled providing the basis for a dropout profile 'map' from which a sub-sample was drawn for in-depth analysis based on answers to a self-administered questionnaire coupled with telephone and face to face interviews. These data were then compared to an 'oblique' sample; drawn from people who were in advantageous positions to know about dropout. These people were parents, partners or teachers of dropouts. Both quantitative and qualitative data were collected. The qualitative data was in narrative form and was used to enrich the meaning derived from the numerical information held in the 'map'.

### The 'foot in the door'

Snyder and Cunningham (1975) developed the 'foot in the door' method. This somewhat devious way of inducing compliance is based on a telephone follow-up interview, reminding the respondent that they have already given their permission for the call, when they completed and returned their self-administered questionnaire.

I particularly favour the telephone as an interviewing tool because it is cost effective, convenient for both the researcher and the respondent, and it is safe. By conferring a degree of anonymity (Dillman, 1978) telephone interviews enable respondents to answer open questions easily and at some length. The interviewer can also keep probing and questioning and give feed back which encourages the respondent to talk (Bradburn and Sudman, 1979). The only obvious drawback is that some 7 per cent of households are still without a telephone (Groves and Kahn, 1979, p. 154). It is also worth considering at this stage how easy it is for a respondent to 'hang-up' if they do not want to talk, but as Ball (1968) points out, the telephone is an 'irresistible intruder' and most people feel they have to pick up the receiver. It is only when they have discerned who their caller is, that they make a conscious decision about hanging-up. I am pleased to say that none of the respondents I telephoned terminated the call. Two reasons can be put forward to explain this. Firstly, they valued the opportunity of being asked about an issue that was salient to them. Secondly, I was giving them a voice, a chance to speak and be heard.

### The 'oblique sample'

This sample was gathered in a rather *ad hoc* manner and data collection was less formally structured than in the preceding surveys. In comparison to the questionnaire, where data was systematically collected or the telephone interviews where an interview schedule was administered, the oblique data, by virtue of its unpredictability, almost presented itself. Parents, spouses, siblings and teachers formed the backbone of this sample. They were interviewed as and when the opportunity arose, sometimes by appointment, usually by chance.

*The biographies — mind the gap!*

Ricoeur (1991, p. 5) said that 'between living and recounting (there is) a gap. . .Life is lived, history is recounted'. However, if we are to make any sense of biographical accounts, we are obliged to understand, that the person who has lived the life, the actor, is probably best situated to recount their own story. The gap created by the respondent's self-reflection and *post-hoc* analysis is a dangerous pitfall for the development of knowledge. It may never be closed, but it can be bridged by triangulating the actor's narrative with statistics, which provide an alternative, external viewpoint for the same events. In this way we can prevent the fatal fall into the gap of misunderstanding.

Denzin (1987b, p. 192) warns us that 'the producer of the oral text' speaks 'the text of his life, but this work is always unfinished, for his story will never be completely told. There are too many ways to tell it'. This is the main problem; the story given today may be interpreted differently tomorrow. The strategy of using external sources of information to corroborate narratives goes some way towards overcoming this difficulty by bridging the historical-contextual gap.

## College enrolment

Before jumping in at the deep end with dropout, it is worth considering why students enrol on college courses in the first place, since undoubtedly enrolment and dropout are linked.

> Students enrol in college with hopes and aspirations of college success. To these students, success means having the opportunity to develop potential, realize ambitions, enhance career options, and increase self-satisfaction. . .a great deal of effort goes into the educational process, and the pay off is seeing the students make progress towards their goals. (Fralick, 1993, p. 29)

Fralick has outlined the socially accepted reasons for people coming to college. Staff, students and the public in general hold these goals as good reasons for college attendance, helping to fuel the idea of social mobility provided by educational achievement (Banks, 1968; Bernstein, 1975). The questions raised by this research cast doubt on the reasons dropouts have for enrolling on college courses and recognize that it is these enrolment reasons, which ultimately give rise to premature withdrawal.

## There are four types of dropout

This study has identified four different types of college dropout (Page, 1996b). Each type having quite different reasons for attending college in the first place and each one offering a very different reason for choosing to leave.

*The early leaver*

The first type of dropout is the **early** leaver. They usually withdraw early in the academic year, certainly no later than November. This type of dropout accounts for nearly 20 per cent of all college dropout. These people enrolled on the wrong course and as soon as they discovered their mistake, they left. They enrolled on the wrong courses because they were given the wrong pre-enrolment advice. This poor guidance may have come from an employer or parent, a schoolteacher, a college lecturer or the careers service. What they all have in common is that the advice they were given completely ignored the plans and ambitions of the student.

Anne told me about her experience, which was so typical of many others, she says —

> I left my course regretfully because it was the wrong course for me — there was no mention of it being the wrong course — even when I specifically asked if it would be OK — I was furious — I'd wasted all that money — it seems to me that the college is only interested in your wallet.

Paula's story is not dissimilar, she says —

> My firm was going to pay for this course — I work in a personnel department doing very varied work — I really feel I was totally misled — I really feel the college have tried something that I don't feel really works — and certainly not for me — I feel this course has been misrepresented.

Tim, an employed young man said that —

> I was told to go on this course by the training scheme that employed me — I needed the money — it seemed particularly pointless as I already had done most of the syllabus at a higher level.

It can be seen clearly from the narratives that these students had been given very poor advice and guidance on choosing their courses. These students were asking the right questions, trying to get the necessary facts to make informed decisions. This information was either being withheld or alternatively, these students were not able to comprehend what they had been told. This latter position seems unlikely from the evidence in this study and that put forward by Green (1962) whose own study in America showed that dropouts included the top 18 per cent of the ability range. This study could not corroborate that figure but the statistics showed that all the dropouts involved in the research were as well qualified as their peers who persisted with the course and in some cases (approximately 9 per cent) they were much better qualified. In terms of ability, it seems unlikely that they would mis-understand the information given. Certainly their own self-reflection on this matter shows that they think they were deliberately misled.

The following example will further help illustrate what I mean by students who are aware of their own ability. Elizabeth explains her thoughts about the hairdressing course she was on —

> I felt the course was of little benefit considering I paid three hundred pounds of it! The course was not as advanced as I thought it would be and I was not learning anything that I did not already know.

There seems to be an historical attitude 'hangover' among some admissions staff who still cling to the 'bums on seats' method of enrolling students. This is based on over-enrolment to ensure the continued running of a course. For instance, if the minimum number of students needed to keep a course going for the full academic year is fifteen, then custom and practice dictates that twenty students are enrolled to allow for dropout.

Today, funding is linked to outcome and achievement. Because of this change in the funding rules it has become increasingly important to enrol students who will stay the course. In the past, when funding was linked only to enrolments, it paid a college to over-enrol, and then lose the extra students. If this meant enrolling people who had no hope of succeeding or desire to complete, then that was a small price to pay. The college did not lose out, it got its funding. The lecturers did not lose out, they kept their jobs. The persisting students did not lose out, they got the full use of the limited resources. The only people who were completely disregarded in all of this were those who were unfortunate enough to get enrolled on the wrong courses, because for them, they lost time, money, effort and sometimes, self-esteem. The statistical evidence in this study shows that a significant proportion of these early leavers (52 per cent) come back and re-enrol on other, more appropriate courses in the following academic year and are then very successful.

### The opportunist dropout

The second type of dropout is the **opportunist**. They have drifted into college because they had nothing better to do, and unsurprisingly, when something that they prefer turns up, they leave. They are more of a drop-in than a dropout. The timing of opportunist dropout is difficult to predict since it is impossible to say when the ideal opportunity that they have been waiting for will present itself. The commonest reason given by dropouts in this category is finding employment. The drive towards getting a job can vary but is often associated with family circumstances. Philip will serve as a typical example, he was mature, married and his wife had recently had a new baby, he takes up his story.

> With a family to support — I had to leave — no decision — I found a job — I found the work difficult — I was slow — the workload was stressful — no time to think — I couldn't do the job and college'.

This example will also serve to illustrate a dilemma posed by dropouts' narrative accounts on the one side, and the statistics provided by college management on the other. The numeric information gathered by the college on dropouts, over an extended timeframe, show quite clearly that mature men never leave for a job. Younger men often gave employment as a reason for leaving and women almost always gave this reason. The point I wish to raise here is that the 'official' reasons given may be more of a convenient excuse rather than a real account of what the person intends to do. Collecting information about dropouts using a *pro forma* completed by a student's tutor inevitably creates an opportunity for incorrect information being introduced. It is much easier for a student to tell their tutor that they are leaving to get a job or for personal reasons rather than say what they really think, which may be that they hated coming to college, or they've just got pregnant. The institutional setting seems to have an in-built set of acceptable justifications that override what the dropout really wants to say. The ancient Greek philosophers were aware of this phenomenon when Heraclitus (c 540–480 BC) explained that 'hidden structure is stronger than visible structure' (Luce, 1992, p. 43). Sociological investigations need to consider these hidden structures too, because they are highly influential in the interpretation of the evidence given. The discrepancy between the data collected by the college and the answers respondents chose to give me during interviews is considerable, it is a further indication of the size of that 'gap' between the real life lived and the story being told. The action of tutors may be motivated by good intentions but undoubtedly it should be recognized that ticking a category of convenience when listing the reason for a student's withdrawal is easier and less likely to generate any repercussions.

Karen is a good example of a student who just drifted into college. She says,

> There were very few jobs around which was what I wanted to do, so I chose to seek a course for extra qualifications.

Another student, Ian, a young man with many personal problems adding to his difficulties, explained his position at length. It is a jumbled account. Part of this confusion stems from the way he uses language, nevertheless it is appropriate to tell his story in his words, in his own way.

> I choose to go to college because I had no other educational choice and my wants were not a low grade job — I was very confused when I left school — I knew I'd wasted my time — I'm a lazy person — when I can't get self-satisfaction from a task and need time to get my head together to do something — when I do get down to something I usually succeed. College was my only escape from going mad — so I went — the lecturer suggested this course and I just said — yes!

Opportunist dropouts come to college as a second best, a way of killing time while waiting for something better to come along. They may not know what they really want and just drift into college because its expected of them, knowing it's not really the right choice for them at the time but what else is there? College staff, employers and sometimes their families too, all ignore their real aspirations. Eventually, they find the opportunity they were waiting or searching for, and having made a very positive decision, they leave.

### The consumer

The third type of dropout never actually becomes a student in the first place. They enrol on a course, but in their terms, what they have done is bought an educational commodity. They are not affiliated to the college and they do not see themselves as a student. This type of dropout is the **consumer**, and accounts for a large number of withdrawals, between 60–70 per cent, particularly from part-time, skills based courses such as foreign languages and computing. These people come to college to learn a skill, they are not interested in the certification; they have simply bought a product. It is difficult to construct a picture of a consumer dropout without recourse to the statistical data. These dropouts are usually already employed; they have a clearly defined learning objective such as wanting to speak French or knowing how to use a word processor. They are also quite clear that they do not wish to sit for any final qualification. This is an unfortunate mixture of reasons for college attendance as nearly all FEFC funded courses have a clear qualification aim to which outcome funding is attached. These dropouts are completely satisfied with the course and the teaching they receive. They liked their lecturers and said that they 'got on great' with them.

It is the scale of this type of withdrawal which gives rise to so much concern. For example, in one academic year, approximately 500 people enrolled on a part-time word processing course, only two qualified, the others all dropped out, having withdrawn, in their own terms, successful. We now begin to understand why it may be useful to create an alternative outcome category based on successful course completion, rather than the usual pass or fail at examination. The comments of one such consumer dropout will help to illustrate these numerical findings. She was a mature student, enrolled on a business course and she explains rather angrily at first,

> Where did you get my name from — what makes you think that I withdrew from college — I have never been a student at this college — I only enrolled on this evening class so that I could use my computer better — but I've never been a student at college — I would like you to make sure that your records are amended accordingly and that my name is removed from your lists.

In this comment we have the whole consumer picture. This is a student who is rather annoyed at the intrusion presented by my questions and the categorization I imposed. In her own mind, she is absolutely certain that she is not a student. She does admit to having enrolled on a course but this action of enrolling in itself does not confer the status of studentship on her, even though it is taken for granted as doing so by all college staff. She defines her own reasons for doing the course and she decides when her task is complete. No other criteria are relevant to her.

### The life crisis dropout

The fourth and final category of dropout is the **life crisis** dropout. These people come to college for all the usual, conventional reasons and then at some point an insurmountable crisis overtakes them and they leave. Car accidents, ill health, a death in the family and sudden financial hardship can create difficulties which some students cannot overcome. Life crisis dropout accounts for about 4 per cent of total college withdrawal and because it is unpredictable it will be impossible to eliminate completely. Curiously, the numeric data shows that life crisis occurs more frequently amongst vocational than academic students. Colin provides a good example of a vocational student hit by a crisis neither he nor his family could overcome. He was a full-time construction student living in an isolated, rural area. Unfortunately for Colin, he had a car crash which although it left him unhurt, wrecked his vehicle. He was unable to pay for the repairs to his car and having no other way of getting to college, he withdrew. He explains,

> I hope to be able to start again next year, when I've earned enough to get a new car.

Although Colin's example is unusual, it does illustrate the double trap of rural poverty. His family could not afford to help him, there were no bus routes he could use, and he was absolutely dependent on his car for travel. With his car written off, he had no choice but to leave.

Another all too common life crisis, which affects young women, is pregnancy, especially if it is unplanned. Tracy was one of these dropouts. She managed quite well in college throughout the gestation period, but when she returned after the baby's birth, it was not long before she realized that her mother, who had taken on the baby-care, was not coping with the infant, and Tracey had to leave. At the time, there was no crèche in college, and Tracy had little alternative but to shoulder the duties of a full-time mother. Local statistics show that each year there are approximately 500 births to teenagers in this college's catchment area.

Illness, particularly long-lasting illnesses or conditions that require hospitalization sometimes lead to students dropping out. This is more common in mature students, particularly if they are on a part-time course. After the prolonged absence, they may come back briefly, but finding themselves behind with their studies they leave. As one mature dropout, Robert put it,

> When I was asked questions that I couldn't answer in class I became increasingly more self-conscious and eventually gave up — I just couldn't face it.

The death of a parent can be very traumatic for students; so much so, that sometimes they fail to cope and choose to leave. If the death of one parent is difficult to handle, the death of two must be particularly stressful, especially when those deaths were suicidal. This is what happened to John. His father killed himself when he suspected that John's baby sister was the result of an incestuous union between John and his mother. John always denied this, but the story was commonplace news both in college and the local community and was the root cause of the harassment that he and his mother had to endure. Eventually, she killed herself, and I think one of the most difficult interviews I have ever had to conduct was this one. John came into my office straight from the coroner's inquest. He was dressed in his best and tried to talk with a strong voice, which kept faltering. He told me how he had found his mother's body hanging from the stairs in their flat. He told me all about the cruelty of his neighbours who had thrown dirt at the family washing as it hung on the line and how they threw stones at him and his mother, and broke the windows of their flat. He explained about the council who said they would re-house the family in another area, but acted very slowly. He described the fights he had fought, inside and outside college, with other students who taunted him at every opportunity they could get.

> I need to get a job now — no money to live on you see — I've got ten quid left — then that's it.

By its very nature life crisis is unpredictable and probably not preventable. The provision of specialist counsellors and agencies may go some way towards alleviating the sudden, personal problems of students, but if the situation is really serious then undoubtedly leaving college is a sensible choice.

### The tangled stories — interpretive interaction[1]

When I started this study I had a vision of helping students succeed. These students were just like the ones sitting in my classroom every day; they were real people with faces I could recognize, personalities, families and stories to tell. I had yet to learn that dropouts had a different measure of success. I had yet to listen to what they had to say.

When the research was at its planning stages I was still a practitioner, and together with many of my staffroom colleagues, I held certain notions and ideas about students to be true and unassailable. One of these was the commonly held opinion that 'study is in all cases directed towards the securing of qualifications' (The AUDIT Commission, 1993) and another was that all dropouts are, in the words of one senior lecturer 'self-selecting failures'. There was no evidence to contradict this, but as the research took shape and grew, it began to encompass an untidy tangle of narratives, none of which seemed to come in an orderly fashion ready to be slotted into these theories. What was really going on and why couldn't I just accept the myths my colleagues had no problem believing? Part of the answer lies in the action of collecting these unusual stories; in making dropout problematic and recognizing that during this process I was drawn into a relationship with these respondents for which I was unprepared. Initially, I tried to gather information in an objective, dispassionate manner, collecting facts and figures. It was not long before I found myself emotionally 'tweaked' by the narratives I was hearing and no matter what counsel I gave myself, I could not switch on the detachment I was looking for. This was the entanglement process, when their lives interacted with mine. Thus the research experience became part of the focus of the study (Usher and Bryant, 1989). Understanding other people is always subjective because, as Berg and Smith recognize, 'we use ourselves as instruments for studying' (1988, p. 11). Engaging in the collection of these narratives was enabled by my instrumental interaction with the research subjects. I was as much a part of the research as they were.

The interpretation of these narratives involves understanding the significance of what Denzin refers to as the 'universal singular' (1987, p. 15). That each drop-out was at one and the same time an individual decision maker conforming to the experiences of all dropouts. Understanding those experiences and lifting them from the background of the individual, that noise of everyday life, and interpreting them as significant in the broader sense, was the purpose of this study. The categorization of dropouts into a group is complex because they are not a group; they are individuals with shared characteristics.

The dropout problem is also partly linguistic. The foundation of the problem is the way dropout is spoken about and the value systems built up around it by those using it as part of their everyday language (Wittgenstein, 1953). The word — dropout — was being used by college staff and other students as a powerful, negative, label. The label had meaning, its definition having to do with social devi-ance, non-conforming, poor self-esteem, criminality and resource wasting. All of these negative attributes were used for their relative power in controlling and mani-pulating the behaviour of students. In other words, persisters, those students who stay the course, are made to feel much better about themselves because they are not dropouts. Thus I came to recognize that the word, dropout, has power and a social function. Dropouts themselves spoke in different words, which were not negative. They used strong language speaking in terms of determination and achievement; 'I wanted to leave', 'I got a job', 'leaving was the right decision for me'.

## Solutions

There are other barriers to successful course completion, which were identified by this study. These barriers were located in the dropout's families, their previous schools and the wider community. Much more research is required before a com-plete understanding of student dropout can be established. However, student retention can be improved, not by tinkering with the statistics, which in effect does nothing except conceal the figures, but by recognizing underlying causal factors. Unfortu-nately, current practice still grossly underestimates the true number of withdrawals, and today's education climate continues to foster a reluctance among staff to accept any responsibility for these students' actions. While college staff continue to believe in the student deficit model of dropout, they will not welcome intervention pro-grammes which shift the responsibility from the dropout to the college. Meaningful intervention is required and it will have to deliver more than a return ticket to the course the student has just left. Ideally, prevention programmes will enable students who find themselves on the wrong course to change, rather than have to leave and then re-enrol on the right course, a year later. Advice and guidance must be accurate, comprehensive and take into account the ambitions and aspirations of the student. It has to be acknowledged that life crisis dropout is not preventable, and it is therefore unlikely that any college will ever be able to improve its retention rates much above 96 per cent. Colleges are also going to have to decide which side of the consumerism fence they are sitting on. If education is going to be 'market forces' driven, as it appears to be today, then colleges should not be surprised that some of their 'customers' are buying their product and just like consumers in other retail outlets, they resent any interference in what they choose to do with that course/product. Finally, we have to admit that for some students, leaving college is the right decision. We need to help them disempower the word, so that dropout is no longer used as a 'stick' with which to beat them.

### The last word

This work was, in part, written for the dropouts, as a token of the expectations implicit to 'potlatch' (Mauss, 1954). Potlatch is a form of archaic exchange of gifts where the recipient of one gift tries to exceed the generosity of the giver by returning a greater gift. All the dropouts in this study gave me the gift of their stories. I have given them the gift of a voice. By bringing their stories to the attention of those who would not normally be listening, I have kept my part of the potlatch bargain. I hope I have represented them without distortion.

> and who can apportion out and dovetail his incidents, dialogues, characters and descriptive morsels, so as to fit them all exactly, without either compressing them unnaturally, or extending them artificially...and then when everything is done, the kindest-hearted critic of them all invariably twits us with the incompetence and lameness of our conclusions. We have either become idle and neglected it, or tedious and over laboured it. It is insipid or unnatural, over-strained or imbecile. It means nothing, or it attempts too much. (Trollope [1815–1882] p. 185)

Trollope expresses both the fears and aspirations I have in relation to this study. It may seem inappropriate to align a serious research study with a work of fiction, but in their own ways they both try to interpret for a wider audience, the lives of those who would otherwise remain obscure and misunderstood.

Finally, I should like to emphasize that in order to protect my respondents, all the names of the people included in this study are fictitious.

### Note

1   Denzin, N. (1983).

### Glossary of terms

FEFC — Further Education Funding Council

## References

AUDIT COMMISSION (1993) *Unfinished Business*, London: HMSO.

BALE, E. and PARKIN, C. (1989) 'Student withdrawal from part-time courses of further education', Paper presented at the International Conference on Research and Development in Vocational Education, Adelaide, March.

BALL, D. (1968) 'Towards a sociology of telephones and telephoners' in GROVES et al (1989) *Telephone Survey Methodology*, New York: John Wiley and Sons.

BANKS, O. (1968) *The Sociology of Education*, London: Batsford.

BERG, D. and SMITH, K. (1988) *The Self in Social Inquiry: Researching Methods*, Newbury Park, CA: Sage.

BERNSTEIN, B. (1975) *Class, Codes and Control, Vol. 3. Towards a Theory of Educational Transmission*. 2nd edition, London: Routledge and Kegan Paul.

BRADBURN, N. and SUDMAN, S. (1979) *Improving Interview Methods and Questionnaire Design*, Chicago: Jossey-Bass.

BURGESS, R. (1982) *Field Research: A Sourcebook and Field Manual*, London: George Allen and Unwin.

DEARING, R. SIR (1994) 'Dearing to focus on A level dropouts', *Times Educational Supplement*, 12 May, p. 2.

DENZIN, N. (1983) 'Interpretive interactionism', pp. 129–146, in MORGAN, G. (ed.) *Beyond Method*, Beverly Hills: Sage.

DENZIN, N. (1987) *The Alcoholic Self*, Newbury Park, CA: Sage.

DENZIN, N. (1987b) *The Recovering Alcoholic*, Newbury Park, CA: Sage.

DILLMAN, D. (1978) *Mail and Telephone Surveys: The Total Design Method*, New York: John Wiley and Son.

DURKHEIM, E. (1964) 'The rules of sociological method', The Free Press. Cited in O'DONNELL, M. (ed.) *Reader in Sociology*, 1987, Walton-on-Thames: Nelson.

FRALICK, M. (1993) 'College success: A study of positive and negative attrition', *Community College Review*, **20**, 5, pp. 29–36.

GREEN, D. (1962) 'A study of talented high school dropouts', *Vocational Guidance Quarterly*, **3**, pp. 171–172. Cited in IRVINE, D. (1987) 'What research doesn't say about gifted dropouts', *Educational Leadership*, **44**, 6, pp. 79–80.

GROVES, R. and KAHN, R. (1979) *Surveys by Telephone: A National Comparison with Personal Interviews*, New York: Academic Press.

LAO-TZU (c.6) *Tao-te-ching*, Book2, Ch. 71, translated by LAU, T. (1963) cited in *The Columbia Dictionary of Quotations*, 1995, Columbia University Press: Electronic version.

LUCE, J. (1992) *An Introduction to Greek Philosophy*, London: Thames and Hudson.

MAUSS, M. (1954) *The Gift: Forms and Functions of Exchange in Archaic Societies*, trans. by CUNNINSON, I. Glencoe: The Free Press.

PAGE, M. (1996) 'A framework for understanding student dropout in the further education context', PhD Thesis (unpublished), June, Southampton University.

PAGE, M. (1996b) 'Don't leave me this way', *FE NOW*, November, p. 29.

RICOUER, P. (1991) *From Text to Action*, London: Athlone Press.

ROBERTS, G. and WEBB, W. (1980) 'Factors affecting dropout', *Adult Education*, **53**, July, pp. 85–90.

SNYDER, M. and CUNNINGHAM, M. (1975) 'To comply or not to comply: Testing the self-perception explanation of the foot in the door phenomenon', *Journal of Personality and Social Psychology*, **31**, 1, pp. 64–67.

TROLLOPE, A. (1953) [1815–1882] *Barchester Towers*. (eds) SADLEIR, H. and PAGE, F., Oxford: Oxford University Press.

USHER, R. and BRYANT, I. (1989) *Adult Education as Theory, Practice and Research: The Captive Triangle*, London: Routledge.

VAN MAANEN, J. (1983) *Qualitative Methodology*, Beverly Hills: Sage.

WITTGENSTEIN, L. (1953) *Philosophical Investigations*, Oxford: Blackwell.

# 8    An Auto/Biographical Account of Educational Experience

*Brian Roberts*

## Stories. . .stories

Through stories we relate our lives to ourselves and others, we attempt to make sense of our experiences and give an account of who we are. For example, when we meet a stranger, perhaps on a long train journey or at a party, we tell stories to say who we are, both to our own self and the other person: about where we are from, what we are doing now and what we will be doing. From the endless incidents and experiences, thoughts and feelings of our lives, we make and remake accounts; through stories we sequence and give meaning to the remembered elements of our past (see Gergen and Gergen, 1984). The shaping of the past, the concerns of the present and the anticipation of the future are intimately related (Mead, 1956, pp. 328–41; Sartre, 1968, pp. 100–9; Schutz, 1971, pp. 214–17). By retrospection (and prospection) stories are constructed; at the most general, one story may summarize our life with a major theme of escape; journey; disappointment; or contentment. There are also subsidiary stories that are distinctive but are usually still connected to other stories we retell. These various stories may well coincide with particular episodes in life or a chronological span (e.g. parts of family, schooling and work life) (Denzin, 1989, pp. 41–43). These subsidiary stories are told and revised according to the situation, new experiences or prospects. Here, we are applying 'story' quite loosely to denote the attempt to write or tell about experience, to ourselves and others — according to some sequence or order containing incidents, persons and responses rather than as a simple, consistent account with a start, beginning and end. In practice, life stories are to some extent provisional and often contain uncertain and even contradictory elements. It is tempting to see such stories as 'personal myths' (see Hankiss, 1981; Peneff, 1990; Samuel and Thompson, 1990); as neither true nor false expressions of experience but, instead, attempts to explain or make sense of the past and our part in it, and how we have become what we believe we want to be.

A significant aspect of the story or the personal myth is that it contains one or more elements which are 'defining' (or 'epiphanies', see Denzin, 1989, p. 70) — the story surrounds something which we regard as important, we return to it; we continue to select the story or subsidiary story since it holds some fascination and significance for us. Perhaps, the meaning or truth of the story is not fully apparent to us because it seems to be hidden or has multiple interpretations. In the story of my education and its outcome I see a puzzle: what are the key elements and how do they connect to produce the particular ending?

My schooling remains something of a mystery to me. By 'mystery' I mean that it is difficult for me to understand how the end point is connected to the start of my path from a working-class background to the world of the professional academic. My education began in a village school, followed by a rather larger small town junior school in the 1950s; it included 11+ failure, attendance at an all-boys secondary modern school and transfer to a new mixed-sex grammar school. On leaving the sixth form I had my two 'A' level passport to a new polytechnic and eventually seven years of higher education. An important part of the mystery of schooling for me lies in the comparison with the different route followed by my two brothers and sister who only went to single-sex secondary modern schools. I joined my older brother for a year at the same school and my younger brother followed some ten years later. Instead of entering the local job market in skilled or semi-skilled factory work or mining — the local jobs available for 'secondary mod' boys — the way became open for me to transfer to a grammar school, and then progress to 'college'. For me, the experience of work on the shop floor in local factories was only a time between courses.

In my social background there seemed little to suggest that I was headed for a different path in education. We were not an aspirant or upper-working class family. My father was a painter and decorator employed in the public sector who had to retire in his fifties after a serious accident at work. My mother was employed in a series of cleaning and domestic help jobs until a work accident and the onset of ill-health, resulting from childhood illness, also brought early retirement.

### The village school: 1955

My early years, until about 9-years-old, were spent in a village beside a main railway line in northern England. The village was rather ordinary looking without particular features although the church spire is said to be unusual. It was a working farming village, with three farms in its centre. It is now primarily a commuter village with one farm now replaced by a housing estate. Everyone really did know each other and popular festivities such as the Summer Fayre and Christmas Show were well attended. The people were generally working class being farm workers, or had jobs in the mine in the next village, or at a local factory.

My family could be described as semi-skilled working class. I was brought up in the Old Vicarage, next to the church with its own gate into the churchyard. It sounds rather grand, but in fact, conditions were relatively primitive, even for the 1950s. It had an outside bucket toilet, a ladder to reach the upper-floor rooms and Calor gas for the cooker. Part of the house dated back to the seventeenth Century and a plaque on a side wall indicated its age and claimed that it had a famous resident four hundred years ago. As part of the rental agreement, the oldest room was set aside as a museum for occasional visitors. The most arrivals I remember were five coach loads of American tourists descending unannounced one day. In addition to my father's parents, who were Welsh in origin and lived in the village, I seemed to know most local people and I was in the habit of saying 'hello' to everyone. I was well-known and when I broke my leg at the age of five the mantlepiece was full of fruit from neighbours. No doubt they remembered that I needed an operation six weeks after birth and, at three months old, nearly died from whooping cough — I was 'given the night to live'. I also had 'fits' which were treated by 'mustard baths' in the tin bath in front of the coal fire. These illnesses and mishaps brought me close to my mother and made me the acknowledged family favourite. The life of the village, particularly the freedom of children to roam, left a strong memory of an idyllic time, a memory shared by my older brother and sister.

My parents had not had an extensive time at school. My father left school at thirteen to sell vegetables with my grandfather around the local villages. My mother was from a single parent family and had grown up in the 1930s. She had to help my grandmother to do paid domestic work to keep the family going. Our family had a strong working-class identity, with my mother having a very keen sense of 'us' versus 'them'. My father was especially fond of argument on most social and political topics at both work and home.

Before reaching school age I was looked after for some time by my grandparents, while my mother worked in the local fields cutting sugar beet or picking potatoes. I remember being taught to tell the time by them and, when at 5-years-old I broke my leg, reading a clock in the hospital while a 'pot' was fitted; I noticed it read 9 o'clock and was way past my bedtime. My grandparents' two up and two down cottage had at least two fascinations for a young child — a shilling coin in the slot television and two large pigs to look after in the allotment.

The village school which I entered as a 5-year-old was set on the edge of the village and was probably built around 1910. It had only two classrooms — one for the infants and one for juniors with two cloakrooms where school dinners were served. The toilets were next to the coal heap across the playground which had wide grass borders on either side. At first sight, the school looked like a rather large bungalow with a steep roof. The school became a private residence many years later.

Each classroom had a large fire at the front. The infants sat around tables, the juniors in rows. There were just over fifty children at the school and it had two teachers. Most of the children came from the village but there were others from the immediate hamlets. My memories of the school are relatively few but clear: I remember the reciting of times tables — I knew the 'tune' but failed to grasp many of the 'words'; and the class dancing to a 'music and movement' programme on the radio and being asked to 'all be trees' when the music stopped — that was a favourite lesson. I also remember the embarrassment of being the most frequent child to put up a hand to request to go to the toilet. Other memories include playing at war fights; being something of a leader of one group; and part of the class going up to the juniors. I also went into the juniors at the same time but I was soon returned to the infants. I did not understand why and felt I had been considered not yet good enough for the transfer. Not long after an eventual promotion, the family left the village. On leaving the school I was asked to select a book as a present; I chose

*Moby Dick* and I still have the copy. I had already been presented with a couple of class book prizes for general knowledge which was always my best subject.

### The town junior school: 1959

The move to the town was a big event for the family. For several years my father had been working as a painter in public works. After the war he had tried to work alone but the income was poor and the family was far from well off. With a regular wage, and my mother's seasonal farm work, my parents somehow managed to get a mortgage on a new three-bedroom house in the local town. So, in spring 1959 I travelled in the back of a removal van with my dad to what seemed a very different world.

The local town had around 20,000 people, whereas my village had no more than 400 or so. On my first day at the new school I walked the short distance with my 'Mam' to see the head teacher. The only thing I remember is being asked a number of times table questions. I was put in the 'B' form and stayed there until the final year when I was promoted. I do not remember any problems settling in. The main differences were the size of the classes which contained everyone the same age, the more formal atmosphere and the large school assemblies. The school had about 360 children and the pile of school milk crates always indicated to me just how much bigger this new context was. In terms of school work it seems I made good progress in the 'B' form although (it was said) I occasionally wasted time 'minding others' business' while trying to be helpful; perhaps here was some indication of a future career in sociology?

My reading ability was high, certainly for the 'B' form. But, my home had very little reading matter, mainly the *Daily Herald*, *News of the World*, and sometimes a woman's magazine. Books were few, usually a prize from school or Sunday School for good attendance, or an annual such as *Rupert Bear* bought with a Christmas book token from a relative. My main reading was comics. As I graduated from *Beano* and *Topper*, to *Tiger* and *Lion*, and on to *Rover* and *Adventure*, the pictures became fewer and the text more prominent. 'Comic day' was awaited with anticipation and after reading mine and my brother's comic there was my sister's *Bunty* and later *School Friend*. The importance of the comics was not simply in terms of helping my reading but also they gave me heroes to identify with, often working-class ones who had overcome adversity.

The times tables, and arithmetic generally, were not my strong point, in fact they were a source of embarrassment; so, in my final year in the juniors I got my mother to write the tables out for me to learn. Another weak point was my awful writing; perhaps partly due to having to adopt a different style in my new school. In any event I had to attend remedial writing classes. More pleasant memories of the junior school were the playground games, including marbles, 'snobs', and adventure games; and collecting cards on soccer, flags of the world and other topics.

I was grateful for the confidence in me shown by the 'B' form teacher prior to my last year. By this time I had gained a great interest in history. I joined the local library and each Saturday I would get out another batch of books. In class I was encouraged to read ahead and also given the job of getting ready what we would now call 'visual aids' such as pictures of Roman soldiers and towns. An important step for me was the promotion to the 'A' form in the final year following my second place in class. This change gave me more self-belief, but in the 'A' form I was very aware of being a new recruit from a lower form and worried about my place in the academic hierarchy within the class. School reports indicated that I was around average in class but my oral work was 'outstanding' and that I had wide interests. Maybe I was willing to say a lot on any topic. Again, perhaps a career in sociology was assured!

The 11+ exam came as something of a surprise. It was not something which was discussed at home and I had little knowledge of it. My recollection is that one day we were organized into unfamiliar exam conditions and given papers containing lists of increasingly difficult 'sums' and English exercises. The exam was in two rounds, with not even all the 'A' form getting into the second. The next memory I have is of all the final year meeting and as our names were read out we learned which school we were to attend. At that stage, I do not even think I really knew the difference between a grammar school and a secondary modern. However, I was soon aware that some children had been successful and that I was not one of them. On leaving the school, my year group was split between a relatively new mixed secondary modern, two single-sex secondary moderns, a girls' high school and a very old boys' grammar school. My boys' secondary modern was next door to the traditional grammar school. In autumn 1961 I started the secondary modern, just as my older brother entered his final year.

### The secondary modern school: 1961

I was always eager to contribute to class discussion. Joining the 'A' form in the last year of the junior school perhaps made me a little less willing to raise my hand to answer questions but I was probably still one of the keen ones. My general knowledge was good. I remember being very happy when praised by a student teacher in the junior school for knowing what the initials FBI stood for; interestingly, I knew this despite our family not having a television to watch the American police imports. My 11+ failure seemed to reinforce an underlying sense of frustration and feeling of lack of recognition. I soon began to realize that the boys at the grammar school were taking a higher path and a distinction had been made between us. It became obvious to me that they were to enjoy superior facilities. For instance, whereas we were bussed to a grass field for athletics, the grammar school pupils had a new running track on site.

In the first afternoon at the secondary modern we were placed in four classes, A to D. My name as read out for the 'A' form. Few boys from my old school were in the form because they lived nearer to the mixed secondary modern school. There was a small group of us at the top of the 'A' form who competed keenly for places. Each end of term report gave our position in each subject and our overall position in class. I worked hard at these tests and got into the regular habit of homework and revision. Of course, I watched the American comedy programmes on our newly acquired television before getting down to work. I was generally well disciplined and cannot remember my parents ever having to remind me to do my homework. Early in the spring term a number of us in the 'A' form were asked at assembly to bring our work to the headteacher. With a mixture of puzzlement and dread I scooped up my neater work and went to the head's office. I was introduced to another headteacher and it soon became apparent that a new grammar school was opening in the next town and recruits were needed. Arithmetic was still not as strong as most other subjects but on the other hand my sporting abilities, including representing the school in cross-country and football, appeared to fit the ethos of the new grammar school. It was explained to me that the school would be playing Rugby Union. In March 1962 my parents received a letter from my headteacher at the secondary modern school to say that I had been recommended for a transfer to the new grammar school. For the remainder of the year those who had been selected, and chose to transfer, were reminded in class that they were destined for the grammar school — while it was a little embarrassing we felt different and I was aware just how pleased for us the class teachers seemed.[1]

## The grammar school: 1962

My parents were delighted by my success. The neighbours were told and gave their congratulations as we passed in the street. For my parents my entrance to the grammar school was a major achievement and source of pride; they understood my later academic successes less and less because they had few points of comparison. It meant that they never put pressure on me to study but gave their support. On the first day at the grammar school three of us from my old form caught the school bus in town to travel the eight mile journey. I had seen my new school once but not from the inside. My initial emotions were very mixed. For the first time I wore a school uniform. At the secondary modern only two of us did not have the uniform in the 'A' form — the wearing of school uniform lessened as you went down the forms. The uniform made me feel uncomfortable in two ways; wearing new clothes felt nice but odd because it did not feel or look like me, and I felt some guilt due to the cost. The payment for the satchel, grey mac, school tie, grey and white shirts, grey socks, two rugby shirts, plimsolls, cap and blazer had been a struggle. I felt concerned because my parents were not well off; there were then two older children still at home and my younger brother had just arrived.

Despite the smart new uniform, frequent comments were made during the first couple of years about my untidy appearance; in addition my written work was almost unreadable. Instead of 'A' and 'B' forms we had those who had passed the 11+ in one form and the rest of us in two others. As a new school it began with only the lower years and about seventy-five pupils in each year. The school was very modern in design, bright, and well-equipped. We all felt some excitement at having something new. The school received attention from a very wide range of visitors who came to observe the new 1960s school architecture. It was set in landscaped lawns with a large playing field, and shared a shale running track and a swimming pool with a new technical school next door. I could not help compare these facilities with those I had recently left in the secondary modern.

At the grammar school my first feelings also reflected an anxiety about my ability. Did I justify a place in a new grammar school? How would I fare? I became more aware of speech and accent. Certain words, forms of address and expression were unfamiliar and I became conscious of my own mode of speech. This self-scrutiny was fostered by meeting other pupils from better off backgrounds, for instance, the sons and daughters of shopkeepers, managers, and professionals. My political views began to mature and I started to argue vigorously in class discussions against those putting forward conservative opinions. In advancing my 'socialist views' I felt I was also defending my family and working-class background. By the sixth form I declared that I was a communist.

Sport was an important part of my school life. Rugby Union was the main winter game. I did not like it much, even less so when we lost to the local private school. It was not the game I had grown up with and had gone to watch with my dad. The fact that we played relatively very few soccer matches against other schools made me resentful. I represented the school at cricket, rugby, soccer, cross-country and athletics, but it was not difficult getting into school teams due to few boys being in each year. My main sporting success was in athletics where I did well against other schools and ran in the county championships. Athletics was also a family tradition. I liked running but did not enjoy competition due to my nervousness before a race.

After arriving home at about five o'clock, watching my favourite American comedy programmes and eating the family dinner, I had the demands of school work. Our modern house had only one living room, and at first it was only heated downstairs. I shared a bedroom with my older brother until the sixth form, which made finding space to work difficult. As homework increased and Saturdays were taken up with school sport I had less in common and less time to mix with my friends in the neighbourhood. By the age of sixteen my close friends were from the local grammar school. The move to the grammar school also meant the beginning of a sense of distance from my parents; an awareness that I had gone beyond their experience and that their help was limited. It gave me a greater feeling of independence than was probably usual in adolescence. They wished me to do well but I do not remember them nagging me to study, in fact, around examination time they were concerned that I was working too hard.

Eventually, the choice of 'O' levels had to be made. My final results were varied but I did gain eight passes and entrance to the sixth form. Since I liked studying and I could not see any alternative, I stayed on to take an unusual 'A' level combination of chemistry, history, geography. My parents did not encourage me to leave and the jobs I knew about did not appeal. Talks about university applications made me think that further study after school was possible but what job could I do? The careers service suggested I consider becoming a probation officer. Probably a teacher mentioned studying sociology and I began to read *New Society* and the *New*

*Statesman* at home. Meanwhile, I was beginning to feel some dissatisfaction with studying at school. This was partly due to some chafing at school restrictions; for instance, comments were being made about my long hair and sideburns and I increasingly resented religion and school assemblies. But, it was also because I wanted to dwell longer on some subject topics and question further. By now I had been scouring along the local library shelves for wider reading and begun to dabble in poetry, philosophy and anything with socialism in the title. I wanted more explanations and to study something that might change the world.

As my years at the grammar school progressed, my view of a future career began to shift. In my early school years I realized that my future would be different from my father, other men from my background, and from many of my friends in the secondary modern. But, I had no clear picture of what to expect and I had no immediate role models. All the men in my family had worked in the mines at some point and were mainly in semi-skilled occupations. Comics provided some idealized career models, for instance, a favourite was the exciting life of a Canadian mountie. Around thirteen joining the army seemed to be a more realistic possibility.

In the sixth form, university prospectuses were sent for and I thumbed the pages for sociology courses. Unfortunately, I applied to some of the most fashionable universities and not surprisingly I received only one offer and failed to get a university place. I had also applied to a handful of the emerging polytechnics and received a couple of interviews and offers. My eventual choice was heavily influenced by being a fan of Manchester United. I had travelled with the 'lads' from about the age of 12 to see United's home matches. Since I knew the city a little and supported United, I chose a course in the same place. During the summer after 'A' levels I worked alongside my brother on the shop floor of an engineering factory. I accepted an offer from Manchester at the last possible moment and arrived on the first day of term in a suit, my hair newly cut short and holding a small blue suitcase. I had nowhere to live. It was a few weeks after my eighteenth birthday. I was to emerge from full-time education one polytechnic, two universities and seven years later.

### Auto/biography and working-class experience

I have told the story of my education in more or less the same outline form countless times. Nearly every time the account is given, at some level, there is the pursuit of comprehension; a need to find the clues and make the connections which may make sense of my educational life and its outcome. I have entitled my account of my schooling an 'auto/biography'.[2] Here, I am using the term as an attempt to stand back from my life while at the same time engage with it. So, the use of auto/biography is a recognition of a double movement we ordinarily make in describing our life events, past influences and relationships. In telling a story we usually include our motives, decisions, acceptances or rationalizations within a description and interpretation of our circumstances. In this way, the retelling of life experience is not only a retrospective process but it is also implicated in the shaping of our current identity. This 'rewriting' of our past does not construct identity completely anew.[3] For instance, some elements of my past are given, such as the dates when I moved from school to school. But, the meanings attached to events may vary in intensity and content over time. What I find surprising when retelling my story is the extent to which the elements selected appear to have remained unchanged over a long period. Why do I choose these elements rather than others and what are their significance? I return frequently to the story as if the signs are there but their meanings and connections are not clear. The clues are given but the case is not solved.

In trying to penetrate and connect the clues which may provide the explanation of educational experience, the starting point must be class. My transition to secondary education came in the period of the late fifties and early sixties when government reports and academic research pointed to the wastage of ability and talent in the educational system. The question of widening educational opportunity was being raised (Marshall, 1992, pp. 36–7). A whole series of home and school factors were identified as perpetuating social disadvantage: the circumstances at home and parental attitudes, the links between the home and school, and the conditions and structure of schooling were all highlighted. Why were some working-class pupils successful at school and others not, even if they had attended grammar school? It appeared that selection was not merely on academic criteria but also had a social class basis.

Social factors were investigated by Jackson and Marsden who were concerned with those working class children in the 1950s who succeeded in grammar school (Jackson and Marsden, 1966; see also, Marshall, 1992, Chapter 3). The successful pupil tended to be from a smaller, upper-working class family living in a more middle-class area. Such academically able children had aspiring, deferential working-class parents, and accepted the values of school. The pressure from an ambitious home led these children to be hard working and to be given positions of responsibility such as prefects (Jackson and Marsden, 1966, p. 171). The identification with the neighbourhood was replaced with a new life with different friends, manners and accent.

For a minority of working-class children who continued through grammar school an attachment to neighbourhood persisted and they developed a significant questioning of the type of education which they experienced (Jackson and Marsden, 1966, p. 172).[4] The adaptation of the latter group to the grammar school seems closer to my own feeling of estrangement brought about by the type of discipline and hierarchy and ethos; I was also irritated by the expectation of loyalty to 'the house' and 'the school', the commitment to rugby union rather than soccer, and the brightly coloured uniform which marked me out as different. Jackson and Marsden also added some research on the unsuccessful — those who entered grammar school but were early leavers. To many of them the grammar school had brought an alien world, demoralization, loss of confidence and other effects (Jackson and Marsden, 1966, pp. 268–69). Conversely, those children from middle-class homes found the transition from home to selective schooling less problematic due to home background and advantages; even if things went wrong for the child, the parents were willing to challenge the school's opinion (Jackson and Marsden, 1966, pp. 56–57).

While my parents were interested in my education, their knowledge of the school system, their assessment of my ability and needs, and their confidence in dealing with the school were restricted due to their own educational experience and relative lack of education.

Entrance to the grammar school for a working-class boy from my background brought a sense of loss and insecurity; the certainties of home life, including an assumption that I would have a job similar to my brother's and father's, were becoming less reliable as guides for the future. I was now different and set on a divergent track and headed for an unknown destination.

Richard Hoggart in *The Use of Literacy* (1958) points to the effects of the grammar school on the 'scholarship boy' brought by the sense of loss generated by the gradual shift from class background begun in school. The effects on me of grammar school life echoes some of Hoggart's account of his earlier experience. He argues that the sense of loss in the working-class child is made greater by a self-consciousness and the emotional and physical uprooting from class. He speaks of an unease resulting from being caught between two cultures. The scholarship boy is said with pride to 'have brains' but as affiliation to the street group of boys fades and his interaction within the family group shifts, the boy becomes increasingly separated from the closeness of his original culture (Hoggart, 1958, pp. 292–95). Underneath, insecurities and anxieties can develop which reflect the persistence of a sense of isolation and possible rejection (Hoggart, 1958, pp. 296–304).[5] The grammar school also brings new experiences and opportunities beyond those of a working-class background. In my case, I became a success by attending grammar school but what exactly did that mean and foretell?

In the last ten years my prime research concerns have been in the processes of identity formation and the study of biography. Interestingly, the study of the 'individual life', in terms of deviant careers and the life history method, was central to my postgraduate work some twenty-five years ago.[6] My return to the study of life histories has brought a more personal edge and has included the study of the role of the researcher's own biography in research, the formation of Welsh identity and the biographical understanding of time. I am beginning to interconnect these research areas and to see them as having a personal origin and motivation related closely to my own biography. More latterly, I have begun to write about myself. This account of my education can be taken as auto/biographical since it contains an account of my past, reflects upon it, and introduces other accounts of working-class education and biographical interpretation. There is an interplay between what is unique in my personal trajectory and what is held in common with the experience of others from comparable male, semi-skilled, working-class positions. In short, my interest in biography has a personal referent, it is part of my own attempt to understand, order and explain how I have come to my current destination and concerns.

I overcame the disadvantages of class background — but how? Certainly opportunities did occur at the right time for me, such as the opening of a new grammar school and the general changes in higher education in the 1960s. But, a deeper explanation is also required to account for my story. For instance, why did I succeed in entering the sixth form as one of the minority of 11+ failures to 'stay on'?

Again, a clue lies in explaining how working-class children respond to grammar school education. Bernstein's work on the transmission of culture is very relevant here (see, for example, Bernstein, 1975).[7] He has been interested not simply in the outcome of inequalities and the structure of educational opportunity but on the structuring and content of communication, how everyday life is lived through 'codes' or 'modalities'. Here, we cannot describe the complexities of Bernstein's work and its conceptual changes. However, a central aspect has been how *codes* are constituted by *classification* — which refers to the degree of insulation between discourses, practices, agents and contexts and the provision of rules of recognition, and *framing* — which refers to the controls on selection, pacing and sequencing in communicative relations and contains further rules. Of special relevance is Bernstein's notion of coding as applied beyond the situation of the classroom and even the school, to the contexts of the family, community and wider class formation.

From their family, neighbourhood and class background working-class children have to negotiate and adapt to the unfamiliar communication coding of the school. I had to make my own adaptation to the world of the grammar school and the wider social structuring it represented. More specifically, I conformed, in Bernstein's terms, to the instrumental culture or order of the school by pursuing the acquisition of skills but was at the very least ambivalent to the expressive culture or order concerned with conduct and character. It was mainly the regulation and maintenance of the moral order of the school and its reflection of a broader social order which posed difficulties for me. I was keen to gain knowledge but found an incompatibility between the ethos and rituals of the school and a loyalty to my social background. For the working-class child the movement between different communication codes of home and school entails choices and compromises; in many cases this can eventually lead to embarrassment, rejection or estrangement in relation to home life as successes increase. Some working-class children find the transition is rather more smooth due to the ambition and values, and the relatively stronger knowledge and resources of their parents. I was caught between the two types of code within the school — conforming to one by being keen to learn and understand, but subversive of the other. I did not feel comfortable with a set of values and loyalties which seemed detached from my experience of home and neighbourhood and which were offered as necessary for success in life. My educational career could be seen as a series of crossings of social boundaries of differing types and strength which define social group, shape social contexts and order life experience. Those crossings which were the most difficult for me were those that required most compromise and loss, and are probably the ones which I continually retell in my story.

The mystery of my schooling remains and probably always will. How was I able to make the boundary crossings? The answer is something more than opportunities being available, such as the opening of a new grammar school. It may well lie in the type of my response to schooling; I wanted to learn and do well but the experiences of streaming and selection produced an anxiety about my academic ability and social worth, including a sensitivity and protectiveness towards family and social background. The instances of rejection left their personal mark but did not deter me. The experience of schooling could have resulted in a routine conformism, an acceptance of a 'B stream' designation or some disruptive behaviour. Onto my initial enthusiasm to learn, a determination to succeed academically, establish my social worth and defend my social background, were grafted. It is here that the answer to the mystery of my academic success must reside. But, whether for those working-class children who succeed academically or those who do not, there are costs to the self. 'Hidden injuries of class' are produced by the measurement of worth and the confirmation of dignity according to class position (Sennett and Cobb, 1973). But, an irony is that in trying hard and excelling in the system of rewards for demonstrated ability, the praise received by the successful individual does not seem to relate to him or her but to the performance (Sennett and Cobb, 1973, pp. 259–60). The common refrain 'You are middle-class now' is not convincing, it does not ring true. My movement between the worlds of class was not complete and left a lasting psychic legacy. The experience of social mobility produced an inner personal dynamic containing a defence of social background, a sense of loss, and an anxiety regarding social worth and social identity.

## Notes

1  Once allocated, transfer between types of school was often limited in the 1950s and 1960s (see Kogan, 1978, p. 32). In my case I believe one or two boys could transfer at the end of the second year from my secondary modern to the adjacent grammar school.
2  For an influential use of the term 'auto/biography' see Stanley, 1992, 1993.
3  For extended use of the idea of 'rewriting' see Freeman, 1993.
4  Jackson and Marsden identified a working-class group of 15 who successfully finished grammar school but remained committed to local loyalties rather than the ethos of the school (see Jackson and Marsden, 1966, pp. 120–22; Marshall, 1992, p. 46).
5  Hoggart (1968) and Marsden (1968) later provided autobiographical accounts of their own educational experience. For a wider study of the experience of social mobility and individual views on class using 'life histories', see Goldthorpe, 1980.
6  I was particularly interested in the work of Matza and his ideas of 'drift' and 'becoming' (Matza, 1964, 1969).
7  For an assessment of Bernstein's use of classification and frame and his 'structuralism' see Atkinson, 1985.

## References

ATKINSON, P. (1985) *Language, Structure and Reproduction*, London: Methuen.
BERNSTEIN, B. (1975) *Class, Codes and Control*, Vol. 1, London: Routledge and Kegan Paul.
DENZIN, N.K. (1989) *Interpretive Biography*, London: Sage.
FREEMAN, M. (1993) *Rewriting the Self*, London: Routledge.
GERGEN, M.M. and GERGEN, K.J. (1984) 'The social construction of narrative accounts', in GERGEN, K.J. and GERGEN, M.M. (eds) *Historical Social Psychology*, New Jersey: Erlbaum, pp. 173–189.

GOLDTHORPE, J.H. (1980) *Social Mobility and Class Structure in Modern Britain*, Oxford: Clarendon Press.

HANKISS, A. (1981) 'Ontologies of the self: On the mythological rearranging of one's life-history', in BERTAUX, D. (ed.) *Biography and Society*, London: Sage.

HOGGART, R. (1958) *The Uses of Literacy*, Harmondsworth: Penguin.

HOGGART, R. (1968) 'Richard Hoggart' in GOLDMAN, R. (ed.) *Breakthrough*, London: Routledge and Kegan Paul, pp. 90–105.

JACKSON, B. and MARSDEN, D. (1966) *Education and the Working Class*, Harmondsworth: Penguin.

KOGAN, M. (1978) *The Politics of Educational Change*, London: Fontana.

MARSDEN, D. (1968) 'Dennis Marsden' in GOLDMAN, R. (ed.) *Breakthrough*, London: Routledge and Kegan Paul, pp. 106–123.

MARSHALL, G. (1992) *In Praise of Sociology*, London: Routledge.

MATZA, D. (1964) *Delinquency and Drift*, New York: John Wiley.

MATZA, D. (1969) *Becoming Deviant*, NJ: Prentice-Hall.

MEAD, G.H. (1956) *On Social Psychology*, Chicago: The University of Chicago Press.

PENEFF, J. (1990) 'Myths in life stories' in SAMUEL, R. and THOMPSON, P. (eds) *The Myths We Live By*, London: Routledge, pp. 36–48.

SAMUEL, R. and THOMPSON, P. (1990) 'Introduction' in SAMUEL, R. and THOMPSON, P. (eds) *The Myths We Live By*, London: Routledge, pp. 1–22.

SARTRE, J-P. (1968) *Search for a Method*, New York: Vintage Books.

SCHUTZ, D. (1971) *Collected Papers, Vol. 1: The Problem of Social Reality* (NATANSON, M., ed.), The Hague: Nijhoff.

SENNETT, R. and COBB, R. (1973) *The Hidden Injuries of Class*, New York: Vintage Books.

STANLEY, L. (1992) *The Auto/Biographical I*, Manchester: Manchester University Press.

STANLEY, L. (1993) 'On Auto/Biography in Sociology', *Sociology* **27**, 1, February pp. 41–52.

# 9    PhD Students and the Auto/Biographies of Their Learning

*Zoë Parker*

Within the qualitative approach to enquiry, narrative enquiry is a significant strand. Within narrative enquiry, auto/biography is a further significant strand. This simple taxonomy allows one to situate auto/biography as a genre of enquiry. This carries with it advantages of clarity and difficulties of over-simplification. These are parallel to those one encounters when attempting to define literary genres and place individual works within specific genres. As soon as one confines a text within a box or boundary, the text defies its placement there. It reveals complexities which question its unproblematic situatedness within the genre; one where it has been trapped. To give one concrete example: *The Dispossessed*, by Ursula Le Guin (1974). Is this written, or to be read as fiction, as science fiction, as fantasy, as feminist, as metaphorical, utopian/dystopian, novel, critique of Western cultural values, all or none of the above? We need categories and genres of enquiry in order to begin to think about the different qualities of diverse forms of text and research. Equally, we need to bear in mind always that these categories should be questioned and revised, revisited and represented. This is so that, as Hatch and Wisniewski say, we may 'break through to the next level of understanding' (Hatch and Wisniewski, 1995, p. 131).

The slash between the two elements in the term auto/biography is a useful reminder that the words we use are problematic. Shared meanings and understandings are not easily come by. The slash also reminds us that there is a gap between self and other. There is a difference in the tone and texture of the accounts we provide as researchers of our own actions and those of others. There is no longer a tenable position which affords the text one writes about another higher status than the text one writes about oneself. There is no longer some hierarchy where the former has greater objectivity. The problematics of postmodernism force one to recognize that any proposition is questionable. Postmodernism critiques research in education as powerfully located in a modern, progress oriented, and humanistic enterprise. Education has been and remains a project which is concerned with the development of each individual's potential (as discussed by Usher and Edwards, 1994, pp. 24–32, for example).

I (sometimes) name and label myself an action researcher. This implies that the research I do is explicitly value-laden and concerned to improve the situation in which I am an agent. I frequently ask myself about my research, 'So what?'. The purpose of my research is to provide a textual space for the voices of doctoral students and discover in conversation what supports our enquiries. The bracketed 'sometimes' implies that I also decry labelling and naming when it constrains the person. Just as Le Guin's novel can be variously named and labelled and never pinned down; so my own researcher persona can be variously defined but should retain always, already (after Derrida) the possibility of escape from a particular set of power relations or a certain discourse. From the outset, I was concerned to develop the notion of the autobiography of one's learning. As the work progressed, I encountered the term auto/biography which highlights the *differance* (a term from certain postmodern discourses perhaps best translated as playful deferral) and/or difference between individuals' experiences. The place of the slash in using the term auto/biography stops the flow of the word which might have the effect of making the reader pause to consider issues of authorship and voice. Phyllida Salmon defines PhD research as authorship which needs personal confidence so that the student can claim ownership and cease to: 'hide behind the skirts of others, fearful of making any statement, any judgment, that cannot be supported by reference to published work' (Salmon, 1995, p. 9). She cites Becker (1986) saying that students have to somehow stop being 'terrorised by the literature'. This focus on authorship underlines the relevance of paying attention to this issue within my project. Grumet (1990, pp. 277–82) highlights the importance of considering whose voice is speaking in educational research.

One cannot raise the issue of voice without considering its feminist roots, or, at any rate I do not wish to do so. The term voice holds within it a concern for inclusion and particularly for dialogue between different voices — conversation. In the context of her research about women managers moving on (which is an exploration of sixteen women's career and life choices) Judy Marshall has this to say:

> Speaking through previous silences feels exciting and also risky. However much I seek to pay attention to the complex processes through which meanings are made, I know that I, as woman and as writer, have no control over what sense anyone makes. I am concerned about rendering this group of women vulnerable through the research, or being so revealing that women generally are made more vulnerable. And yet I believe that women now need to speak more openly about their lives. I think that some women want to hear each other speak in this way; some want to be understood; and some feel a sense of duty to disclose their experiences, despite their pain or embarrassment, as warnings or comfort to others. Speaking out is partly to break through the isolation that many women managers feel. But it is also done in a spirit of exploration, wanting to create a different world, to encourage new ways of managing, organizing and being by opening to critique current organizational practices revealed through some women's eyes. (Marshall, 1995: 20)

I quote at some length because to express the term 'voice' it feels right to set out such a cumulative array of ideas. Also, the reasons and feelings Marshall expresses are close in tone to my reasons for constructing auto/biographies of learning. In the case of my research, it is the voices of part-time researchers which I wish to hear speaking from within their contexts. The idea of the isolation of the PhD researcher is often expressed and discussed and finds its parallel in Marshall's writing about and for women managers. Marshall's research account weaves her own voice into the chorus in a way which challenges the traditional, positivistic or objectivist accounts I criticize elsewhere in this text.

The term auto/biography of learning denotes a specifically educational form of auto/biography. The purpose of this kind of auto/biography is to narrate an edited version of one's life which focuses especially upon articulation and explanation of what it means to each individual to learn. This may mean focusing upon values which underpin particular forms of practice. It may also entail exposing one's doubts, difficulties, uncertainties and vulnerabilities in order to explore strategies for surviving and thriving despite and because of such constraints. From my own value position, this is important because I believe that as educators we should acknowledge the authority of experience and try to maintain authentic relationships with others. The notion of the authority of experience comes from the work of Munby and Russell (1995, pp. 172–84) who place it in contrast to the authority of reason and the authority of position. The idea that one may have a duty to expose some of the difficulties in one's learning is connected to the notion of empathy as central to teaching. By this I mean that we may as educators fulfil some of our duty of care (after Noddings, 1995, pp. 137–48) by revealing our own frailties and thereby showing an understanding of the similar difficulties our students may experience. If this sounds too high-minded there is the simpler and more basic human desire to communicate with others something of one's own story in order to go on creating one's self. Along these lines, Stephen Rowland has written recently about the need to develop forms of writing about education which resist positivistic pressure and may: 'enable us to reflect [upon] our teaching in ways which reclaim love as the heart of our professional practice' (Rowland, 1997, p. 243). This suggests a way forward in reclaiming our professionalism in a manner which celebrates whole heartedly our situatedness in a critical community of educators. It also highlights the notion of education as a richly emotive and subjective enterprise.

Rowland's work, particularly his introduction of the word 'love' into the discussion, chimes with recent work by McWilliam (1996, pp. 305–17) which makes an interesting case for the analysis of pedagogy as an erotic field. By this, McWilliam seems to mean that as educators we need to reclaim teaching and learning as embodied activities which take place within a mutual search for the pleasure of knowledge. A complex and difficult interaction and exchange of desires which is much more than simply potentially abusive. Hers is a necessarily layered and subtle argument which I cannot fully explore here; but my simple reading of it is that she is calling for the whole person and the delicate flow of social relation to be taken into account in our ways of thinking about and experiencing pedagogy. At one point she puts it like this:

> Clearly, inquiring into pedagogy as an erotic field is much more complex (and transgressive) than arguing that teacher authority in itself is seductive, or even acknowledging that pedagogical power involves a conflict of motives, recruiting the desires of potential learners in the interests of maintaining teacher pleasure/

authority. It entails exploring pedagogy as a field in which the sexed and inscribed social bodies of teachers and learners engage in a range of oral and other perform-ances in pedagogical spaces over time. These performances produce ongoing change in as much as they *relate* the gendered bodies of the teacher and learner. (McWilliam, 1996, p. 315, original emphasis)

This emphasis on the word 'relate' highlights the different meanings of the word; those concerned with telling and narration and those concerned with connection and kinship. This is important for the notion of the auto/biography of learning because I see it as necessary to tell the story in order to establish points of connectedness and contrast in the similar and different ways in which we learn.

I am not just an advocate of the individual against the social as I believe the social has often more political significance than the personal and individual (*vide* action researchers' call for collaboration towards emancipation or liberation as found in the work of Luce-Kapler, 1997, pp. 321–29, discussing post-structural feminist form of action research; Lomax proposing principles for educational action research, 1994a, 1994b; Winter's six principles for action research, 1989). However, one might echo the call which comes from inside a history of autobiographical writing. It is possible to see Augustine and Rousseau as heroes of the personal, throwing down the individual gauntlet against the hegemony of group understandings imposed by large and powerful political institutions (as discussed by Griffiths, 1995, pp. 75–87). It is also important to remember the feminist standpoint that the personal is political. The idea of individuals in conversation, creating a multi-faceted dialectic which has both inter-personal and intra-personal understandings within it (see Lomax and Parker, 1995, for a discussion of these two forms of dialectic) is one way of escaping from the false dichotomy of the individual versus the social.

The term auto/biography moved me to rephrase the autobiography of learn-ing as the auto/biography of learning. I re-presented my initial concern in this way and introduced this new problematization of self/other and a consonant celebration of relatedness and distance or difference (as I saw it). The kind of action research I embrace is explicitly educational. It takes place within the field of education but also aims to be educational in and of itself. Drawing on Polanyi's work, I wish to explore the relation between epistemology and ontology: knowing and being (Polanyi, 1969). But I wish to overturn that order and place being first and give it more importance than knowing. This hierarchy is apparent in the phrase auto/bio-graphy of learning. The lived life comes first and the knowledge or wisdom (after Maxwell 1984, in particular, who sees wisdom as more significant than knowledge and defines the former as inclusive of the notion of love) one acquires is a second-ary product of the primary process of living.

The genre of action research within which my enquiry is located is a par-ticularly personal one. It is possible to see action research as lying on a continuum which has at one end any practical enquiry which takes place in the 'real' world of practice (as in much of what is called action research in the United States). At the other end of this continuum one could place action research that is a peculiarly personal endeavour which generates living educational theory (after McNiff, Lomax and Whitehead, 1996, pp. 123–47; Whitehead, 1989, pp. 41–52). This end of the continuum is concerned with praxis (simply definable as morally committed action). This choice of focus upon living theory resonates loudly with the phrase auto/biography of learning. This is theory both generated from a life (grounded and situated in practice) and dynamic and changing, tentative and problematic because it (theory) is itself alive. Educational action research often requires the researcher to write herself into the accounts of her research. This requirement highlights an auto/biographical element in action research. As is apparent below in the extract from the auto/biography of my learning, I was pleased to try and incorporate myself into my research accounts as I explicitly rejected the specious objectivity of many research texts, particularly those from within the field of psychology where I had first begun to carry out research. It seems important to be consciously aware of one's own learning in the research process and to make this process explicit. It is often disempowering and disheartening to encounter research texts which make the process of research sound smooth and tidy and write out the emotional aspects of doing research. One needs a certain confidence to shore oneself up against the struggle of being in a recurring state of 'not knowing'. Hearing that others have coped and survived against difficulty and distress can strengthen one's own resolve. As educators, we may have an unfortunate tendency to believe in right answers and the need to produce and elicit these. As researchers we need to cultivate the ability to ask the right questions and accept that a definitive answer is often naive oversimplification.

My PhD explores the experience of a number of doctoral students in different fields and 'disciplines', with a particular focus on action researchers in education. I am action researching my experience and placing this research in dialogue with the experiences of others studying in different research paradigms. I chose to focus upon PhD study for the practical reason that this was to be a central element in my own practice at the time. The PhD was where I was most formally doing my learning as I learnt to become a teacher educator. It interested me that it is the highest level of examined work which seems to demand a kind of individual expression in the oft quoted criterion that it should make an original contribution to knowledge. It is also a *rite de passage* which can mark acceptance into the academy and as such often constrains the student within a set of obligations to communicate in certain formally (and often formerly) acceptable ways. One has to produce and defend a thesis which locates itself within, or in opposition to, certain intellectual traditions in order to be intelligible. To use my PhD enquiry in order to study the experience of doctoral research seemed an appropriate way to embrace the problem of reflexivity.

In order to show some of the qualities of an auto/biography of learning, I want to present fragments from my own and from others' stories. The extracts are drawn from our published work and from my unpublished journal. I wanted to show a contrast in tone between the carefully prepared stories of research which are for public consumption and my recent struggles in my journal when I was writing this chapter. You may note that we are all female, although as Spelman (1990) pointed out, this is not an homogenous category of person. I think it matters, however, that we are women in education and that this emerges in the texts below. I present the auto/biographies as fragmented in order to remain true to the position put forward by Packwood and Sikes (1996, pp. 1–11) when they consider their

> particular notion of experience. . .experience depicted as problematizing the world and acting as the catalyst for further research. (op cit. p. 1) They point out that: Experience is viewed as fragmentary from a postmodernist perspective. Our ability to predict and thereby control phenomena through knowledge is severely limited because experience is in principle chaotic and prone to fracturing. A narrative approach attempts to recognize and capture the fragmentary, fractured and chaotic reality of the research process for all of the individuals concerned. It embeds that process within the textual product. . .Adopting a narrative approach in which both the researcher and the researched contribute to the story encourages a deep reading of the text, for it positions the reader as a co-constructor of the realities of both researched and researcher. (Packwood and Sikes, 1996, pp. 8–9)

Therefore, the gaps and fractures in the following texts are not meant to annoy or unsettle the reader, but like the slash in auto/biography, to give pause and to allow time for the reader to play her part in constructing the meaning of the story (after Iser, 1972, pp. 211–28).

A plea and an apology: I want to say clearly that I may have misrepresented others' words by taking them out of context. This is the challenge of editing — how dare one disembody or dismember texts by taking and re-presenting only certain parts? Please, if any of the ideas in this chapter interest you, go back and read the original texts in their entirety — restore to them their integrity.

### Pam's voice — fragments from the auto/biography of her learning

> In this paper I put the case for an *educational* research that is different from the discipline's approach to education and different from social science. . .As part of my argument I will try to link what is unique and personal in our work and lives as educators and educational researchers with what is patterned and general and communicable to others. I want to demonstrate the central place of the subjective in educational research, both in the form as well as in the content of this paper. To do this I use the narrative of my own educational journey, which I represent as a snakes and ladders chart and as a sub-text through the main paper. It is the narrative of a personal journey that locates my educational values within my personal biography; but it is also the narrative of a public journal which links my own biography with what we have learned from research about education over the last three decades, touching on social class, gender and the control of knowledge. . .The track which I have struggled along in my personal journey is Education, with its seductive yet *improper* promise of never having to venture off into a real world. As a young girl in a convent school I considered (and rejected) life as a nun which I thought might lead me to a life of books and reading, removed from the housework my mother made me do. Later I believed that scholarship would fulfil my

dream and I studied hard, amassing various qualifications. Still later, I thought that being a professor in the ivory tower of a university could finally do the trick. What confusion about the meaning of education!

I came from a working-class home. My parents were divorced so that we never conformed to the norm of the nuclear family presented in most of the school books of the time. Then it was considered shameful to be divorced and shameful not to have both parents. Children were blamed. As a teacher trainer I have always been careful to alert student teachers to the dangers that lurk in reading books. . .not to embarrass children as happened with the old Janet and John books, and their compulsory two parent, two children. . .all white. . .family.

I passed the 11+ and my mother insisted I went to the convent school rather than the grammar school. . .I did not see that my mother had ambitions for me. . .she was offering me a ladder, rather I thought she was a snob. This is what I mean by looking back along the track. We see things that we missed at the time. I went to the convent with much trepidation, the wrong accent, the wrong school uniform and as a 'day bug'. When I tried hard to please, as in English, my report told me I should try harder. This confused and angered me. I have since learned. . .how difficult it is to know the quiet shy individuals in a large class. . .I did not understand what was expected of me. I was good at games. . .but the shy 11-year-old that stood in front of the class at the weekly games kit inspection and was publicly shamed for having dirty socks was also me. . .The dream of university was planted just before I left school by a new. . .teacher. . .instead I left school. . .[Pam describes her early career in a bank where she was shunned by colleagues for reading in her lunch breaks; then how she went to university as a mature student and eventually trained as a teacher] The importance of my training for me was that I met the first great teacher in my life, Basil Bernstein, and he was to direct my studies for the next five years and enable my first real understanding of what education was about. . .[Pam describes her years as a teacher in school and how she went into teacher education] My early days at Gipsy Hill College of Education were personally traumatic as my marriage disintegrated and I was left as a single parent with two young children. It is at such times that one learns to appreciate the support and kindness of a community. I will be eternally grateful to my colleagues, my head of department and the principal. My career as a teacher trainer spans 25 years. . .for 20 years I had the same line manager. . .[who] supported my aspirations to do research but once he said when I was trying for a promotion: 'What do you women need more money for?'. . .For many years I failed, like many women in my position, to recognize that I was being denied opportunity by the very paternalism that supported me in my personal difficulties. Paternalism is a form of social discrimination against women that is invisible to its perpetrators. . .so subtle that those discriminated against have difficulty seeing it in operation because it is accompanied by loving care. I only came to recognize the destructiveness of paternalism once my children had grown up. Many women do not recognize it once they are in the middle. I am constantly amazed when very bright women, who are still at the bottom of their career ladders, say that they have never experienced discrimination at work. This is why my metaphor of re-crossing the track is so important; why it is important to be able to stand back and re-assess the situation from more than one perspective. . .my battles seem always to have been against closure and elitism. (Lomax, 1994a)

*A partial commentary on the fragments from the auto/biography of Pam's learning*

I have chosen to present the most personal aspects of the text from which the fragments are drawn in order to underline the most obviously autobiographical elements in the story. I want to demonstrate how these personal matters are presented by Pam as educationally significant and therefore why this is an auto/biography of learning. Interestingly, Pam's text, written before I embarked on writing this chapter, critiques and challenges some of the ideas I have presented thus far. The word love is introduced in the context of paternalism, against the backdrop of Pam's very personal engagement with gender issues. This challenges the positive light in which pedagogy as involving desire and the need to incorporate love into consideration of professionalism have been presented above. Pam's voice warns the reader that love may disguise a discriminatory act in education, it may have an abusive effect. From the inside of her experience as a woman in education, Pam is relating how she herself has learnt through looking back and re-viewing what she did not see at the time, when she was 'in the middle' of her experience. Her argument is for inclusion of the disadvantaged in education, she feels she has fought against closure and elitism in her career and encouraged teachers to consider children from less privileged backgrounds. On an abstract level, perhaps partly between the lines of what she says, there is an argument for inclusion of new and original ways of thinking about education: particularly in the use of metaphor and different ways of representing ideas. I see this as relating to work that she and I went on to do together that concerned ways of representing research (Lomax and Parker, 1995).

This pre-figuring of future work is one of the purposes of auto/biography of learning. It is not enough to look back and remember what one has achieved or how one's thinking has changed over time: the events that one struggled to overcome in an heroic fashion. The serious purpose needs to be educational in that it informs one's future practice. Pam's text has this intent in that she uses it to clarify her value position and sets herself an agenda for future work. This aspect is most apparent in the opening lines of her text above, but it is elaborated on throughout the main body (hence my request for readers to consider the original texts to which this piece refers; also my plea to consider texts as embodied and embedded in larger projects: to hear the voices I can present here as only partial representations). This seriousness of intent echoes for me with Michael Erben's view (Erben, 1996, pp. 159–74) of biographical method as not simply a means of accumulating information and interpreting data; but far more significantly as an educative exercise which promotes: 'development in the moral reasoning of the researcher' (op cit. p. 159). Seriousness of purpose is foregrounded by Nielsen (1995, pp. 4–12) when she alerts us to the nature of seduction in the context of scientific texts. She makes the point that: 'If the text does not have serious intentions, the seduction does not tempt us' (Nielsen, 1995, p. 11). I believe that both Erben and Nielsen here underline the importance of seeing research, and in these cases narrative research in education particularly, as significant and meaningful when it constitutes praxis.

## Zoë's voice — fragments from the auto/biography of my learning

What are the main things I can express that I have learnt so far in studying for my PhD? I have spent five years enrolled as a part-time student and that span of time is the first thing I want to discuss. It is not a long time in the context of my auto/biography as a learner, yet it is the longest time I have spent focused upon one set of issues. Worrying away at the same questions and all the new ones which keep occurring makes me long for the shorter, more concentrated span of a three year full-time degree. I have a sense of shame that I have not got further faster, especially since I was incautious enough to let far too many people know that I was doing a PhD on the subject of PhDs. That well-meant question 'How is your research going?' can provoke me to snap back like a cornered dog. I have a strong sense of putting up with learning slowly, in the interstices between all my other activities. Of course, I don't only learn inside my PhD. In fact that part of my work often feels coldly lonely and sterile compared to the warm, companionable fruitfulness of teaching. But it is really the not getting anywhere fast enough which gets me down and makes me paint my research in such a negative light. (Journal entry 28.9.97)

As I write this chapter now, I am aware that it constitutes only one version of the auto/biography of my learning. One can only ever write authentically from the position one holds as one writes: I cannot claim to know that which is as yet unknown to me and my writing reveals the current state of my art of knowing. The version I write now should bear some resemblance to past and future attempts to communicate thoughts and feelings around the content — but the problem with learning is the need to recognize that if I am to continue to learn I shall have to accept my current account as partial and relatively naive. Yet although I have blithely used the word 'knowing' frequently so far in this text, I do not feel sure that I know what it means to know. (Journal entry 1, 28.9.97)

I have never struggled so much with a particular piece of writing as I struggle now to write this chapter. One problem is that I have too many purposes for the chapter: it meets an obligation, a professional commitment which I made a year ago; I hope that it might be of help or interest to others who are interested in the place of auto/biography as a way of doing research in education; I need it to ring true to my real self/selves as I cope with a bereavement; I do not want to sound as confused, or just plain silly, as I am, but nor do I want to pretend this is all easy or unproblematic, nor present some inauthentic account, etc. . .(Journal entry 2, 28.9.97)

*Fragmentary comment on Zoë's voice*

The three fragments in the section above constitute both the public and the personal. Public in the sense that I intend to share and discuss them with others and open them out for critique; personal in that they are an attempt to convey what it feels like to do this piece of writing from inside. They are therefore written to some extent in the same tone of voice as the rest of this piece. However, there also creeps in a contrasting tone of voice which expresses more overtly some of the struggle of coming to terms with learning, some of the difficulties in producing a reasonable and rational, polished text.

I want to move on to present these two voices (Pam's and mine) in concert with a third voice; another PhD student who has now completed her doctoral study, who works in a large comprehensive school and embodies a particular form of partnership between a school and a university in much of her work. Moyra Evans is employed both by her school and by my home university in a way which celebrates as new a form of inclusion of perspectives between different kinds of educational institution (and carries with it, incidentally, new problematics which concern how we can view each other as partners — but that is a different story). The following conversation is an extract from a joint self-study, where each of us attempted to explore, explain and understand our different perspectives on and in education. Pam has supervised both my and Moyra's work and perhaps therefore embodies the university as gatekeeper in this text and in conferring awards to others within and outside the university. However, her explicit concern for inclusion (as expressed in the extract from her auto/biography of learning above) undermines and challenges my placing her in such a potentially invidious role.

*Moyra, Zoë and Pam's voices — harmony or discord in an educational setting?*

Our particular interests as action researchers involve finding unique ways of representing what we come to know about our practice and locating our knowledge within an autobiography of our own learning so that we find authority in our own experience (Belenkey, Clinchy, Goldberger and Tarule, 1986; Carter, 1993; Clandinin, 1992; Convery, 1993; Evans, 1996; Lomax, 1994a; Lomax and Parker, 1996). . .[in the paper this is extracted from we are exploring our practice as tutors facilitating a Masters award in education, trying to see whether we know ourselves as educators, if we live up to our espoused values, we wrote stories to reflect upon our work and discussed these using a version of memory work]. . .

Pam:    Your story [Moyra]. . .focuses very much on you and your fear of the unknown, and that's quite useful. . .because it shows us as being vulnerable as teachers, and the teachers' stories are about their fear of the unknown.

Moyra:  What about your vulnerable stories?

Pam:    Well I haven't got one. I'm not as vulnerable as you are.

Moyra:  Why is that?

Pam:    I don't know.

Moyra:  Well let's explore it.

Pam:    I think it's because I'm quite removed from it.

Moyra:  Aren't you vulnerable at all?

Pam: Yes, but I don't consider my work part of my basic me. I don't consider it that way. I'm incredibly vulnerable about some things, but doing a job of work as best I can, I don't have myself in it in that way.

Does exposing our vulnerabilities to others increase the possibility of empathy between people? Moyra's immediate thought was that her story exposed her own vulnerability. But why should she feel vulnerable? She had been teaching for long enough to feel confident in what she was doing. Were her fears of the unknown or were they fears of people? Might teachers hold views of teaching which she might find difficult to connect with? If so, how would they build the relationships necessary between teacher and learner?

Moyra: Just explore vulnerability. Why don't you think it's a bad thing? What do you mean by that?

Pam: If you can afford to be vulnerable, you can also be strong, I think. If you can afford to let other people see the weakness or the tenderness about things you value strongly, then I think you're being strong. You're more or less saying I'm showing you this because I'm so strong myself that whatever you do I'll only change if you really persuade me and not because you bully me or do anything else.

Moyra: I like this idea but I need to develop the courage if it is to be an idea to which I can wholly subscribe. Perhaps the answer hinges on whether one can afford to let other people see the weakness. . .Is the whole situation fraught with political implications? Is that why people cannot afford it? Might they lose credibility in their job if they expose their vulnerability? Can we engage in self-study if we are not willing to expose vulnerability?. . .[Later in the conversation]

Zoë: This is to do with how we see things differently and why. . .to do with our experience. . .how we've been differently socialized.

Pam: What you've just said. . .makes a really important central point doesn't it? That the difference of people in a group is as important as their similarity?. . .Power relations are key because we do, as teachers, take over the minds of our students and they think our thoughts. How do you get away from that and still help them over the hurdles because you know the answers? It's a terrible dilemma.

Zoë: I think that's one of the things we might find a clue to. . .through understanding that we've got different ways of doing things but they are OK in their different ways. And through understanding that our students might have a different way of doing things and it might get them to a better place than we had imagined them getting by the route we suggested?

. . .[later still] What have we learnt? That we know so little? That we have excluded so much in the past because it did not fit neatly into the dominant paradigm? That we have paid too little attention to individual difference?

Zoë:    A turning point in my learning happened during the collective memory work because it felt to me as if we had reached a new way of working together, a way which integrated our friendship into our joint inquiry into professional issues. This went together in my mind with the moment where Pam endorsed an idea I had about working together. . .that we all bring different styles to our teaching and we could learn from our differences. I understand now that this turning point was a liberating moment. I believe that my understanding of my own development as an action researcher is a key element which informs my practice. In exposing my process of learning, which includes my points of vulnerability, doubt and difficulty, I believe I can be a better teacher and my students can learn better. I have been developing the idea of an autobiography of learning to help explain this process. . .an edited version of a life, focusing on the specific concerns which have been chosen to describe and explain the values that underpin a particular practice. There are certain special moments which I see as turning points which change my understanding of my learning. The incidents we have individually chosen [to discuss in the paper this is extracted from] are probably such turning points and as such may reflect our uniqueness as teachers.

Moyra:  But how can I decide which part of the autobiography of my learning I should share with others? How do I come to understand my own autobiography? Why should I inflict it on other people? Do they want to know or do they need to know in order that they can get on with some learning about improving their teaching? Do they have time to listen?

Pam:    I like a point Mel Lever makes in her response to a draft of our paper: 'It is important that we do not separate aspects of our learning life. . .any part of our life or our development must have a bearing on our research. If we constructively and openly criticize our own life this must be part of the knowledge of ourselves and our development'.

## Concluding comment — how many voices will enter the chorus?

The voices in the preceding section echo some of the concerns throughout this chapter. But, yet again, they do not simply underline the arguments I have presented; they present other dissenting viewpoints. I find it interesting that the final section above concerns work we were doing with special needs educators. I conceive of this group of educators as particularly concerned with hearing divergent voices which disrupt our norms. It seems to me that in examining our teaching of this group, we clearly celebrate what we are learning from them: to acknowledge the different and difficult. Another lesson we appear to be learning in this extract from our work is to recognize and perhaps protect vulnerability. Love does not appear in the text, friendship makes a brief appearance, perhaps hinting at ways we might support each other and yet others politically? There is a preponderance of question marks in the conversation and the interweaving text. This stresses the tentative and highlights the dialogical element because the question always invites a response. Or are these rhetorical questions? I hope not, as our intent was to try and engage a wider audience with our dilemmas.

## References

BECKER, S. (1986) *Writing for Social Scientists: How to Start and Finish Your Thesis, Book or Article*, Chicago: University of Chicago Press.

BELENKEY, M., CLINCHY, B., GOLDBERGER, N. and TARULE, J. (1986) *Women's Ways of Knowing*, New York: Basic Books.

CARTER, K. (1993) 'The place of story in the study of teaching and teacher education', *Educational Researcher*, **20**, 1, pp. 5–12, 18.

CLANDININ, D.J. (1992) 'Narrative and story in teacher education', in RUSSELL, T. and MUNBY, H. *Teachers and Teaching: From Classroom to Reflection*, New York: Falmer Press, pp. 124–137.

CONVERY, A. (1993) 'Developing fictional writing as a means of stimulating teacher reflection: A case study', *Educational Action Research*, **1**, 1, pp. 135–151.

ERBEN, M. (1996) 'The purposes and processes of biographical method', in SCOTT, D. and USHER, R. (eds), *Understanding Educational Research*, London Routledge, pp. 159–174.

EVANS, M. (1996) 'An action research enquiry into reflection in action as part of my role as a deputy headteacher', PhD thesis, Kingston: Kingston University.

GRIFFITHS, M. (1995) '(Auto)Biography and epistemology', *Educational Review*, **47**, 1, pp. 75–88.

GRUMET, M. (1990) 'Voice: The search for a feminist rhetoric for educational studies', *Cambridge Journal of Education*, **20**, 3, pp. 277–282.

HATCH, J. and WISNIEWSKI, R. (1995) 'Life history and narrative: Questions, issues and exemplary works', in HATCH, J. and WISNIEWSKI, R. (eds) *Life History and Narrative*, London: Falmer, pp. 113–135.

ISER, W. (1972) 'The reading process: A phenomenological approach', *New Literary History*, **3**, pp. 211–228.

LEGUIN, U. (1974) *The Dispossessed*, New York: Harper and Row.

LOMAX, P. (1994a) *The Narrative of an Educational Journey or Crossing the Track*, Kingston: Kingston University.

LOMAX, P. (1994b) 'Action research for managing change', in BENNETT, N., GLATTER, R. and LEVACIC, R. (eds) *Improving Educational Management through Research and Consultancy*, London: Paul Chapman Press/Open University Press, pp. 156–167.

LOMAX, P. and PARKER, Z. (1995) 'Accounting for ourselves: The problematic of representing action research', *Cambridge Journal of Education*, **25**, 3, pp. 301–314.

LOMAX, P. and PARKER, Z. (1996) 'Representing a dialectical form of knowledge within a new epistemology for teaching and teacher education'. Paper presented at the American Educational Research Association Conference, New York.

LUCE-KAPLER, R. (1997) 'Becoming a community of researchers', *Educational Action Research*, **5**, 2, pp. 321–329.

MARSHALL, J. (1995) *Women Managers Moving On: Exploring Career and Life Choices*, London: Routledge.

MAXWELL, N. (1984) *From Knowledge to Wisdom: A Revolution in the Aims and Methods of Science*, Oxford: Basil Blackwell.

McNIFF, J., LOMAX, P. and WHITEHEAD, J. (1996) *You and Your Action Research Project*, London: Hyde Publications/Routledge.

McWILLIAM, E. (1996) 'Touchy subjects: A risky inquiry into pedagogical pleasure', *British Educational Research Journal*, **22**, 3, pp. 305–315.

MUNBY, H. and RUSSELL, T. (1995) 'Towards rigour with relevance: How can teachers and teacher educators claim to know?' in RUSSELL, T. and KORTHAGEN, F. (eds), *Teachers who Teach Teachers: Reflections on Teacher Education*, London: Falmer Press, pp. 172–184.

NIELSEN, H. (1995) 'Seductive texts with serious intentions', *Educational Researcher*, **24**, 1, pp. 4–12.

NODDINGS, N. (1995) 'Care and moral education, in KOHLI, W. (ed.) *Critical Conversations in Philosophy of Education*, London: Routledge, pp. 137–148.

PACKWOOD, A. and SIKES, P. (1996) 'Adopting a postmodern approach to research', *Qualitative Studies in Education*, **9**, 3, pp. 1–11.

POLANYI, M. (1969) *Knowing and Being*, London: Routledge and Kegan Paul.

ROWLAND, S. (1997) 'A lovers' guide to university teaching?' *Educational Action Research*, **5**, 2, pp. 243–253.

SALMON, P. (1992) *Achieving a PhD – Ten Students' Experience*, Stoke-on-Trent: Trentham.

SPELMAN, E. (1990) *Inessential Woman: Problems of Exclusion in Feminist Thought*, London: The Women's Press.

USHER, R. and EDWARDS, R. (1994) *Postmodernism and Education*, London: Routledge.

WHITEHEAD, J. (1989) 'Creating a living educational theory from questions of the kind: How do I improve my practice?', *Cambridge Journal of Education*, **19**, 1, pp. 41–52.

WINTER, R. (1989) *Learning from Experience*, London: Falmer Press.

# 10 A Biographical Approach to the History of Education: Nineteenth Century Nonconformist Lives and Educational Expansion

*Diana Jones*

For the historian who seeks to understand the social complexities of educational expansion throughout the nineteenth century, the ethics of Christian Nonconformity, cannot be ignored. While it would be inaccurate to claim that these were the only significant determinants for the multitudinous educational initiatives which burgeoned throughout that century, there is strong evidence that the influence of Nonconformity (not least through the auspices of powerful Nonconformist businessmen), was pervasive and far from inconsequential in the unprecedented development of education, particularly that provided for the ever growing numbers of the working classes.

Within the context of Max Weber's highly influential thesis regarding the relationship between ascetic Protestantism and the foundations of modern vocationalism,[1] this chapter examines the singular contributions of three nineteenth century Nonconformist businessmen, William Allen (1770–1843), Sir Edward Baines jnr MP (1800–1890) and Jeremiah James Colman MP (1830–1898),[2] to an emerging system of popular education. Combined, their highly influential activities span almost the whole of the nineteenth century. In their own particular spheres, Allen, Baines and Colman, were all outstandingly effective in pioneering popular education, in establishing a vocationally focused curriculum which, while not infrequently stressing the importance of education for the growth and personal advancement of the individual, simultaneously and without any apparent consciousness of inconsistency, emphasized the need to provide the working classes with opportunities to develop practical skills and habits of industry. As a result of efforts by many who, like the subjects of this study, were influenced by the ethics of ascetic Protestantism,[3] a system of mass education was established, unequivocal in its intention of moulding the attitudes and behaviour patterns of the working classes, of producing industrious and compliant workers, essential to the needs of an increasingly successful industrial society. In order to appraise the social significance of the contribution of these three representative members of a clearly defined industrial elite, a collective biographical approach has been adopted.

The acceleration of concern with biographical research in recent years, has given rise to a new growth of interest in prosopography, or collective biography, as an appropriate methodological tool for investigating, what Lawrence Stone has identified as the two fundamental problems of history — a) the source of political action; b) social structure and social mobility. Within a further sub-set of problems which Stone cites, and of particular relevance for this study, is 'the correlation of intellectual or religious movements with social, geographical, occupational, or other factors' (Stone, 1987, pp. 45–46).

The purpose of prosopography, as defined by Stone, is to investigate 'common background characteristics of a group of actors in history by means of a collective study of their lives' (1987, p. 45). There are two distinct approaches, the 'Mass' school, concerned with gathering data from large numbers, and the 'Elite', concerned with small group dynamics and the gathering of evidence from a wide variety of sources. In both approaches the overriding purpose is to focus attention on the group in order to demonstrate the extent of cohesiveness in terms of particular social phenomena, say, gender, class, education, personal interests, religious belief, politics, attitudes, prejudices, ideals, economic interests, business enterprise, public activities. . .(Stone, 1987, p. 46).

The researcher who adopts a biographical approach is, sooner or later, faced with the task of examining auto/biographical material itself. It is necessary, therefore, to refer to the genre of modern biography and implications which arise from employing such a methodology. Of particular significance here is the puritan tradition, which persisted well into the nineteenth century, of biographies and autobiographies having a declared purpose of serving as a model for the good of others. A not unrelated factor, identified by Erben, is that the modern biographer emerged during the eighteenth century 'as part of the Enlightenment's commitment to understanding the relationship between morality, ethics and the vagaries of everyday existence. . .a textual space in which to present a discourse on the nature of the public and the private. . .with their tensions between verisimilitude and subjectivity' (1993, p. 15).

Tensions between a perceived need for objective research and the problem of bias, the recognition of the inevitably partial and subjective nature of evidence, is an ever present reality for the social historian. It is essential, therefore, that biographical researchers should, not only accept the selective and interpretative nature of their role, but also recognize and take responsibility for the fact that out of auto/biography, biography is, in turn, being created. In other words, the individual under investigation is inescapably observed, not to say *constructed*, through a series of filters. While the 'body', the subject remains unchanged, the filter process through which a particular life is examined causes the images received to vary. As Stanley asserts, 'the "reconstruction" of a biographical subject is an intellectual non-starter'. Questions have to be addressed 'the past from *whose* viewpoint?', 'why *this* viewpoint and no other?', and 'what would be the effect of working from a *contrary* viewpoint?' (1992, p. 7). In considering the 'accuracy' of a particular construct, or construction, the extent and partial nature of filters must be confronted.

The lives of Allen, Baines and Colman, their attitudes and actions, their respective roles in regard to the development of mass education, are accessible only through the documentation (much of it biographical), that has survived. These include, Allen's detailed personal diary which he kept from the age of eighteen until the end of his life,[4] letters and speeches from the pen of Baines himself and Helen Colman's comprehensive memoir of her father, J.J. Colman.

*En passant*, it is interesting for this socio-historical analysis to note that, while Weber made only limited use of auto/biographical material in developing his Protestant ethic thesis, he drew particular attention to what he called 'the fascinating task of presenting the characteristics of ascetic Protestantism through the medium of the biographical literature' (1985, p. 259) and expressed regret that he was unable to utilize such material himself.[5]

In using biographical writings it is important to remain fully aware of the relationship between biographer and subject. For example, Helen Colman had intimate knowledge of her father's private, business and public life, together with an undoubted filial regard. In addition, she had extensive knowledge and understanding of social, economic and political issues of the day. It is also important to take note, not only of selectivity of material and mode of presentation, but the biographer's own personal biography and its social context. Even when the narrative is specifically autobiographical, the filter process is at work. The content of letters, speeches, notes, reports, would originally have been composed for a particular audience, or, *as may* be the case with, say, a personal diary, no audience at all. Both the purpose and the target audience cause the author to select certain subjects and reject others, to voice certain opinions and views and suppress or remain silent on others. The Allen diaries provide an almost complete autobiographical account of his adult life. The Colman memoir includes material directly from the pen of the subject himself. Baines's own prolific writings provide much important autobiographical material. Again account must be taken of selectivity. Material will have been included to confirm or elucidate particular points or facets of life, which from the writer editor's point of view, were perceived to be of interest and/or importance for the intended readership.

As well as acknowledging limitations in data, the biographical researcher must also have regard for the inescapable complexity of roles adopted by individual members of the group under investigation: the inherent uniqueness of each character. To find perfect congruence, Stone asserts, is rare (1987, p. 60):

> The individual is moved by a convergence of constantly shifting forces, a cluster
> of influences such as kinship, friendship, economic interests, class prejudice, political
> principle, religious conviction. . .all play their varying parts. . .(Stone, 1987, p. 65)

Nonetheless, if the fact of 'the baffling complexity of human nature' (Stone, 1985, p. 65) is accepted, prosopography can be utilized as a serious methodological tool, not as a panacea for all socio-historical problems but, more appropriately, as an explanatory tool of the cohesive strength of a particular social grouping (Stone, 1987, pp. 57–65), for example, the role of a Nonconformist industrial elite in establishing an ethic of work and system of mass education.

A central pillar in Weber's argument for a relationship between the development of modern capitalism and the ideology of ascetic Protestantism, is the belief that the sixteenth century Reformation and the birth of Protestantism, contained within it clear, unambiguous convictions concerning the place and importance of work in the Christian life. Within this context, it can be argued that throughout the period of industrialization, in the widening of consciousness of the need to provide education for the working-class labourer and his progeny, religion, not least Christian Nonconformity, played a conspicuous role in controlling the direction in which it developed (Jones, 1989, p. 93). 'The children of the Reformation and the descendants of the Puritans', proclaimed Baines, 'cannot but value an instructed people. . .' (1853a, p. 2).

Individualism, a fundamental concept of the Reformation and burgeoning Nonconformity, arose out of a perceived need for religious autonomy of the individual. From this point, it was a natural step to the conviction 'that all should learn to read the Bible for themselves. . .to free mankind from the blind dependence on authority. . .' (Simon, 1976, p. 137) and the idea, which came to fruition during the years of the Protectorate, that education was 'a fundamental human right in which all should share' (Simon, 1976, p. 137). A century later, as the realities of industrialization arrested middle-classes' consciousness, there was, as stated, a further awakening to the need to provide increased educational opportunities. Throughout this cataclysmic period, 'whether at the national level on policy formation and legislation or at the local level in the provision of infant, elementary, technical, adult education, Nonconformists were prominent, both through individual activity and, increasingly, as an influential corporate body' (Jones, 1996, p. 72).

In seeking answers to motivational causes, Vaughan and Archer (1971, p. 227), attribute historicized sociological factors in applying 'Weber's concept of domination and assertion. . .in terms of a conflict between the dominant established church and the assertive middle class [invariably Noncomformists] for the control of education' (Webster, 1976, p. 208). While, both groups held unswervingly that mass education involved the imparting of religious values, 'preserving law and order, teaching respect for property and the existing economic structure and giving children practical instruction of a kind useful to future workmen' (Goldstrom, 1972, p. 7), there were fundamental, not to say conflicting, ideological differences — *subordination versus self help and improvement; sectarian versus non-sectarian education; state education versus voluntaryism.* Evidence is strong that popular education developed, not only against a backdrop of polemic but was specifically shaped as a direct result of the antithetic position which the establishment and that increasingly powerful body of religious dissenters took on such issues.

### Subordination versus self-help and improvement

A dominant concern of the nineteenth century establishment was to curb social unrest and maintain the status quo by upholding values such as deference and respect for rank. As Andrew Bell, founder of the National Society, declared:

> the improvement of the subordination and orderly conduct, and general behaviour of the children, has been particularly noticed and must be regarded as infinitely the most valuable part of its character. (Rule, 1986, p. 236)

Conversely, Nonconformists regarded education as the means of rescuing the lower classes 'by encouraging thrift, temperance and industry; self-help was to them a virtue' (Goldstrom, 1972, p. 34). Anomalies, however, must not be overlooked. As Blaug (1975) points out, 'manufacturers came to appreciate that schooling bred "attitudes of punctuality, persistence, concentration, obedience", with the result that it could be regarded as a sound investment' (Webster, 1976, p. 208). Nonetheless, respect for law and order, did not include 'abasement before social superiors' (Goldstrom, 1972, p. 34). As Colman stated in 1857:

> In these days of progress, that man is sure to be left far behind, who has neglected the cultivation of his intellect while he who strives to improve his mind stands a fair chance of raising himself in the social scale. (Butcher, nd, p. 366)

### Sectarian versus non-sectarian education

While religious teaching was universally regarded as the central pillar of popular education, on the form it took the establishment and nonconformity were diametrically opposed. In 1811 the National Society for the Provision of Education of the Poor in the Principles of the Established Church, was formed. Its rival the British and Foreign Schools Society (BFSS), held firmly to the belief that religious education should be based on biblical teaching alone. Indeed, the rules of the BFSS required that:

> the lessons for reading shall consist of extracts from the Holy Scriptures, no catechism or peculiar religious tenets shall be taught in the schools. (Sylvester, 1970, p. 288)

Within the context of Weber's theory for a correlation between religious ethics and the demands of an industrialized society, it is relevant to note the uncompromising position of Nonconformists, that non-sectarian religious instruction was integral to, not to say the foundation of, a practical, utilitarian education (Jones, 1996, p. 407).

### State education versus voluntaryism

Throughout the middle years of the nineteenth century, the question of state versus voluntary systems of education was a persistent cause of controversy. Nonconformists held the view that secular instruction and religious teaching should go hand in hand, and that in no circumstances should state aid be accepted for the latter. Broadly speaking, the voluntaryist position was 'that the State should leave the work of education to the spontaneous efforts of Christian benevolence' (Anon, 1879, p. 620). The voice of voluntaryism was most vociferous during the middle years of the nineteenth century. 'We will not be dragooned into a State Religion', declared

Baines in 1843, 'our children shall not be taught what our own consciences do not approve' (Baines, 1969, p. 29). Three years later, he argued:

> It is the duty of parents to provide education for their children. . .It is the duty of the rich to help the poor. . .Government interference to educate the poor would destroy voluntary efforts. (Baines, 1846, p. 49)

In similar vein, Colman declared in 1858 'We have quite enough of Government intermeddling, and the more it is allowed to interfere, the worse for the independence and progress of the nation' (Colman, 1905, p. 164).

Before examining contributions which Allen, Baines and Colman made to a developing system of mass education, it is germane to compare other biographical details. First, Allen, Baines and Colman were all born into families moderately successful in business. Allen's father was a silk weaver. Baines's grandfather was, alternatively, an officer of excise, a grocer, a cotton manufacturer and coal merchant. His father, like himself, was a newspaper proprietor. For two previous generations the Colmans had been manufacturers of flour and mustard.

There is considerable evidence that all three subjects espoused Christian Nonconformity. Allen was a committed Quaker. His diaries are prolific with reference to the demands of Christian morality and to his own personal faith. Baines was a Congregationalist who not infrequently drew public attention to 'the high principles of duty to God and man' (Baines, 1846, p. 132) and the value and 'happiness of personal religion' (Baines, 1846, p. 36). Colman was alternatively, a member of the Baptist and Congregational denominations. His words sum up the attitude of all three:

> our Nonconformity should be not an accident of our birth, but the conviction and principle of our lives. . .let us not be ashamed of our Nonconformity, but rather glory in it. (Colman, 1905, p. 144)

In addition to Nonconformity, success in business enterprise was a prerequisite for membership of this research group. Allen was associated with business enterprise for a period of some forty-eight years. At the age of 16 he became an apothecary's clerk. Three years later a partner in the business, remaining so until his death. Colman's forty-five years in business began at the age of 21 when he became a partner in J. and J. Colman. Four years later he assumed complete control which he retained until 1896, two years before his death. Baines joined his father's newspaper business, the *Leeds Mercury*, at the age of 15. At 18 he was promoted to editor, at 27 he became a partner. From his father's death in 1848 until his own in 1890, he was the chief proprietor. He was, therefore, active in business enterprise for an impressive sixty-three years.

While there is substantial evidence that through rational, systematic and devoted attention to business all three accumulated considerable personal wealth, there is, conversely, no evidence which suggests that wealth was pursued for its own sake, rather the converse is true. As Weber points out, 'asceticism looked upon the pursuit of wealth as an end in itself as highly reprehensible; but the attainment of it as a fruit of labour'. . .(1985, p. 172):

the religious valuation of restless, continuous, systematic work in a wordly call-ing, as the highest means of asceticism. . .When the limitation of consumption is combined with this release of acquisitive activity, the inevitable practical result is obvious: accumulation of capital through ascetic compulsion to save. (1985, p. 172)

Attitudes to wealth do seem to correspond to those identified by Weber. Colman, for example, is unequivocal in his attitude towards avarice:

Let the merchants and tradesmen of England remember that riches are not the true mark of nobility any more than title is. . .The race for riches must not be the mov-ing spring of action. . .Enterprise is wholesome enough but it must have a good foundation to rest on. (Colman, 1905, p. 433)

A Nonconformist conscience, with its attendant notions of *duty* and *responsibility*, is demonstrably present in the public lives of Allen, Baines and Colman[6]. 'Part of the Colman creed' it is asserted, 'was a belief in the obligation to accept respons-ibility from whatever direction the summons should come' (Edgar, nd, p. 7). In relation to his desire to further education of the poor, Allen is recorded as saying 'I long to see all the world employed in doing good to man' (Hall, 1953, preface). On his fiftieth birthday, Baines wrote 'I must not shrink from the steadfast and zealous maintenance of my principles. . .I am bound to act charitably and humbly' (Baines, 1850). 'Moral justification of worldly activity was', asserts Weber, 'one of the most important results of the Reformation' (1985, p. 81).

Personal educational experiences of Allen, Baines and Colman, were not untypical of the practical, utilitarian education widely received by sons of the mer-cantile middle classes. As Davidoff and Hall comment, there was a tendency amongst the middle classes to expect an 'economic return from their children's education' (1987, p. 291), particularly boys'.

Allen's education began with private instruction. Later he attended a Quaker boarding school in Rochester. Following this, he took responsibility for his own learning. 'A grand object with me' he wrote, 'is to perfect myself in the study of medicine also in Latin' (Chapman-Huston and Cripps, 1954, p. 282):

he usually had some work in French on hand and read a portion of it every day. He also made considerable progress in German. In drawing. . .he engaged the services of a Master — some few years later he began the study of Algebra. . .and when on holiday was 'pretty busily engaged in taking angles and in calculating them.' (Chapman-Huston and Cripps, 1954, p. 282)

Baines was educated first at a private school in Leeds, then at the Protestant Dis-senters' Grammar School in Manchester.

It is not without interest to note that both Allen and Baines were educated in Nonconformist foundations, which 'employed rational teaching methods [and] strove to satisfy the needs of the upper middle classes for a practical, modern education' (Barnard, 1961, p. 30). 'This factor' states Brown, 'has led some historians to see

Nonconformity as an important training ground in "achievement motivation" leading to entrepreneurial enterprise and technological innovation' (1991, p. 80).

Colman was first tutored by his mother, then at an infant school and later by a personal tutor. From the age of 17, in common with Allen, he took responsibility for his own education, attending mutual improvement societies and evening classes.

### William Allen

As eminent scientist, philanthropist, man of business and ardent promoter of useful knowledge and mass education, the life of the Quaker, William Allen, was many faceted. In many respects parallels can be drawn between his life and that of Benjamin Franklin (1706–1790), cited by Weber as a paradigm for the spirit of capitalism. Both were scientists and businessmen. Both had an influential involvement in politics and reform. Both demonstrated pacifist tendencies and were strong supporters of the abolition of slavery. Both adopted a utilitarian approach to life. Order, resolution, frugality, industry, justice, moderation, were characteristics which each displayed. Both were philanthropic and keen promoters of education, particularly for the working classes. Allen's strong commitment to an ethic of work is widely acclaimed. He was, declared Sherman, 'eminent for *industry and perseverance in useful objects.* . .his mind was not distinguished by any showy attributes; it was pre-eminently practical' (1857, p. 455), a statement reminiscent of Weber's interpretation of the ideal type capitalistic entrepreneur as one who 'avoids ostentation. . .as well as conscious enjoyment of his power' (1985, p. 71).

The influence of Allen was immense, if not without precedent — through ceaseless campaigning for the abolition of slavery and capital punishment; through numerous philanthropic endeavours; as confidant of politicians and royalty; through intimate involvement with the British and Foreign School Society (BFSS); as partner in the New Lanark experiments of Robert Owen; through extensive continental journeyings as ambassador for the Society of Friends and the BFSS, which took him as far as the emperor's court in Russia; as editor of *The Philanthropist*; in the establishment of an agricultural colony and industrial school at Lindfield in Sussex.

To present the minutiae of Allen's remarkable contributions to education is impossible. A review of his main activities must suffice, beginning with his long and intimate involvement with the British and Foreign School Society (formerly the Royal Lancasterian Society for Promoting the Education of the Children of the Poor). Allen first met Joseph Lancaster (1778–1838) (universally acclaimed for his pioneering of the monitorial system), in 1808. In that year the Lancasterian Society was formed. Allen became its treasurer, a position he held (later for the BFSS), until his death in 1843. Doncaster records that 'probably no other single concern occupied so much of William Allen's time and energy' (1965, p. 24). For more than twenty years Allen was the leading and *most active* member of the BFSS, both at home and abroad. 'Without his efforts' states Bartle, 'the BFSS would surely not have survived' (1992, p. 25). His niece talks of the heavy demand upon his time of extensive correspondence and 'the ardent zeal which he ever manifested in this great cause' (*Life* I, 1846, p. 109). She also notes his considerable monetary contributions, stating, 'his anxious desire for the improvement and elevation of the labouring classes of society. . .enabled him cheerfully to sustain a burden which would otherwise have been insupportable' (*Life* I, 1846, p. 100).

It was not only financial affairs with which Allen busied himself. His diary for June 1816, records, along with numerous other activities:

> *Sixth Month 6th* Went to the great school meeting at Shadwell; upwards of one thousand persons were present. The Duke of Kent in the chair. . .
> My examination on the subject of the education of the poor, by the Committee of the House of Commons, has occupied much of three days. . .
> *14th* Attended first meeting, at Spital Square, of the Auxiliary School Society for the north-east district of London. . .
> *20th* School committee; numerous attendance and very satisfactory.
> *23rd*. . .I am getting on with the manual of the Borough Road School. . . ; it is the most important thing that has been done for a long time. . .
> *27th*. . .to Walworth, to attend a meeting of the first school association there
> *28th*. . .school concerns, &c.; . . . .(*Life* I, 1846, p. 269)

All this immediately prior to his first continental journey under the auspices of the Society of Friends. As on all his journeyings[7], Allen sought to further the cause of popular education. To cite just one example, in Rotterdam he visited 'schools of public utility, where upwards of two thousand six hundred children were taught' (*Life* I, 1846, p. 273), using Lancaster's system. Doncaster notes that it was largely through Allen's own work on behalf of British schools, that by 1820 he was able to write 'There is hardly a country in the world where they do not exist' (1965, pp. 24–25).

During 1816 Allen was examined by a Committee of the House of Commons on the subject of education for the poor. His diary for 20 May 1816, notes:

> I received a note from Brougham, to inform me that he was about to move for a committee of the House on the subject of the education of the poor, with notice that he should call me up to give evidence. (*Life* I, 1846, p. 268)

In 1818, he provided evidence to the Parliamentary Select Committee appointed to inquire into the Education of the Lower Orders in the Metropolis and Beyond (Maclure, 1965, p. 22). In 1838, on behalf of the BFSS, he responded, in a 'Memorial' addressed to Lord John Russell, to a Select Committee on the Education of the Poorer Classes paper, entitled *Suggestions for the Advancement of Education*. This paper described the subject of education, as 'one of the most interesting and important to the great mass of the people of this country which can ever be discussed in Parliament', a sentiment with which Allen wholeheartedly concurred. The 'Memorial' urged upon the Government:

> the paramount importance of establishing, as preliminary to every other measure, a *Board of Education*, enjoying the confidence of the various religious denominations of the country. The Committee [BFSS] strongly feel that on the degree in

which such confidence is reposed will mainly depend the efficiency of all efforts in favour of education. (Stanley, 1839, pp. 3–4)

A chronicle of Allen's contribution to working-class education must make some reference to his involvement in Robert Owen's (1771–1858) paternalistic pioneer work within the cotton mills at New Lanark. In 1814, together with a number of others, he entered into partnership with Owen. Although Allen's influence was considerable, particularly on the educational side, and lasted for more than twenty years, it was, from the beginning, an uncomfortable liaison. Of his first visit to New Lanark, Allen observed:

> I found the arrangements. . .excellent, and even beyond my expectations; but, alas! Owen, with all his cleverness and benevolence, wants the *one thing*, without which, parts and acquirements and benevolence are unavailing. (*Life* I, 1846, 209)

This *one thing* referred to Owen's lack of Christian faith. When the contract of partnership was initially signed, Owen had agreed that the Bible would be used in his schools and specific religious instruction given. 'In 1817, however, he publicly declared his hostility to religion' (Bartle, 1992, p. 21). In 1822 Allen wrote to Owen:

> . . .I have ever felt for the benevolent part of thy character. Sorry indeed am I to see, that our *principles* are diametrically opposite; . . . .(*Life* II, 1846, p. 238)

Owen, not surprisingly, resented Allen, whom he regarded as 'a man of great pretensions in his sect, a very busy, bustling, meddling character, making great professions of friendship to me, yet underhandedly doing all in his power to undermine my views and authority' (Owen, 1867, p. 141). Nonetheless, it was not until 1835 that Allen finally severed his connections with the work at New Lanark.

Another initiative in which Allen immersed himself was at Lindfield in Sussex where, in 1824, he purchased land in order to establish a School of Industry (*Life* II, 1846, p. 385). His intention 'was to improve the temporal, moral and social state [of the agricultural community], by inducing habits of industry and independence' (*Life* II, 1846, pp. 401–2). By 1831 the schools were providing education for some 300 children, who were taught 'reading, writing, and arithmetic, with other branches of useful knowledge. . .taught on the liberal principles of the British and Foreign School Society' (*Life* II, 1846, p. 402). Allen's adherence to the principles of self-help are apparent in the practical contributions which children made to the expenses of their own education. In addition to school work, pupils engaged in farming, shoemaking, tailoring, weaving, printing, knitting, needlework, patchwork and straw plaiting (Bartle, 1992, p. 24 and Chapman-Huston and Cripps, 1954, p. 109). Bartle suggests that the curriculum was probably wider 'than any other school of industry of its period' (1992, p. 28). As with the BFSS and his numerous other benevolent activites, Allen's personal involvement at Lindfield was ubiquitous. As the school prospectus unambiguously stated, 'the whole concern will be under the super-intendence of William Allen' (*Life* III, 1846, p. 183).

### Edward Baines jnr, MP

It is as protagonist in the cause of retaining the voluntary principle in education that Baines is best remembered. One of his earliest recollections, it is recorded, was at the age of 9 when he attended a lecture by Joseph Lancaster on the subject of the monitorial schools system. An unnamed biographer writes that from that time:

> the interest of Mr Baines in the cause of popular education has never ceased. He has laboured longer, probably, than any other public man, to place a sound and thorough education within the reach of every English child. (Anon, 1881, p. 250)

In 1880, Baines himself stated, 'the universal spread of education among the humbler classes of the people, and the improvement of education among the higher classes, have always seemed to me the surest methods of advancing the prosperity and welfare of our country' (Baines, 1880, p. 24).

Baines was directly involved with a number of educational movements. At the age of 15 he became a Sunday School teacher, continuing as such for over forty years, until his election to parliament in 1859. In 1818 he was, with his father, a founder member of the Leeds Philosophical and Literary Society. As a young man he visited Owen's New Lanark experiment. While in London in 1824, he visited the London Mechanics' Institution, founded a year earlier. In describing this experience fifty-six years later, he referred to it as:

> a crisis in my life, when, having heard of the strange novelty of teaching science to mere mechanics, I went to hear Dr Birkbeck. . .lecturing and experimenting before five or six hundred 'unwashed artificers'. It was as surprising as it was gratifying to see the intelligent comprehension and enjoyment. . .I felt certain that a great discovery had been made, which might be of immense value to the manufacturers of England. . .The Lesson was eagerly learnt. . .and Mechanics' Institutions were formed at Leeds and Manchester. I thought it my duty. . .to lecture in many of the towns and villages of Yorkshire, and to explain and recommend the new system. (Baines, 1880, p. 30)

Baines formed a life long commitment to the work of Mechanics' Institutions. In 1837, at his suggestion, a West-Riding Union of Mechanics' Institutes was formed, of which he was president for more than fifty years. By 1851 there were 119 Mechanics' Institutions throughout Yorkshire with 20,000 members. In that year Baines published an address to working men on the advantages of Mechanics' Institutions, in which he advocated the virtues of industry, thrift and self-help, by contrasting the characteristics of the 'undeserving' poor with those who demonstrated:

> self-denying habits in the acquisition of useful knowledge in which the industrious husband brings his wages to a thrifty wife: the humble home is clean. . . : on their shelves are a few books, and no bottles. . .a little money has been laid by in a Savings' Bank. . . : the boys enter the Mechanics' Institution, and spend those evenings in reading which others spend in drinking and riot: industry, prudence

and economy, under a kind Providence, at length make the man the proprietor of a house — a freeholder, and a voter. (Baines, 1851, pp. 3–4)

In his eightieth year Baines declared, 'I believe our Mechanics' Institutions are doing a great preparatory work in laying the foundations of knowledge for the operative classes, and fitting them to enter our higher schools and colleges' (Baines, 1880, pp. 25–26).

On the voluntarist position the stance of Baines was, for more than two decades, without compromise. In 1843 he published an influential booklet *The Social, Education, and Religious State of the Manufacturing Districts* in which he argued the case for:

the power of *voluntary Christian zeal*, to provide the means of Education and Religious Instruction, even for a rapidly increasing population. (Baines, 1969, p. iii)

Ten years later he published *Strictures on the new Government measure of Education*, in which he stated:

Of the benefits of Education, there is happily no question. . .For myself, my principle and my practice are now, as they ever have been, to promote the universal instruction of the people. . .I maintain that knowledge is one of the first of blessings to individuals and to communities. The controversy is as to the means, not as to the end. Principles of the first importance, social, political, and religious, are involved. . .The rights of conscience and the interests of religion are among those sacred things; and of secular interests I esteem the spirit of independence one of the most precious. (Baines, 1853b, p. 2)

Later, in the same publication he claimed:

I do not know of one single improvement in the educational system that was not originated by private individuals or public societies. The training of teachers was one of the very earliest operations both of the British and Foreign School Society and the National Society. The practice of inspection was begun by them. They made grants in aid of school buildings and of school books and apparatus. They improved the methods of tuition. . .Government just took up what others had begun. . .I unhesitatingly declare my belief that the interference was not needed, and that. . .and in the long run the education of the people would have a healthier character, and be quite as extensive, if left entirely to the people themselves. (Baines, 1853b, p. 15)

In 1864 Baines was appointed to the Taunton Commission as a representative of voluntaryism. By 1868, however, his position had shifted sufficiently to enable him to sign 'its report as an advocate of state aid' (Aldrich and Gordon, 1989, p. 16). Gradually he came to the conclusion that voluntaryism alone was an inadequte basis for a national system of education. In 1870 he gave general support to Forster's Education Bill, his view being that 'though necessarily a compromise and not altogether free from reasonable objection, [it] was perhaps the only measure on which Parliament could have agreed' (Baines, 1880, p. 34). Historians have suggested that this change of heart by Baines exemplified the shift which had taken place in public opinion (Lawson and Silver, 1973, p. 314).

That religion was a conscious motivator of Baines, in relation to educational expansion for the manufacturing poor, in the morality he unrelentingly sought to impose on the working classes, is repeatedly demonstrated. As he himself expressed it:

> Great as is the value which I attach to education. . .I cannot for a moment compare it to the value or the happiness of personal religion. . .As such I bequeath it to all the youth who may ever hear my name. (Baines, 1880, p. 36)

### Jeremiah James Colman, MP

Colman's interest and involvement in education was extensive. He held strong views and acted upon them, as evinced by the position he took on national issues, his prominent role in education in the City of Norwich and, not least, the various educational initiatives provided for his own workforce. On educational matters he was unrelentingly individualistic. At Norwich YMCA in 1858, he declared: 'What we do for ourselves we generally do well; what is done for us by our Government is as universally ill done' (Colman, 1905, p. 164).

While Colman never lost his preference for voluntaryism and was active in the Nonconformist protest against many of the provisions of the 1870 Education Bill, later, in common with others, he modified his views. 'In the light of practical politics' states his daughter, he came to believe that 'Government interference is the only general solution of a very difficult question'. Nonetheless, his dislike of sectarian education never abated. In 1872, explaining reasons for supporting a Resolution condemning the Education Act and censuring the use of public money for denominational teaching, he declared:

> . . .the time will come when Education will be free from sectarian boundaries. . .It is because I fear some portion of the recent Act tends to delay this time, and meanwhile promotes sectarian differences, that I feel bound to record my vote for the Motion. . .(Colman, 1905, pp. 168–69)

Towards the end of the 1880s Colman was voicing concern at increasing central control of education and what he saw as attendant checking of useful experiment at the local level. In 1888, while admitting the usefulness of some examinations for scholarships — valuable 'as a ladder by means of which the poor boy of brains and diligence can gain for himself the highest educational advantages', he made clear his dislike of 'Payment by Results', believing in the breadth of study rather than cramming for one special examination (Colman, 1905, pp. 170–71).

Colman's involvement in education within the City of Norwich, included: the development of technical education and provision of a free library; increasing provision for the education of women and girls; administration of city charities which included educational provision such as the Boys' and Girls' Hospital Schools; an association with Norwich Grammar School of forty years. From 1880 he was vice-chairman of the governors and from 1890 chairman (Colman, 1905, pp. 172–77).

Colman's attitude towards education, its importance, its appropriateness for the working classes, its conduct and its curriculum, is summed up in a letter he wrote to his workforce in 1857:

> In announcing the commencement of a School at Carrow, I wish to state. . .the reasons for its being opened, and the manner in which it will be conducted.
>
> . . .[We]. . .are sensible that great difficulties lie in the way to prevent your giving a good education to your children. . .and we hope you will receive the help in the friendly spirit with which it is offered.
>
> Many persons in establishing schools put them under Government inspection, in order to receive Government grants, but wishing our School to be entirely untrammelled, we shall conduct it on the purely voluntary principle.
>
> . . .as regards religious subjects, the Bible. . .alone will be taught, nothing that bears the stamp of sect, party or denomination will intrude.
>
> . . .[weekly payments 1d for ONE, $1\frac{1}{2}$d for TWO from one family, 2d for THREE. . .] will go towards a Prize Fund, to be distributed in books and useful articles. . .amongst the most industrious and deserving scholars. . .
>
> I hope many of you will avail yourselves of the advantages the School offers, but I wish you to most distinctly understand that the use of it is perfectly voluntary. . .only let me impress upon you the importance of education. . .somewhere.
>
> Remember the motto of your Reading Society 'KNOWLEDGE IS POWER', power for advancement, power to be good and to do good, power to be happy and to cause happiness to others. . .
>
> . . .Those of you who send your children, will I hope give your aid at home. . .for bad example or bad management in your homes may neutralise the best possible training at School. It is of the utmost importance that you should teach your children to be punctual, neat and industrious.
>
> . . .we shall rejoice to find that the School helps you to educate your children and train up a set of men and women who will go into the world qualified for any duties they may be called upon to discharge. (Butcher, nd, pp. 366–68)

The curriculum included, 'reading, writing, spelling, arithmetic, grammar, geography, English history, drawing. . .the diligent and careful teaching of the sacred scriptures' (Butcher, nd, p. 368) and for girls, needlework. Colman was committed to the concept of technical education. In 1887 he stated:

> The cry that has been raised over the country for Technical Education. . .We need the adoption of some scheme by which those in Schools, from the Elementary School up to the Universities, shall be taught practically and soundly those things which will at once make them good scholars and intelligent workers. (Butcher, nd, p. 238)

Colman saw his schools as pioneering manual work. Ultimately the curriculum included, cookery, gardening, bee keeping, bent iron work, sloyd, laundry work, modelling in clay, basket weaving, chip carving, leather work, brush drawing, domestic economy (house cleaning), first aid and nursing. In 1880 he wrote:

> We try to give the best all-round education we can to some 500 or 600 scholars ...work which will cultivate manual dexterity thereby fitting the children for the various handicrafts by which they will hereafter gain their livelihood. (Colman, 1932, p. 71)

Of all inducements to industry, popular education must arguably be regarded as the most pervasive, in engendering a nineteenth century working class with habits conducive to industrialization. As is well documented, at the beginning of the nineteenth century educational provision for the labouring classes was at best haphazard and at worst non-existent. By the end, a national system was well established. In the intervening decades, while as acknowledged Nonconformists were not alone in pioneering educational schemes, evidence (not least biographical) supports the view that their influence was not without consequence. As previously noted, of particular significance within the context of Weber's theory, is their obdurate belief in nonsectarian religious instruction as an integral part of a practical, utilitarian education. This dualism resulted in a paradoxical situation where education, the principal vehicle through which the lives of working men, women and children were *improved*, simultaneously and unambiguously prepared them for a life of labour.

Again, as not infrequently argued by social historians, Nonconformist involvement in promoting technical education gave rise to a further incongruous set of circumstances, in which social control and inducements to self-help are juxtaposed. Such persuasive control is graphically illustrated by Baines in his addresses to working men on the advantages of the Mechanics' Institution and in urging them, through 'self-denying habits' to 'the acquisition of useful knowledge' (Baines, 1851, p. 3).

The practical ethics of Nonconformity permeated nineteenth century educational initiatives. As Bebbington states, it was education which 'brought Nonconformity most prominently into the political arena' (1982, p. 127). Allen, Colman and Baines, all used the political platform to advance their educational ideals. Allen had the ear of many leading politicians of his day — Peel, Russell, Morpeth, Brougham. In 1872 Colman in seconding the Address to the Queen, took the opportunity to present his own position on education:

> As a Nonconformist I cannot but say I regret certain portions of our recent legislation, but, as a citizen, I regret them still more because they tend to promote sectarianism rather than to place education on a broad national basis. . .I hope that when the education question comes on we may discuss our differences fairly and temperately with the view of promoting education, and bringing it home to every child in the kingdom. (Anon, 1872)

For Allen, Baines and Colman, the subjects of this necessarily short biographical study, religion and the secular life were a unified whole. By the beginning of the twentieth century, as Weber prophetically declared, Protestant ethics and the spirit of capitalism had gone their separate ways, leaving the utilitarian 'gods' of materialism and consumerism to reign supreme, 'material goods [having finally gained] an inexorable power' (Weber, 1985, p. 181).

The question at the close of the twentieth century remains one of ideology. What kind of society, what kind of educational system do we want for the future? Do we go into a third millennium with materialism remaining the dominant form of social organization? Or, do we search for change? Perhaps, taking a biographical approach, we, like Janus, look forward with enterprising hope, at the same time pausing to look back, to reflect upon and learn from the lives, the social experiences of previous generations?

### Notes

1   In 1905, in the wake of some 150 years of industrial revolution, Max Weber published *The Protestant Ethic and the Spirit of Capitalism*, what he called at the time, 'a sort of spiritualistic construction of the modern economy' (Weber, 1975, p. 356), and in which he propounded an argument for ascetic Protestantism 'as the foundation of modern *vocational civilization* [Berufskultur] (Weber, 1975, p. 356).

2

| William Allen | Quaker | Scientist and manufacturer of pharmaceuticals, London |
| Edward Baines | Congregationalist | Newspaper proprietor, Leeds |
| Jeremiah James Colman | Baptist/ Congregationalist | Manufacturer of mustard, starch, flour etc., Norwich |

3   Examples of Nonconformist businessmen who held ubiquitous control over their workforce and were active in promoting vocational education schemes, abound. In addition to the subjects of this study, the following are illustrative of a significant and much larger group:

*Evans*, Richard (1778–1864) and his sons, Joseph (1817–1889) and Josiah (1820–1873), Congregational coal proprietors;

*Greg*, Samuel (1758–1834) and his sons, Robert Hyde (1795–1875), Samuel, Jnr (1804–1876) and William Rathbone (1809–1881), Unitarian cotton manufacturers;

*Pilkington*, Richard (1795–1869) his brother William (1800–1872) and successive generation of Congregational glass manufacturers;

*Rathbone*, William II (1696–1746) to William VI (1819–1902), Unitarian shipping merchants;

*Rylands*, John (1801–1880) Baptist/Congregational cotton manufacturer and merchant;

*Wills*, Henry Overton I (1761–1826), his sons William Day (1797–1865) and Henry Overton II (1800–1871) and grandsons Henry Overton III (1828–1911), William Henry (1830–1911), Congregational tobacco merchants.

*Source*: Jones, Diana K. 1996 *The relationship between religion, work and education and the influence of eighteenth and nineteenth century Nonconformist entrepreneurs*, unpublished PhD thesis, University of Southampton.

4  Following his death in 1843, Allen's niece, Lucy Bradshaw, edited his diaries and letters and in 1846 published the *Life of William Allen with Selections from his Correspondence*.

5  While Weber's recourse to biographical literature was limited, his repeated reference to the life and writings of the eighteenth century American patriot Benjamin Franklin (1706–1790) must be noted. For Weber, Franklin represented the quintessential, 'ideal type' of capitalistic entrepreneur (1985, p. 71).

6  *Allen*: Public activities centred on philanthropic, rather than overtly political activity. As a young man he was an ardent anti-slavery activist working closely with Wilberforce and Clarkson. He was involved in a variety of schemes devoted to improving conditions for the poor. For example, as an active member of societies such as that formed to investigate the causes of increase in juvenile delinquency in the metropolis. Another society to which he belonged concentrated its efforts on the improvement of prison discipline (Tallack, 1893, pp. 51 and 64).

*Baines*: Liberal; 1859–1874 Member of Parliament for Leeds; Free Trader; supporter of the reduction of the borough franchise, catholic emancipation and the disestablishment of the church of Ireland; abolition of compulsory church rates and university tests; 1880 received knighthood; magistrate; Deputy-Lieutenant of the West Riding of Yorkshire.

*Colman*: Liberal; 1871–1895 Member of Parliament for Norwich; 1859–1871 member Norwich Town Council; 1862–63 sheriff of Norwich; 1866 elected trustee of Norwich Municipal Charities (General List); 1867–68 mayor of Norwich; 1869 appointed magistrate for Norwich; 1869 elected vice-chairman of the Trustees of the Norwich Municipal Charities (General List); 1872 appointed magistrate for Norfolk; 1872, elected chairman of the Trustees of the Norwich Municipal Charities (General List); 1893 Honorary Freedom of the City of Norwich; 1896 Elected an alderman of the City of Norwich.

7  Between 1816 and 1840 Allen travelled widely on the continent:

| | |
|---|---|
| 1816, 1/7 — 18/10 | France, Belgium, Holland, Germany, Switzerland, France |
| 1817, 23/6 — 24/8 | France |
| 1818–1820 | Norway, Sweden, Gulf of Bothnia, Finland, Russia, Turkey, Asia Minor, Greece, Ionian Isles, Malta, Italy, Switzerland, France |
| 1822, 6/9 — 29/12 | France, Belgium, Germany, Austria, Tyrol, N. Italy, Switzerland, Tyrol, France |
| 1832, 4/7 — 21/10 | Holland, Germany, Saxony, Austria, Bavaria, Wurtemberg |
| 1833, 25/1 — 18/4 | France, Bay of Biscay, Spain, France, Pyrenees |
| 1840, 26/2 — 14/5 | Belgium, Holland, Germany, Belgium |
| 1840, 19/8 — 28/10 | France, Germany, Switzerland, Germany, Belgium |

## References

ALDRICH, R. and GORDON, P. (1989) *Dictionary of British Educationists*, London: Woburn Press.

ALLEN, W. (1846) *Life of William Allen with Selections from His Correspondence*, 3 Vols., London: Charles Gilpin.

ANON (1872) unattributed newspaper extract of J.J. Colman seconding Address to Her Majesty the Queen.

ANON (1879) 'Mr Edward Baines', *The Congregationalist*, **8**, pp. 617–22.

ANON (1881) 'Sir Edward Baines', *Biography and Review*, **5**, 27, pp. 249–256.

BAINES, E. (1850) 'E. Baines (Jun) Reflections on his fiftieth birthday', in papers of Edward F. Baines, 36(d), West Yorkshire Archives, Leeds.

BAINES, E. (1880) *The 'Edward Baines' Memorial*, Presentation of Address, 3 December, Leeds.

BAINES, E. (1846) *Letters to the Right Hon. Lord John Russell, First Lord of the Treasury, on State Education*, London, Simpkin, Marshall.

BAINES, E. (1851) *Address to Working Men on the Advantages of Mechanics' Institutions*, Leeds, Edward Baines and Sons.

BAINES, E. (1853a) *The Duty of Congregationalists to Popular Education*, 25 October, Leeds, Baines.

BAINES, E. (1853b) *Strictures on the New Government Measure of Education*, London, John Snow.

BAINES, E. (1969 [1843]) *The Social, Educational, and Religious State of the Manufacturing District*, London, Woburn Press.

BARNARD, H.C. (1961) *A History of English Education*, 2d Ed., London: University of London Press.

BARTLE, G.F. (1992) 'William Allen — Friend of Humanity: His role in nineteenth-century popular education', *History of Education Society Bulletin*, **50**, pp. 15–28.

BEBBINGTON, D.W. (1982) *The Nonconformist Conscience — Chapel and Politics 1870–1914*, London: George Allen and Unwin.

BLAUG, M. (1975) 'The economics of education in English classical political economics: A reassessment', in WEBSTER, C. (1976) 'Changing perspectives in the history of education', in *Oxford Review of Education*, **2**, 3, pp. 201–213.

BROWN, R. (1991) *Society and Economy in Modern Britain 1700–1850*, London: Routledge.

BUTCHER, R.H. (nd) *A Fortune from the Side of a Plate 1805–1973*, Norwich, privately published.

CHAPMAN-HUSTON, D. and CRIPPS, E.C. (1954) *Through a City Archway: The Story of Allen and Hanburys 1715–1954*, London: John Murray.

COLMAN, H.C. (1905) *Jeremiah James Colman: A Memoir*, Chiswick, privately printed.

COLMAN, H.C. (1932) 'Carrow School pioneer handicraft work' in *The Carrow Works Magazine*, July, pp. 70–72.

DAVIDOFF, L. and HALL, C. (1987) *Family Fortunes: Men and Women of the English Middle Class, 1780–1850*, London: Hutchinson.

DONCASTER, L.H. (1965) *Friends of Humanity with Special Reference to the Quaker William Allen: 1770–1843*, Friends of Dr. Williams's Library Nineteenth Lecture, London, Dr. Williams's Trust.

EDGAR, S.H. (nd) *The History of J. and J. Colman*, Norwich, published privately.

ERBEN, M. (1993) 'The problem of other lives: Social perspectives on written biography', *Sociology*, **27**, 1, pp. 5–25.

GOLDSTROM, J.M. (1972) *The Social Content of Education 1808–1870*, Shannon: Irish University Press.

HALL, H. (1953) *William Allen 1770–1843*, Haywards Heath: Charles Clarke.

JONES, D.K. (1989) 'Nonconformist ethics in the first half of the nineteenth century: A study of the relationship between religion, work and the provision of working class education', unpublished MA thesis, University of Southampton.

JONES, D.K. (1996) 'The relationship between religion, work and education and the influence of eighteenth and nineteenth century Nonconformist entrepreneurs', unpublished PhD thesis, University of Southampton.

LAWSON, J. and SILVER, H. (1973) *A Social History of Education in England*, London: Methuen.

MACLURE, J.S. (1965) *Educational Documents: England and Wales: 1816 to the Present Day*, London: Methuen.

OWEN, R. (1867) 'Life of Robert Owen written by Himself', in BARTLE, G.F. (1992) 'William Allen — Friend of Humanity: His role in nineteenth-century popular education' in *History of Education Society Bulletin*, **50**, pp. 22 and 28.

RULE, J. (1986) *The Labouring Classes in Early Industrial England: 1750–1850*, London: Longman.

SHERMAN, J. (1857) *Memoir of William Allen FRS*, London, W. and F.G. Cash.

SIMON, B. (1976) *The Two Nations and the Education Structure: 1780–1870*, London: Lawrence and Wishart.

STANLEY, L. (1992) *The Auto/Biographical I — The Theory and Practice of Feminist Auto/Biography*, Manchester: Manchester University Press.

STANLEY, L. (1839) *Model Schools, Return of Expenditure of the Grant for Model Schools and Copies of Applications for Aid*, London: House of Commons.

STONE, L. (1985) *Past and Present Revisited*, London: Routledge and Kegan Paul.

STONE, L. (1987) *The Past and the Present Revisited*, London: Routledge and Kegan Paul.

SYLVESTER, D.W. (1970) *Educational Documents: 800–1816*, London: Methuen.

TALLACK, W. (1893) *Peter Bedford: The Spitalfields Philanthropist*, London: Edward Hicks.

VAUGHAN, M. and ARCHER, M.S. (1971) *Social Conflict and Educational Change in England and France: 1789–1843*, Cambridge: Cambridge University Press, in WEBSTER, CHARLES (1976) 'Changing perspectives in the history of education' in *Oxford Review of Education*, **2**, 3, pp. 201–213.

WEBER, M. (1988 [1975]) *Max Weber: A Biography*, translated and edited by Harry Zohn, London: Transaction.

WEBER, M. (1985 [1905]) *The Protestant Ethic and the Spirit of Capitalism*, London: Unwin.

WEBSTER, C. (1976) 'Changing perspectives in the history of education' in *Oxford Review of Education*, **2**, 3, pp. 201–213.

# 11 The Autobiographical Account of the Education of an African Slave in Eighteenth Century England

*Peter Figueroa*

Social being is accomplished through many forms of social interaction, of which the word is particularly pivotal. To gain an understanding of how such social being is accomplished and how social identities are constructed it is essential to enter into the lives of social actors. Historical autobiography, the recorded word through which some social actors have themselves attempted this return journey into their own experience, as a way of turning towards others, is a particularly rich ground for our own journey of discovery and of reaching out. This hermeneutics of autobiography is particularly important in the study of ethnicized and racialized relations, and in developing and promoting a sophisticated understanding of citizenship in a plural society.

The present chapter thus focuses on the eighteenth century autobiography of Olaudah Equiano or Gustavus Vassa, an African settled in Britain, an ex-slave. This autobiography, written as part of the abolitionist movement, provides unique materials for studying the development and critical role of an outstanding black person at a formative time in modern British history. An important historical document, it has been, along with its author and his contribution to the development of human rights in Britain, all but effaced by amnesia from mainline British education and culture. This forgetfulness speaks volumes about the construction of modern British identity.

Olaudah Equiano tells us that he was born the youngest boy of seven surviving children in 1745 in a 'charming fruitful' Ibo village in the Kingdom of Benin — which is now part of Nigeria (Edwards, 1989, p. 2). He and his only sister were kidnapped when he was about 10-years-old. He was sold into African slavery, from one master to another, moving constantly towards the Atlantic coast. Finally separated from his sister, and reaching the coast some six months after being kidnapped, he was thrown onto an English slave-ship and transported to the West Indies, and thence to the colony of Virginia in North America, where he was bought by an Englishman, Lieutenant — later Captain — Pascal, who forcibly renamed him Gustavus Vassa, after a Swedish king, the name he was mainly known by for the rest of his life.

After serving many years as a slave, mostly at sea, often with the Royal Navy, during which time he managed to accumulate enough money by hard work and trade on the side to buy back his freedom, he was manumitted in 1766 when about 21. Having through the years made good use of any opportunity to learn English and to gain some education, he now lived as a free black man, taking on many roles, including those of a barber, a servant, and a commissioner for stores to the expedition (1787) to resettle black people in Sierra Leone. He also returned several times to sea, for instance as a steward. He became an ardent Methodist.

He published the autobiography, *The Interesting Narrative of Olaudah Equiano or Gustavus Vassa, the African, Written by Himself*, in 1789. It was probably the most eloquent of a growing black literature in English (1760–1787) (Costanzo, 1987), and immediately became a best seller, being translated into Dutch, German and Russian during Equiano's lifetime.

He married a white English woman, Susanna Cullen, in 1792. They had two daughters, Ann Maria, in October 1793, and Joanna, in April 1795. His wife died in December 1795, and he on 31 March 1797. Ann Maria died in July that very year, but Joanna lived into adulthood. Granville Sharp, the leading abolitionist, visited Equiano 'when he lay upon his death bed' (Edwards, 1989, p. xiii) (See also, Carretta, 1995).

The question underlying this chapter is how Olaudah Equiano became the person that he did become. My interest lies mainly in how, from being an Ibo boy who spoke no English, who was uprooted from a society and culture very different from that of England, and who endured the potentially destructive experience of slavery, he grew into an ardent Christian, an educated, knowledgeable, hardworking and active citizen of England, committed to humane, democratic values, to liberty, equity and respect for others, and into the polished author of his autobiography written in a rich, compelling and pleasing English style. Everything in the autobiography could be analysed for its contribution. He gained knowledge and wisdom through his travels, personal experiences, hard work and reflection (Costanzo, 1987). He says himself, '. . .almost every event of my life made an impression on my mind and influenced my conduct' (Edwards, 1989, p. 170). Alternatively, one could investigate exclusively any formal schooling received.

In this chapter I will focus somewhere between these two extremes, but pay particular attention to any formal education which Equiano reports having received. Also, although his early upbringing before his capture certainly contributed much to his formation, I am not concerned with that here. Space will not permit me to treat the issues exhaustively.

### Issues of methodology

My approach has been to rely essentially on the text of the autobiography itself, using a 'phenomenological' method (Moustakas, 1994). The text has thus been read and re-read. Units of meaning within it relating to Equiano's education have been identified and analysed, and relevant themes articulated.

This textual approach clearly involves important limitations. First, there is the fundamental issue of the status of any (autobiographical) text and its subject. For instance, Denzin (1989) seems to accept the self-defeating postmodern view that the subject of the autobiographical text is simply a 'fiction'; that there is a multiplicity of stories, and nothing else; that we are simply submerged in a sea of words. But do people only create themselves in telling, or also in doing? Can their telling report, however interpretively, their past — or present — or can it only create a new 'fiction' about it? In fact, Denzin speaks of lives and their experiences as 'represented in stories' (1989, p. 81) and says that stories 'like the lives they tell about are always open-ended' (1989, p. 81), thus implying an identifiable distinction and difference between lives and stories about them.

Denzin (1989) has also developed the notion of 'epiphanies' in the study of biographies. There are:

> interactional moments and experiences which leave marks on people's lives. . .In them, personal character is manifested. They are often moments of crisis. They alter the fundamental meaning structures in a person's life. (Denzin, 1989, p. 70)

Although these ideas are helpful, there seems again to be some ambiguity. Is 'epiphany' to be taken just as a subjective shining whether in the text of a narrator or in that of a listener or reader? Or are there turning points, critical events, that actually impinge on the author's life beyond the text which gives the reader access to that life?

I acknowledge that any window unto a life '. . .is always filtered through the glaze of language, signs, and the presence of signification' (Denzin, 1989, p. 14). Care needs to be taken, however, not to collapse all distinction between window, glaze and the life targeted; not everything seen through the window is but a figment of the imagination, nor only a construct of language.

Inevitably an autobiography must be selective and involves interpretation (see Spacks, 1976); but it is in principle, and often in fact, possible to mount a reasonable argument based on internal and external evidence as to whether the picture portrayed by this selection and interpretation is a fair picture or not of the author's life. If 'fiction' were taken to mean that this is impossible in principle, then we could not in the end even say anything about this fiction, for whatever we said about it could itself only be treated as fiction, and so on. The very notion of fiction would lose all force.

Indeed, it must be possible to distinguish between degrees of fiction, between, for instance, gratuitous invention, heuristic construct, interpretation, fact. . .Utterances can, of course, be mistaken, misinformed, distorting, partial or downright deceitful, and it is often difficult to draw a sharp line between truth, lies, distortion, gratuitous invention, interpretation, fact and fiction. However, concepts such as, 'mistaken', 'misinformed', 'distorting', 'partial' and 'deceitful' remain empty unless language has some referential power. If all distinction between language and non-language, between truthful and non-truthful language, between language about reality and language about fiction were nugatory, then the virus would attack language itself and destroy it. The magic and mystery of language is that although we cannot 'stuff a real-live person between the two covers of a text' (Denzin, 1989, p. 83), that text can nevertheless in some way actually give us access to that real-life person.

The textual approach, relying on the author's own public statements about himself and his educational experiences, also raises more specific issues of authenticity, honesty, accuracy and self-presentational bias. Paul Edwards (1968) argues strongly in support of the thesis of authenticity, in particular on the basis of linguistic commonalities between the autobiography and a manuscript letter by Equiano (see also Edwards, 1989). Besides, Equiano includes in his text some documents, such as the manumission document and letters to the press, which can be verified independently. He also cites authorities of his day as sources or corroborators, and many facts can be corroborated from independent evidence (see Shyllon, 1977; Edwards, 1989 and especially Carretta, 1996). Furthermore, the detail of description and incident, and the dramatic force and emotional tenor of the narrative of Equiano's kidnapping and transportation to the African coast and across the Atlantic, along with the eyewitness quality of many other events, plus incidental references in the text, such as to his not having been scarified, also provide the story with the stamp of truth and authenticity.

Yet, some question has been raised about Equiano's place of birth, which was, according to him, in the Kingdom of Benin. He also tells us that, through the elder of the two Guerin sisters, whom Pascal had sent him 'to wait upon' (Edwards, 1989, p. 43), he was baptized 'in St. Margaret's church, Westminster, in February 1759, by my present name' (Edwards, 1989, p. 44). There is, in fact, an entry in the parish register for St. Margaret's church for 9 February 1759 which verifies this; but it reads: 'Gustavus Vassa a Black born in Carolina 12-years-old' (Carretta, 1996, p. 300 ftn. 113). However, 'born in Carolina' can be explained, since Equiano was on a plantation 'about Virginia county' (Edwards, 1989, p. 29) when Pascal bought him.

A further complication is that, following the fourth edition of the autobiography, two hostile letters were published in *The Oracle* and *The Star* in April 1792 claiming that Equiano was actually born in the Danish West Indian island of Santa Cruz, and had never set foot in Africa. This, however, seems a scurrilous attack by people in the pro-slavery camp. Equiano robustly rejects this 'invidious falsehood' in a note 'to the reader' in all the further editions (5–9) before his death, appealing 'to those numerous and respectable persons of character who knew me when I first arrived in England, and could speak no language but that of Africa' (Carretta, 1996, p. 185).

Indeed, Equiano's truthfulness is upheld by Granville Sharp who described him in a letter some years after Equiano's death as 'a sober, honest man' (Edwards, 1989, p. xiii; see also Carretta, 1996). Thomas Clarkson, too, termed him 'a very honest, ingenious, and industrious African' (Carretta, 1996, p. 317 ftn. 320). Also, Equiano's contemporaries were offered the following view of his autobiography:

> We entertain no doubt of the general authenticity of this very intelligent African's interesting story; though it is not improbable that some English writer has assisted him in. . . , at least, the correction of his book: for it is sufficiently well-written. The narrative wears an honest face; and we have conceived a good opinion of the

man, from the artless manner in which he has detailed the. . .vicissitudes which have fallen to his lot. . .

The sable author. . .appears to be a very sensible man; . . .guided by principle; . . .his publication. . .has been encouraged by a very respectable subscription. (*The Monthly Review*, June 1789, pp. 551–52; see Costanzo, 1987, pp. 43–44)

Not surprisingly, it was difficult for people at the time to believe that an ex-slave could have written as elegantly as Equiano had done. But Edwards (1968) has rejected the notion that some English writer must have assisted him.

## The context

Even in focusing primarily on the text itself, it is essential to place it in context. Written at a time of widespread debate about the slave-trade, it sought to persuade especially those in power, and was a timely and effective weapon in the abolitionist struggle. However, it was written not long after Equiano's controversial dismissal from a public post, which gave rise to claim and counter-claim in the media of the day. So part of his purpose might also have been to vindicate himself.

Indeed, the 'artless manner' of some of the narrative can actually be seen as a very fine and effective achievement. Equiano needed to impress and win over his readers — mainly white, English, educated, and to a large extent politically active and influential. He needed to show that he had good knowledge of the realities and issues of which he spoke, and that he was an upright and trustworthy person committed to the best public values of the time. Hence, the autobiography is a skilful combination of different styles, including: straight narrative, rich adventure, personal experience, feelings, reflection, questioning, preaching, moralizing, haranguing, reasoning, mocking. . .He starts the narrative on a factual, positive, idyllic note, describing Africa, and referring, not only to his own life there, but to the well-known authority of the day, Benezet. He soon moves into heavy emotion, building up great sympathy for himself, kidnapped as a vulnerable boy, and torn from his mother, family, village, and in particular his sister. Then there is more deep emotion relating to, but also factual observation of, the transatlantic slave-trade and the middle passage. He is not overtly judgmental, even praising the English, including his own slave-masters, stressing his friendliness towards those who were harsh on him. He also flatters, saying, for instance, that in so far as he was 'a stranger to terror of every kind' (p. 43), he was almost English. He attacks 'nominal Christians' (p. 27), but focuses substantially on his own conversion to Christianity, and on the case for spiritual and moral freedom, along with that for physical and civic liberty. He stresses his own honesty, integrity, commitment to hard work, his striving even in the face of severe difficulties, his thrift, bravery and adventurousness. He highlights, too, his ardent desire for education and self-improvement, and displays his economic informedness, using respected economic arguments of the day. And all this he does in a modest way, soliciting as was conventional, 'the indulgent attention of the public', since he was but 'a private and obscure individual' (Edwards, 1968, p. 1). As Costanzo says (1987), he knew how to argue powerfully against slavery, using both intellectual arguments and emotional appeal, so as to pursuade rather than alienate his white English audience of the day.

### Eighteenth century society

Noted for such thinkers as Montesquieu, Rousseau, Kant and Hume, the eighteenth century has been dubbed 'the age of enlightenment'. There were also many other outstanding people, such as: Adam Smith; Jeremy Bentham; Robert Owen; Thomas Paine; the Wesley brothers, who brought about religious revival in Britain; and Benjamin Franklin, the American statesman, scientist, publisher, autobiographer and abolitionist, who advocated thrift and hard work (see Becker and Barnes, 1961; Jones, 1947; Thomas, 1997). The second half of the century was a time of radical social change: the Industrial Revolution; the American Revolution (1775–1783); and the French Revolution (starting in 1789). This century was also 'a cold-hearted and violent era' (Gerzina, 1995, p. 25).

The total population of England and Wales in the eighteenth century was under 9,000,000 compared with 49,861,600 today (*Encyclopaedia Britannica*, 1855, Vol. VIII, p. 753; Owen, 1992). The population of London (metropolitan district and suburbs) was less than 1,000,000 in 1801 — against 6,679,700 today (*Encyclopaedia Britannica* 1857, Vol. XIII, p. 660; Owen, 1992). Despite London's wealth, it had a large pauper population (*Encyclopaedia Britannica* 1857, Vol. XIII, p. 665). The great railway developments, the bicycle and general illumination by gas all lay in the future.

The black population of London in the second half of the eighteenth century has been estimated at about 10,000–15,000 (Shyllon, 1977; Fryer, 1984) — being 534,300 today (Owen, 1992). According to Walvin (1973, p. 72) by the nineteenth century black people were to be found throughout Britain and in 'all walks of life'. Shyllon (1977) has argued that the black population in London formed a community which came together both socially and to work actively against slavery. Black people were also to be found in many other parts of Europe, because of long-standing trade with Africa: the Portuguese, Spanish, Dutch, French and Danes were all active in the slave-trade (Fryer, 1984; Shyllon, 1977; Thomas 1997).

It was fashionable in the eighteenth century for the well-to-do to have black servants or slaves. These were often given outlandish names, dressed up and treated as pets (Little, 1948). The eighteenth century was also a time of racist ideology (Fryer, 1984). Already in 1753 Hume wrote that he was 'apt to suspect the negroes, and. . .all other species of men. . .to be naturally inferior to the whites' (quoted by Fryer, 1984, p. 152). Edward Long expressed many of the familiar views of modern-day racists, and opposed black people being 'invested with English rights' (Long, 1772, quoted by Shyllon, 1977, p. 98–99).

The slave-trade, this translantic genocide, the Black Holocaust, in which altogether some 11,000,000 or more Africans were transported, had already been going on for over two centuries when the young Equiano was kidnapped — although Africans had been slaves in Europe for much longer (Thomas, 1997). By the end of the eighteenth century England had succeeded Portugal as the world's leading slave-trader (Fryer, 1984; Thomas, 1997). It is estimated that 'Britain's slave-merchants netted a profit of about £12,000,000 on the 2,500,000 Africans they bought and sold between *c*.1630 and 1807, and perhaps half of this profit accrued between 1750 and 1790' (Fryer, 1984, p. 36). The earliest record of slaves being sold in England was in 1621.

The abolitionist movement in England came almost a century-and-a-half later. This could be dated from Granville Sharp's action after helping Jonathan Strong, a battered black youth of about 16- or 17-years-old, in London in 1765. The murderous event of 1781, when 133 Africans were thrown live from the *Zong* slave-ship into the sea for the sake of some insurance money, brought the whole matter sharply before the British public (Fryer, 1984; Shyllon, 1977). In 1783, the year of the *Zong* insurance hearing, 'the Quakers established a committee on Abolition and pre-sented a petition to Parliament' (Shyllon, 1977, p. 229). The Society for the Aboli-tion of the Slave Trade was formally instituted in 1787 by Granville Sharp, Thomas Clarkson and ten Quakers (Shyllon, 1977). In 1788 over 100 pro-abolition petitions were sent to Parliament (Fryer, 1984; see also *Encyclopaedia Britannica* 1854, Vol. V). Olaudah Equiano, vigorously opposed, like other black people in England and the Americas, to slavery, worked actively with other black and white people in this cause.

An examination of publications of the 1780s shows that the abolition of slavery, or at least of the slave-trade, was being widely discussed, for and against. For instance, in 1784, James Ramsay published a pro-abolitionist book, and James Tobin and Gordon Turnbull responded with pro-slavery texts. In 1788 *The Public Advertiser* (28 January and 5 February) published Equiano's letters rejecting Tobin's and Turnbull's views (Shyllon, 1977, pp. 231 and 232; Carretta, 1995, pp. 328–32 reproduces Equiano's letters). This is the context in which Equiano's autobiography appeared.

However, the battle was not, of course, immediately won. It was Wilberforce who in 1789 opened the debate in Parliament, stressing the horror and wickedness of the slave-trade, although his motives have been questioned (Shyllon, 1977). There was much support for abolition of the trade, but also much opposition on economic grounds, and on grounds of 'the alleged depravity of the Africans, which rendered them incapable of civilization' (*Encyclopaedia Britannica* 1854, Vol. V. p. 533). The net result was simply to confirm for a limited time the regulation of the trade which had been agreed in the previous year. It was not until 1807 that the slave-trade was outlawed, and 1833 that slavery itself was legislated against through-out the British Empire.

## Education in the eighteenth century

Although there were some long-standing and noteworthy educational institutions for the privileged, a state system of education was not instituted in England until the nineteenth century (see Barnard, 1947). However, there were precursors in the provision of education for the people; but this was the work of 'individual benevolence' (Bartley, 1871, p. 311), 'different religious denominations. . .voluntary associations. . .landlords occasionally. . .and the apprentice system' (Lecky, 1892, VII, quoted by Cordasco, 1973, pp. 7–8).

It was the parochial charity school that really started to provide some education for the poor from about the early eighteenth century (see Bartley, 1871). The emphasis was on catechism, plus writing and arithmetic especially for boys, and household matters for girls (Aldrich, 1982, pp. 70–71). The Sunday School movement also grew rapidly from about the 1780s (Aldrich, 1982; see *Encyclopaedia Britannica*, 1854, Vol. V; 1855, Vol. VIII and 1858, Vol. XV).

### The education of Olaudah Equiano

The question, then, is: how did Olaudah Equiano become the person that he became? This encompasses at least two sets of questions: one about the person he did become, consciously or unconsciously; and the other about how that happened. The prime concern here is at the level of his conscious self-identity, and especially with the educational experiences explicitly highlighted in relation to this.

Olaudah Equiano was undoubtedly a remarkable man, 'intelligent, clever, and complex' (Costanzo, 1987, p. 90). My reading of the autobiography suggests the following major elements of his mature identity: African, black, ex-slave, free, male, abolitionist, Christian, converted, a person seeking knowledge and education, one who questions, educated, hardworking, a seaman, English resident and subject, having a good command of the English language, a stranger, bicultural, an ordinary person, having a strong belief in himself and his cause, 'never defeated despite the great travail he undergoes' (Costanzo, 1987, p. 64). It also seems manifest from his narrative, its contents and style, that he had an eye for detail, was a reflective person who learned from experience, but likewise was a man of action, application, and ambition. He was both an idealist, a humanitarian committed to liberty, equality and fraternity, and a pragmatist.

Equiano's text is certainly rich in 'epiphanies' or events and experiences which were significant in his life, influencing its course, challenging or changing its direction, or indeed reinforcing it. These events, turning points or experiences, retold in the autobiography, simultaneously revealed his being and helped to forge it. Some of the most notable ones include: being kidnapped as a boy; being torn from one culture and socio-historical situation and forced into another quite different; the middle passage; being sold into slavery; friendship with Dick, a white slave-owner a few years older than himself; boarding with an English family; serving two sisters; his schooling; receiving instruction; being re-sold into transatlantic slavery; his buying back his freedom and his manumission; taking over as the 'sable' captain in an emergency; conversion to Christianity. . .Then there was the process itself of writing and publishing the autobiography. Being forced into new, tough experiences and strong contrasts, and then going back over them would undoubtedly have sharpened his awareness, being inherently a reflective process. Space permits me to explore here only some of the themes concerning the education and development of Olaudah Equiano which my reading of the autobiography identified.

Equiano remarks several times on the strangeness of his new experiences, his wonderment at them, and his desire to learn about and from them, and to understand the new things he experienced. Looking back in his forties to the year 1761, when he was about 16, he tells us for instance, 'I had a mind on which every thing uncommon made its full impression, and every event which I considered as marvellous' (Edwards, 1989, p. 51).

He relates how, at about the age of 10, he was thrust into transatlantic slavery.

> The first object which saluted my eyes when I arrived on the coast was the sea, and a slave ship. . .These filled me with astonishment, which was soon converted into terror when I was carried on board. . .I was now persuaded that I had gotten into a world of bad spirits, and that they were going to kill me. Their complexions too differing so much from ours, their long hair, and the language they spoke. . .united to confirm me in this belief. (p. 22)

We can imagine how his awareness was heightened in this situation, and how thoroughly he must have been shaken to his core. Not only was he being thrown into an unfamiliar situation and being confronted with people very different from himself, but this was being done through compulsion and violence, and the situation was superlatively nasty.

He also recounts his impressions when he first arrived in England at about the age of 12.

> I was very much struck with the buildings and the pavement of the streets in Falmouth; and, indeed, any object I saw filled me with new surprise. One morning, when I got upon deck, I saw it covered all over with. . .snow. . . : . . .I thought it was salt; so I immediately ran down to the mate and desired him, as well as I could, to come and see. . .He. . .desired me to bring some of it down to him: accordingly I took up a handful of it, which I found very cold indeed; . . .he desired me to taste it. I did so, and I was surprised beyond measure. I then asked him what it was; . . .the use of it, and who made it; he told me a great man in the heavens, called God. . .After this I went to church; and. . .I was again amazed at seeing and hearing the service. I asked all I could about it; and they gave me to understand it was worshipping God, who made us and all things. I was still at a great loss, and soon got into an endless field of inquiries. . .(pp. 33–34)

Reflecting on his situation two or three years later, when he was maybe 14 or 15, and had been in England for two or three years, he writes:

> I could now speak English tolerably well. . .I now. . .felt myself quite easy with these new countrymen. . .I no longer looked upon them as spirits, but as men superior to us; and therefore I had the stronger desire to resemble them. . .I therefore embraced every occasion of improvement; and every new thing that I observed I

> treasured up in my memory. I had long wished to be able to read and write; and for this purpose I took every opportunity to gain instruction. . .(p. 43)

This suggests that part of his motivation to learn was that he was keenly aware of the power over him of those in whose hands he was. He realized, too, that they had knowledge and technological developments that his people did not have. But we can almost hear the ruefulness in his mature voice as, looking back, he sets out how he felt and saw things at the time of his youth after having spent some years with these his new masters. At that youthful point he might have seen these people as superior; but, in his maturity, at the time of writing, he knew better. Thus, developing an argument to counter 'prejudice. . .against the natives of Africa on account of their colour', he wrote: 'Let the polished and haughty European recollect that his ancestors were once, like the Africans, uncivilized, and even barbarous. Did Nature make *them* inferior to their sons?' (p. 14). In other words, just as the forefathers of present-day Europeans could hardly have been inherently inferior to their own offspring, so Africans, including himself, he is asserting, are not inferior to Europeans. Indeed, his very writing of a full-length autobiography in an elegant, sophisticated and varied style showed *de facto* that he had a very high command of English, and, moreover, that he could enter, as the equal of others in the political community of the day (like a good citizen), publicly and fully into the debate about abolition.

Equiano was not only curious about his surroundings and all new things, and did not only want to travel so as to have new experiences and see new places, but was particularly interested in learning practical skills, and especially in learning to read and write, as well as to carry out computations. Thus, he tells us, when looking back to his situation at about the age of 17:

> I thought now of nothing but being freed, and working for myself, and thereby getting money to enable me to get a good education; for I always had a great desire to be able at least to read and write; and while I was on ship-board I had endeavoured to improve myself in both. (Edwards, 1989, pp. 56–57)

He did not hesitate to explore, to try out things and to seek help and information. Writing about his first voyage to England at the age of about 12, he recounts the following.

> I had often seen my master and Dick employed in reading; and I had a great curiosity to talk to the books, as I thought they did; and so to learn how all things had a beginning; for that purpose I have often taken up a book, and have talked to it, and then put my ears to it, when alone, in hopes it would answer me. . . (pp. 34–35)

Dick (Richard Baker) was about four or five years older than Olaudah, who writes warmly of him. He was a well-to-do and 'most amiable' (p. 31) American with 'many slaves of his own' (p. 32). He 'had received an excellent education' (p. 31), and had 'a mind superior to prejudice' (p. 32). They became 'inseparable', and, for two years he was Olaudah's 'constant companion and instructor' (p. 32). Equiano also tells us that, when he got into his 'endless field of inquiries',

> . . .my little friend Dick used to be my best interpreter; . . .and he always instructed me with pleasure; and, from what I could understand by him of this God, . . .I was much pleased. . . .(p. 34)

This young man is the first person that Equiano identifies, after his enslavement, as his 'instructor', and that over a substantial period of time. There can be no doubt that Equiano learned much from him in a largely informal way. Dick died about three years later, and Equiano referred to this as 'an event which I have never ceased to regret, as I lost at once a kind interpreter, an agreeable companion, and a faithful friend' (Edwards, 1989, p. 32).

There are also several other people who Equiano mentions as being subsequently his 'instructors'. First, there was the wife of a ship-mate of Equiano's master, Captain Pascal. She, her husband and their 5- or 6-year-old daughter lived in Guernsey. Captain Pascal lodged Olaudah (aged about 12) and Dick with this family for some months in 1757. Olaudah writes:

> This woman behaved to me with great kindness and attention; and taught me every thing in the same manner as she did her own child, and indeed in every respect treated me as such. (p. 35)

Next, he mentions two sisters, the Miss Guerins, relations of Captain Pascal. They lived in London, and Olaudah was sent to wait upon them in 1759 when he was about 14. He says: 'They often used to teach me to read, and took great pains to instruct me in the principles of religion and the knowledge of God' (p. 44). Olaudah also mentions two other people who instructed him on board the *Aetna*, on which he served, about 1760–62: the captain's clerk and Daniel Queen. He says, 'the captain's clerk taught me to write, and gave me a smattering of arithmetic as far as the rule of three' (p. 57). The Oxford English Dictionary (2nd edition, 1989, Vol. XIV) defines the rule of three, or 'the golden rule', as 'a method of finding a fourth number from three given numbers, of which the first is in the same proportion to the second as the third is to the unknown fourth'. In Lancaster's improved method of instruction in elementary arithmetic, the rule of three comes at the end, after the combination of figures, addition, subtraction, division, reduction and compound addition, subtraction and division (Lancaster 1805, edited by Cordasco, 1973).

Olaudah particularly mentions Daniel Queen,

> about forty years of age, a man very well-educated, who. . .attended the captain. Fortunately, this man soon became very much attached to me, and took very great pains to instruct me in many things. He taught me to shave and dress hair a little, and also to read in the Bible, explaining many passages to me. . .(p. 57)

Olaudah also learned other practical or vocationally useful skills besides hairdressing. For instance, in 1757, when his master was made first lieutenant of a large Royal

Navy war ship, the *Roebuck*, Dick and himself and the ship-mate they were staying with in Guernsey, were summoned to go aboard. Here Olaudah (aged about 12) learned 'many of the manoeuvres of the ship. . .and. . .was several times made to fire the guns' (p. 37).

Also, years later, in the late 1760s, after he had returned a freeman to England, his old friends, the Miss Guerins, helped him find a placement with a master hairdresser in the Haymarket. About this time too, a neighbour taught him to play the French horn; and, while on a voyage in the Mediterranean, he 'learned nagivation of the mate' (p. 124).

Equiano also received instruction of a more formal nature. His first mention of school relates to the year 1759 when he was about 14. He writes:

> . . .when I went to London with my master, I had soon an opportunity of improving myself, which I gladly embraced. . . .he sent me to wait upon the Miss Guerins, . . .and they sent me to school. (p. 43)

Some months later his master had to get ready again for sea,

> . . .and, to my no small grief, I was obliged to leave my schoolmaster, whom I liked very much, and always attended while I stayed in London. . .(p. 44)

He was then on board the Royal Navy ship, the *Namur*, for some two or more years, and there he learned some reading and writing 'as there was a school on board' (p. 50). Gerzina (1995, p. 154) states that, 'many ships had tutors for their numerous boy sailors'. Rodger (1986, p. 68 cited by Edwards 1989, p. viii) confirms that 'a line-of-battle ship might have on board fifty or more boys aged from six to sixteen'. Olaudah himself remarks about the *Roebuck*: 'There was a number of boys on board. . .and a great part of our time was spent in play', he being about 12 (p. 36).

After he had regained his freedom, Equiano still yearned for a good education. For instance, he also narrates the following about the late 1760s when he lived in the Haymarket;

> I agreed with the Rev. Mr. Gregory, who lived in the same court, where he kept an academy and an evening-school, to improve me in arithmetic. This he did as far as barter and alligation. (p. 123)

The Oxford English Dictionary (1989, vol. I) defines barter as the method of computing 'the quantity or value of one commodity, to be given for a known quantity and value of another', and alligation as the 'method of solving questions concerning the mixing of articles of different qualities or values'.

Olaudah continues:

> In February 1768 I hired myself to Dr. Charles Irving, in Pall Mall. . .here I had plenty of hair-dressing to improve my hand. This gentleman was an excellent master; . . .and allowed me in the evenings to attend my schools. . .I. . .used all my diligence to improve the opportunity. This diligence. . .recommended me to the

notice and care of my three preceptors [i.e. teachers], who on their parts bestowed a great deal of pains in my instruction. . .(p. 123)

Finally, it is interesting to see that Olaudah Equiano, the ardent convert to Methodism, himself took on the role of a teacher. Thus Dr. Irving asked Olaudah to accompany him to Central America in 1775 to look after a new plantation there. Four Amerindians were returning in the same boat after a year in England. Equiano recounts that he was:

. . .mortified. . .that they had not frequented any churches. . .nor was any attention paid to their morals. . .I took all the pains that I could to instruct the Indian prince in the doctrines of Christianity. . .I taught him in the compass of eleven days all the letters, and he could put even two or three of them together and spell them. (pp. 142–43)

### Conclusion

It is clear that Olaudah Equiano was a lively, resourceful, intelligent person, questioning, thoughtful and thirsty for learning, and that he gained much from formal and informal teaching. He experienced many events that were significant for him, but that also had wider significance. In writing his autobiography he must have reflected deeply on some of these. They constituted the pulses of his development: the influences and the flow of life. By recounting them in his autobiography, and by engaging with his readers emotionally and intellectually in doing so, he not only presented a powerful case *against* slavery, physical and spiritual, and *for* freedom, justice and constructive, humane inter-relationships; but also set an example and raised issues for us today as citizens of a plural society and a plural world with its own problems.

In a fuller study I would explore the social, historical, political and personal context of this autobiography much more extensively. I would also go into greater depth on a wider range of aspects of the autobiography itself, including the development of his character, his religious conversion, life and battles at sea, the horrors of slavery, his arguments against it, his abolitionist activities, the social and political values he espoused, relations between him and others, prejudice, culture contact . . .I would also attempt to look at his life from many different perspectives: a black person's, a white person's, a slave-master's, a slave's, an abolitionist's, an anti-abolitionist's. . .

This, however, is not because: 'There is no truth in the painting of a life, only multiple images and traces of what has been, what could have been, and what now is' (Denzin, 1989, p. 81). Rather, in doing so a fuller view and understanding could be gained, a richer truth — incomplete, open and ambiguous as it might remain.

The coherence of Equiano's life is not just an 'invention'. At least because of kidnapping and slavery and his subsequent anti-slavery work, his life did have a large measure of coherence. Also, as with all lives, it had the coherence of being his experiences, his life — existential coherence, a coherence which his autobiography, with its multitude of detail, experiences and argument, suggests to us. This is so, even though, of necessity, at the time of writing, his life remained unfinished and therefore open, though not totally, for whatever was yet to come, it could not have completely escaped from its past.

A text is a material object, a fact, paper with marks upon it. Yet, the mystery of the text is that it gives us access to a reality beyond itself. To call this into question by reducing everything to 'fiction' and to 'story' is to call the text itself into question. It is a false dichotomy to pitch truth against fiction. Against Denzin (1989), Olaudah Equiano's autobiography does provide us with a real author and a real subject in a real world. Of course, it is selective. Of course, there are question marks. Of course, it is thoroughly informed and shaped by interpretation — his and mine. Of course, I have access to his life and reality only through texts, the text of his autobiography and other relevant texts, especially other texts of the time, written by himself, or written by others, whether about him or about any of the matters of which he wrote. That does not negate the historical reality of his autobiography and its real import. As the editor of the 1814 (Leeds) edition of the *Narrative* wrote, 'no statement was made by him, for which he had not some voucher or authority' (quoted by Shyllon, 1977, pp. 237–38). Olaudah Equiano's text provided fact and affect as well as argument. It provided many and varied warrants for its claims, and is, like any biography, a text, a material object, which both presents, *par excellence*, a story of a particular (real) individual, and, at the same time, presents a social story, a story of other (real) individuals, of their lives, interactions, discourses — a story of actual, eighteenth century, English society. Every human person is an individual inextricably 'bound to' others, and language, a text about, which is separate from that about which it is, inherently mediates that reality, is discourse, not only of one speaker with their text and one speaker with another speaker, but of speaker with spoken-about and of text with its 'object'. . .

This text of Olaudah Equiano's, placed in historical context and in the context of the present time, provides a rich resource for education for citizenship in a plural society. It provides evidence of the legitimacy of contemporary plural Britain. It offers arguments for the respect of difference and of the basic democratic values of justice, equity, rationality and human warmth. It offers much food for thought, for reflection and for constructive passion.

### References

ALDRICH, R. (1982) *An Introduction to the History of Education*, London: Hodder and Stoughton.

BARNARD, H.C. (1947) *A Short History of English Education from 1760 to 1944*, London: University of London Press.

BARTLEY, G.C.T. (1871) *The Schools for the People: Containing the History, Development, and Present Working of Each Description of English School for the Industrial and Poorer Classes*, London: Bell and Daldy.

BECKER, H. and BARNES, H.E. (1961) *Social Thought from Lore to Science*, (third edition, in three volumes) New York: Dover Publications.

CARRETTA, V. (ed.) (1995) *The Interesting Narrative and Other Writings: Olaudah Equiano*, (with an introduction and notes) New York: Penguin Books.

CARRETTA, V. (ed.) (1996) *Unchained Voices: An Anthology of Black Authors in the English-speaking World of the Eighteenth Century*, Lexington, Kentucky: The Universal Press of Kentucky.

CORDASCO, F. (ed.) (1973) *Improvements in Education as it Respects the Industrious Classes of the Community, by Joseph Lancaster (third edition with additions [1805])*, (with an Introduction) Clifton, NJ: Augustus M. Kelley.

COSTANZO, A. (1987) *Surprising Narrative: Olaudah Equiano and the Beginnings of Black Autobiography*, New York: Greenwood Press.

DENZIN, N. (1989) *Interpretive Biography*, (Qualitative Research Methods Series 17) Newbury Park, CA: Sage.

ENCYCLOPAEDIA BRITANNICA (1854) Britain, or Great Britain, (eighth edition) Edinburgh: Adam and Charles Black, Vol. V. pp. 372–672.

ENCYCLOPAEDIA BRITANNICA (1855) England, (eighth edition) Edinburgh: Adam and Charles Black, Vol. VIII, pp. 656–792.

ENCYCLOPAEDIA BRITANNICA (1857) London, (eighth edition) Edinburgh: Adam and Charles Black, Vol. XIII pp. 658–80.

ENCYCLOPAEDIA BRITANNICA (1858) National Education, (eighth edition) Edinburgh: Adam and Charles Black, Vol. XV, pp. 806–28.

EDWARDS, P. (1968) '...Written by Himself': A manuscript letter of Olaudah Equiano, *Notes and Queries*, June, pp. 222–25.

EDWARDS, P. (ed.) (1989) *The Life of Olaudah Equiano, or Gustavus Vassa the African Written by Himself*, (with an introduction) Burnt Mill, Harlow: Longman.

FRYER, P. (1984) *Staying Power: The History of Black People in Britain*, London: Pluto Press.

GERZINA, P. (1995) *Black England: Life before Emancipation*, London: John Murray.

JONES, W.T. (1947) *Masters of Political Thought: Machiavelli to Bentham*, (Vol. 2) London: Harrap.

LITTLE, K.L. (1948) *Negroes in Britain: A Study of Racial Relations in English Society*, London: Routledge and Kegan Paul.

THE MONTHLY REVIEW (1789) June, pp. 551–52.

MOUSTAKAS, C. (1994) *Phenomenological Research Methods*, Thousand Oaks: Sage Publications.

OED (1989) *Oxford English Dictionary*, 2nd Edn., Oxford: Oxford University Press.

OWEN, D. (1992) *Ethnic Minorities in Great Britain: Settlement Patterns*, (National Ethnic Minority Data Archive 1991 Census Statistical Paper no. 1) Coventry: Centre for Research in Ethnic Relations, University of Warwick.

THE PUBLIC ADVERTISER (1788) 28 January and 5 February.

RODGER, N.A.M. (1986) *The Wooden World: An Anatomy of the Georgian Navy*, London: Collins.

SHYLLON, F.O. (1977) *Black People in Britain 1555–1833*, London: Oxford University Press.

SPACKS, P.M. (1976) *Imagining a Self: Autobiography and Novel in Eighteenth-Century England*, Cambridge, MA: Harvard University Press.

THOMAS, H. (1997) *The Slave Trade: The History of the Atlantic Slave Trade, 1440–1870*, London: Picador.

WALVIN, J. (1973) *Black and White: The Negro in English Society, 1555–1945*, London: Allen Lane.

# Notes on Contributors

**Gill Clarke** lectures in physical education, sociology and biographical studies at the University of Southampton, prior to this she was field leader for physical education at Chichester Institute of Higher Education after having taught in secondary schools in Hampshire. She is an officer of the British Sociological Association Study Group on Auto/Biography and on the editorial boards of *Pedagogy in Practice* and the *European Journal of Physical Education*. She has co-edited *Researching Women and Sport* (Macmillan) and published articles on lesbian physical education students and teachers.

**Hilary Dickinson** lectures in sociology in the School of Social Sciences at the University of Greenwich. Her current research is on the sociology of auto/biography, and on biographies of learning disability in the nineteenth century. Previous research and writing has included the sociology of vocational education and training. She has published widely and is currently on the editorial board of *Auto/Biography*.

**Michael Erben** is Director of the Centre for Biography and Education at the University of Southampton. He is a convener of the British Sociological Association Study Group on Auto/Biography, a member of the editorial boards of *Auto/Biography* and *Memory and Narrative* and has published widely in the area of biography and sociology.

**Peter Figueroa** is Reader in the School of Education, University of Southampton. He has taught at Oxford University, the Australian National University, and the Universities of Frankfurt, Dar-es-Salaam and the West Indies. His publications include: *Education and the Social Construction of 'Race'*; *Education for Cultural Diversity* (edited with A. Fyfe); and 'Multicultural Education in the United Kingdom: Historical Developments and Current Status' in J.A. Banks and C.A. McGee Banks (eds.) *Handbook of Research on Multicultural Education*, pp. 699–726.

**Diana Jones** lectures in education and sociology within the School of Post-Compulsory Education and Training at the University of Greenwich. Using a prosopographical (collective biography) approach, her current work focuses on the socio/historical analysis of relationships between religion, work and vocational education with special reference to nineteenth century Nonconformist and Jewish entrepreneurs. She has published widely in this area, a representative example of which is 'The Juxtaposition of Lives: Benjamin Franklin and Edward Baines' in *Auto/Biography* (1995, Vol. 3, Nos. 1 and 2).

**Chris Mann** is a researcher based at the Faculty of Social and Political Sciences, University of Cambridge. She is currently adopting biographical approaches to a wide range of studies investigating such areas as: the academic performance of

Cambridge University undergraduates, the values and practice of key educational-ists in state 'democratic' schools in the 1970s, and the impact of military service on the identity of young Israeli women.

**Mich Page** is an international training consultant specializing in equality issues and the analysis of student achievement. Her teaching background is very broad and includes a Krishnamurti International school and one of Her Majesty's prisons. She spent a decade at Bournemouth and Poole College of Further Education as a lec-turer, equal opportunities co-ordinator and later as research manager. During this time she successfully completed a part time PhD at the University of Southampton.

**Zoë Parker** is a lecturer in the School of Education at Kingston University. She is also a member of the BSA Auto/Biography Study Group. She is an action researcher, interested in facilitating practitioner research.

**Brian Roberts** lectures in sociology at the University of Huddersfield. His research interests include biographical study, community studies, the work of Dickens and Welsh labour history. He has published widely and is active in the BSA Auto/Biography Study Group and research committees on biography within the Euro-pean Sociological Association and the International Sociological Association.

**David Scott** is Lecturer in Educational Research at the London University Institute of Education. He has carried out numerous research projects and published widely. He has recently edited *Control and Accountability in Educational Settings* and *Understanding Educational Research* (1996). He is the current editor of *The Curriculum Journal*.

**Robin Usher** is Reader in Education at the School of Education in the University of Southampton. He is the author, with Richard Edwards, of *Postmodernism and Education: Different Voices, Different Worlds* (Routledge, 1994), of *Adult Learning in Postmodernity* (Routledge, 1996) with Ian Bryant and Rennie Johnston, and is editor, with David Scott, of *Understanding Educational Research* (Routledge, 1996).

# Index

*Index*

Richardson, L., 68
Ricoeur, P., 7, 12–16, 23, 35, 72–3, 92
Roberts, B., 103–14
role models, 49, 62, 110
Rousseau, J-J., 119, 154
Rowland, S., 118
Russell, J., 138
Russell, T., 118

Salmon, P., 117
Sartre, J-P., 8
Scott, D., 32–44
secondary modern schools, 107–8
sectarianism, 134
Section 28, 59–61
self, 18–30, 59–61
sexuality, 59–61
Sharp, G., 150, 152, 155
Sherman, J., 137
Sikes, P., 121
slavery, 149–62
Smith, K., 98–9
Smith, P., 20
Snyder, M., 91
sociality, 6–7
sociology, 13–14, 54, 95, 106, 109
Spacks, P.M., 151
Spelman, E., 120–1
sport, 62–3, 109
Stone, L., 131
stories, 18–30
Strauss, A.L., 9

Stronach, I., 23, 44
student deficit model, 88
subject specialisms, 5–6
subversion, 65–7
surveillance, 59–61

Thatcher, M., 59
time, 22–3
totalization, 8
Trollope, A., 100
Turner, V., 83

Usher, R., 18–30, 43

Valéry, -, 8
Van Maanen, J., 89
Vassa, G., 149–62
Vaughan, M., 133
Vico, 11
village schools, 104–6
voluntaryism, 134–7

Walwicz, A., 29
Warnock, M., 10
Weber, M., 7, 130, 132–3, 135–7
White, H., 14
Whitehead, J., 120
Wilberforce, W., 155
Wisniewski, R., 116
Wood, D., 43

Zimmerman, J., 52–3